THE CHANGING FACE OF WELFARE

Consequences and outcomes from a citizenship perspective

Jørgen Goul Andersen, Anne-Marie Guillemard,
Per H. Jensen and Birgit Pfau-Effinger

First published in Great Britain in October 2005 by

The Policy Press
University of Bristol
Fourth Floor
Beacon House
Queen's Road
Bristol BS8 1QU
UK

Tel +44 (0)117 331 4054
Fax +44 (0)117 331 4093
e-mail tpp-info@bristol.ac.uk
www.policypress.org.uk

British Library Cataloguing in Publication Data
A catalogue record for this book is available from the British Library.

Library of Congress Cataloging-in-Publication Data
A catalog record for this book has been requested.

ISBN 1 86134 591 7 paperback

A hardcover version of this book is also available

Cover design by Qube Design Associates, Bristol.
Printed and bound in Great Britain by Hobbs the Printers, Southampton.

Contents

List of tables and figures

Tables

Figures

Preface

This book is an outcome of COST Action A13, 'Changing Labour Markets, Welfare Policies and Citizenship'. The purpose of COST Action A13 has been to examine the effects of social security systems and welfare institutions on the processes of political and social marginalisation and exclusion. So far, COST Action A13 has published or is in the process of publishing the following books and articles in journals:

Jørgen Goul Andersen and Per H. Jensen (eds) *Changing labour markets, welfare policies and citizenship*, Bristol: The Policy Press.

Jørgen Goul Andersen, Jochen Clasen, Wim van Oorschot and Knut Halvorsen (eds) *Europe's new state of welfare: Unemployment, employment policies and citizenship*, Bristol: The Policy Press.

Tony Maltby, Bert de Vroom, Maria Luisa Mirabile and Einar Øverbye (eds) *Ageing and the transition to retirement*, Aldershot: Ashgate.

Jean-Claude Barbier and Wolfgang Ludwig-Mayerhofer (eds) 'The many worlds of activation', *European Societies*, vol 6, no 4, Special issue on activation policies.

Harriet Bradley and Jacques van Hoof (eds) *Young people in Europe: Labour markets and citizenship*, Bristol: The Policy Press.

Birgit Pfau-Effinger and Birgit Geissler (eds) *Care and social integration in European societies*, Bristol: The Policy Press.

COST is an intergovernmental organisation for the coordination of scientific and technical research, aiming at the coordination and formation of networks on a European level between nationally funded research projects. Some 80 experts, appointed by 17 countries, have participated in COST Action A13. The COST Action A13 network was in force for five years (1998-2003). For further information about COST Action A13, see www.socsci.aau.dk/cost.

Glossary

Activation
Job training (in the form of a subsidised temporary job) or education, with the strongly emphasised aim of bringing people back to employment. However, it is sometimes suggested that, in a broader sense, 'activation of social protection' should designate all sorts of restructuring social policies that aim to enhance employment.

Active citizenship
A new ideal of citizenship or a new set of rights and duties based on a conception of a claimant (eg an unemployed person) as an active citizen. The active citizen is granted more autonomy and choice but in return is assumed to be self-responsible, flexible and mobile.

ALMP
This abbreviation stands for 'active labour-market policy', which includes activation but may also include proactive measures, such as education for those employed.

Decommodification
An individual's right to maintain a reasonable standard of living during periods without employment, such as unemployment, retirement and illness – to live as a citizen relatively independent of one's labour-market position. This is a key concept in much comparative welfare research that focuses on the variations between welfare regimes.

Discourses
The presentation and discussion of an issue. This is an institutionalised way of thinking; a social boundary defining what can be said about a specific topic. Discourses are seen to affect our views on all matters.

Empowerment
This term means enabling citizens to control their own lives and being able to exploit opportunities for participation. It has both an institutional aspect (opportunities) and an individual aspect (knowledge, skills, experience and subjective competence).

European employment strategy	The European employment strategy (EES) was launched at the Luxemburg Job Summit in November 1997 and became a key component of the broader strategy launched at the Lisbon summit in 2000. It emphasises the commitment of the European Union to promote employment and includes a process that defines common objectives in relation to employment policy, together with guidelines for the development of the employment policies of member states.
Human resource management (HRM)	This is a management philosophy focusing on the development of co-workers, strategies for the individual, career planning, competence assessments and relevant tools for the development of the self.
IAP	The 'individual action plan' is an element of activation policies in the Danish welfare state. The IAP explicitly accounts for the content and purpose of the activation. It is negotiated in dialogue with a social worker or employment officer and signed as a contract by the unemployed person.
Male breadwinner model	The model of a household unit with a male breadwinner and a female housewife and home carer, on which most welfare policies are historically based, especially in continental European welfare states.
Marginali-sation/social exclusion	Social exclusion usually means cumulative social deprivation leading to exclusion from most of what is understood as a normal, everyday life. Marginalisation refers to a process or to a marginal position in relation to various arenas in society such as work, and social and political participation.
PARE	*Plan d'aide au retour à l'emploi.* This is the standard unemployment insurance 'individual plan'. From July 2001, PARE has been the standard provision for all new unemployed people who claim unemployment insurance in France. Along with access to the benefit, it comprises an individualised 'project' (involving the negotiation of an action plan, or *'projet d'action personalisé'* (PAP)).

Path dependency	In the broadest sense, path dependence refers to the fact that certain policy choices are more likely because of the prior choices made. More narrowly, it refers to mechanisms (positive feedback) that drive policies in a particular direction that is very difficult to escape from, because of the political or practical costs of doing so.
Policy closure	A policy closure occurs when problems are formulated in a way that restricts alternative means of handling them. It excludes the possibility of other ways of thinking and talking about the issue.
Poverty	This term usually refers to relative poverty measured in relation to median equivalent disposable income. The relative poverty level is typically operationalised as 50% or 60% of median equivalent disposable income. Equivalence is established by correcting for differences in household size and composition. Competing equivalence scales are applied in making this correction.
RMI	*Revenu minimum d'insertion* – the standard assistance minimum income in France, which, since 1988, has also been associated with a personal plan – *contrat d'insertion*. A distinctive RMI feature has been – despite its current 2004 reform – the absence of any work obligation.
Social policy agenda	In 2000 the EU published its first social policy agenda which emphasised the dynamic interaction between economic policy, employment policy and social policy.
Social quality	The extent to which people are able to participate in the social and economic life of their communities under conditions which enhance their well-being and individual potential. That is, the extent to which the quality of social relations promotes both participation and personal development.
SSO	Social security, Denmark.

The Third Way	Efforts to formulate a new, more centrist and more market-oriented social democratic political formula, inspired by Tony Blair's New Labour, but appearing in a variety of forms.
The Transatlantic consensus	Proponents of this position support free markets and trade liberalisation as the mechanisms to promote growth and improve living standards. They assume that the poorest will automatically benefit from global economic growth.
Welfare regime	Esping-Andersen's concept of a welfare model encompassing particular, mutually reinforcing configurations of welfare state, the labour market and the family.
Workfare	An approach to reducing poverty and at the same time reducing 'welfare dependency'. The US and the UK represent the purest form of workfare programmes. A workfare approach emphasises individuals' duty to work, restricts their access to benefits, and reduces the levels of compensation paid and restricts the duration of payments to them.

Notes on contributors

Jørgen Goul Andersen is Professor of Political Sociology, Director of the Centre for Comparative Welfare Studies, Aalborg University, Denmark. He was the working group coordinator of COST Action A13: 'Changing Labour Markets, Welfare Policies and Citizenship', leader of the Danish election programme and the Danish International Social Survey programme, and a member of the Board of the Danish democracy and power programme. His research fields include comparative welfare state research, election research, and political power and democracy.

Jean-Claude Barbier is Directeur de recherche CNRS (Centre national de la recherche scientifique) at the Centre d'études de l'emploi (Noisy le Grand, France). He works on the international comparison of social policies, social protection systems and employment policies. He is also currently studying the European employment strategy from the point of view of the dissemination of ideas. He also does research on the epistemological and methodological issues of cross-national comparative research. A member of the COST Action A13 unemployment group, he participates in many European networks, and particularly in the TLM.net project funded by the DG Research of the European Commission.

Asmund W. Born is Associate Professor at the Copenhagen Business School, Denmark. He has published extensively on risk and power in organisations and on the connection between language and power.

Marina Calloni is Professor of Social and Political Philosophy at the State University of Milano-Bicocca and the director of the International Network for Research in Gender. She has participated in several international research projects and cross-borders networks, collaborating with universities, research centres, NGOs and supranational institutions. She has published widely as the author of books and articles in several languages and countries.

Anne-Marie Guillemard is Professor of Sociology with a chair at the University of Paris-Sorbonne, Department of Social Sciences. She is a member of the Institut Universitaire de France and of the European Academy of Sciences, and is also on the editorial board of *Revue*

Française de Sociologie and Vice Chair of the European COST Action A13 Network entitled, 'Changing Labour Markets, Welfare Policies and Citizenship'. She is the author of numerous articles on the sociology of social policies and the welfare state, and the sociology of ageing and the life course. Her latest book is, *L'âge de l'emploi. Les sociétés à l'épreuve du vieillissement.* Among other publications she was co-editor of the book *Time for retirement.*

Rune Halvorsen is a Research Fellow in the Department of Sociology and Political Science, Norwegian University of Science and Technology, Trondheim, Norway. Social marginality has represented the common denominator in his research on family policy, social movements and welfare policy.

Per H. Jensen is Associate Professor in comparative welfare studies at Aalborg University, Denmark. He is director of the Danish post-graduate research school on 'Welfare State and Diversity', and he was Chair of the COST Action A13 Network. He has published widely around the topic of labour markets and welfare states in a comparative perspective.

Jørgen Elm Larsen is Associate Professor at the Department of Sociology, University of Copenhagen. He is coordinator of the graduate school of 'Integration, Production and Welfare'. His current fields of research are social inclusion and exclusion, activation policy and social work with marginal people. His publications in English include 'Gender, poverty and empowerment' in *Critical Social Policy* (with John Andersen), 'Lone mothers: how do they work and care in different welfare state regimes?', in T. Boje and A. Leira (eds) *Gender, welfare state and the market. Towards a new division of labour?* and 'The politics of marginal space', in J. Andersen and B. Siim (eds) *The politics of inclusion and empowerment. Gender, class and citizenship.*

Birgit Pfau-Effinger is Professor of Sociology and Director of the Centre for Globalisation and Governance, University of Hamburg. She has published widely in the fields of comparative welfare state analyses, comparative labour market analyses, welfare culture, social care, sociology of the family and gender relations, and the sociology of transformation. She was working group coordinator of the COST Action A13 programme 'Changing Labour Markets, Welfare Policies and Citizenship' and co-editor of *Work, Employment & Society*, and is coordinator of the international EU 5th Framework research project on 'Formal and informal work in Europe' (FIWE).

Laura Saurama is a Research Fellow in the Department of Social Policy at the University of Turku. She has studied the reasons for and consequences of early retirement in Finland and other Nordic countries. She was working on a Nordic research project, 'Unemployment, Early Retirement and Citizenship: Marginalisation and Integration in the Nordic Countries'. She was a member of COST Action A13 programme in the working group, 'Ageing and Work'.

Birte Siim is Associate Professor in the Institute of History, International and Social Studies, Aalborg University. She was coordinator of the national Danish research programme 'Gender, Empowerment and Politics' (1997-2002) and contributed to the Danish Commission of Democracy and Power with a project on 'Changes in Gendered Power Relations' (2001-03). Her recent publications include co-editing *The politics of inclusion and empowerment: Gender, class and citizenship* and *Contested concepts in gender and social policy,* and she is the author of *Gender and citizenship. Politics and agency in France, Britain and Denmark.*

Adrian Sinfield is Professor Emeritus of Social Policy at the University of Edinburgh, where he has worked since 1979. He has written mainly on the topic of social security, poverty, unemployment and the social division of welfare. He has been both Chair and President of the Social Policy Association. He was a co-founder of the Unemployment Unit and is Vice Chair of the Child Poverty Action Group.

Philip Taylor is Executive Director of the Cambridge Interdisciplinary Research Centre on Ageing, University of Cambridge. He has researched and written in the field of age and employment for 15 years. His current major research projects include one funded by the Social Sciences and Humanities Research Council of Canada which is looking at ageing and life-course issues in the information technology sector, and another funded by the European Social Fund which is looking at age barriers in small and medium-sized enterprises and developing interventions. He is a member of the Age Concern Cambridgeshire trustees committee and a member of the committee overseeing the Age Concern-sponsored 'Regions for all Ages' programme.

Alan Walker is Professor of Social Policy at the University of Sheffield, UK and co-founder and Chair of the European Foundation for Social Quality, Amsterdam. His research focuses on social policy and social gerontology, particularly with reference to the European Union. He is currently Director of the European Research Area in Ageing and, previously, was Director of the Economic and Social Research Council's 'Growing Older' programme on extending the quality of life, the UK National Collaboration on Ageing Research and the European Forum on Population Ageing Research. He has published more than 20 books, 200 reports and research monographs and 300 scientific papers. Recent books include: *Social quality: A vision for Europe* (co-edited with W. Beck, L. van der Maesen and F. Thomèse) and *Growing older: Quality of life in old age* (co-edited with C. Hennessy).

ONE

'Active' citizenship:
the new face of welfare

Per H. Jensen and Birgit Pfau-Effinger

In the course of the 1990s, the welfare states of modern western societies were confronted with new and changing challenges that were, in part, contradictory. These challenges were caused by exogenous processes, including globalisation and EU integration, as well as endogenous processes involving social and economical change within European societies (Esping-Andersen, 1999, Esping-Andersen et al, 2002). As a consequence of such processes, social security systems came under pressure (Ferrera and Rhodes, 2000; Scharpf and Schmidt, 2000; Hinrichs, 2001). At the same time, new demands pertaining to social security developed as a result of changes in the life histories of individuals (Naegele et al, 2003; Guillemard, Chapter Four, this volume). Processes such as increasing rates of unemployment in the 1990s, increasing labour-force participation of women, increasing migration to EU member states, demographic developments (particularly an increase in the proportion of older people) and the proliferation of unstable forms of employment, together with the related prospect of insecure income, have contributed to these changes (Lind and Møller, 1999). At the same time, new discourses concerning the legitimacy of welfare state spending have emerged at the cultural level. These have often been based on neoliberal and communitarian thinking and have led to the active alignment of welfare states towards the market, resulting in part in the questioning of the state's role in redistribution.

As a consequence of the processes by which welfare states have attempted to find solutions to these new challenges, many European welfare states were restructured in the 1990s and at the beginning of the new millennium. The nature of these changes is a contested issue among social-policy researchers. Some argue that European welfare states are converging towards a neoliberal type of welfare regime in which the welfare state assumes a more marginal role in relation to the market (Gilbert, 2002). Alan Walker (Chapter Three) argues that neoliberal economic globalisation has led to a transformation of

European welfare systems along at least two dimensions: firstly, in deregulation, privatisation and marketisation and secondly, in the shift from social justice to economic investment (the productive role of welfare) in the guidance of social policy. Other things being equal, these new developments may increase the risk of poverty and social exclusion. According to another type of argument, the restructuring was path-dependent and the institutional design and the underlying principles of welfare regimes were not questioned in principle (Barbier, 2004).

A broad debate has also developed in relation to citizenship and the issue of how citizenship was redefined in these processes. This development, it would seem, was somewhat contradictory: while some elements of citizenship were weakened during the restructuring processes, other elements were improved, such as social rights in relation to social care and elements of participation in the governance structures of welfare states.

Processes of social integration, marginalisation and exclusion have partly changed albeit in ambiguous ways, as a consequence of changes in the structures of welfare states, in welfare state policies and citizenship, as well as changes in underlying cultural values and ideals (Pfau-Effinger, 2004a, 2004d). On the one hand, members of some social groups, such as women and immigrants, were integrated to a greater degree into the labour market, which is the core institution for social integration in European welfare states (Siim, Chapter Ten). On the other hand, however, European societies are increasingly hosting new social groups of immigrants without legal status who are completely excluded from citizenship (Calloni, Chapter Six). Furthermore, the patterns of labour-market integration for older people have also changed in ambiguous ways: in part, the instrument of early retirement has been used by employers as a medium for the reduction of the number of workers; while on the other hand, older workers have also been increasingly integrated into labour markets (Maltby et al, 2004). During these processes, new patterns of social marginalisation have also developed.

Changes in the patterns of social integration are not restricted to the labour market. New forms of work and social integration have also increasingly developed outside labour markets, primarily within the private household. This has been associated with the development of new types of social rights in relation to social care. The manner in which these contribute to social integration, however, remains a contested issue in social policy research (Knijn and Kremer, 1997; Pfau-Effinger and Geissler, 2005).

In order to understand all these changes, it is important to include in our analysis the field of actors who are involved in these processes, as well as the changing nature of the constellations of actors. This has often been based on changes made to governance structure in welfare states. Contemporary welfare state policies aret multilevel polices, as policies and regulations at the local, national and supranational level are intertwined. Interrelated with these changes are changes in governance structures. This means that, in particular, the types of actors, institutions and organisations involved in the policy-making process have been extended. New private-public types of policy making have since developed, civil society is more involved in policy-making processes, and grassroots movements participate to a greater degree. The basic assumption put forward by Rune Halvorsen (Chapter Fourteen) is that established welfare institutions are now challenged by an increasing number of voices among individuals and groups belonging to the target group of 'activation', that is, those who are the victims of financial and social exclusion.

This also leads to the question as to the ways in which cultural change, in relation to the definition of citizenship and attitudes towards the welfare state, has influenced the development of welfare states in terms of their actual policies. Can these cultural changes explain differences between individual states in terms of these policies, and how do they contribute to explaining the ways in which citizenship is constructed?

As it turns out, the traditional concepts and approaches of welfare state research are not always adequate when attempting to analyse the changes outlined above. Thus, together with analysing these changes in welfare states and the notion of citizenship on which they are based, it has also been found necessary to analyse the concepts and approaches that have been applied in social policy research.

How can change in welfare states be analysed?

There is broad consensus in the literature that the welfare state is undergoing a process of change. However, the literature is marked by differing interpretations of the direction and strength of the change that is underway. This is due to the inadequate foundation of our conceptualisation(s) of the changes affecting the welfare state. Hall's (1993) distinction between first, second and third order change is often utilised, as are Pierson's (1994) conceptualisations of systemic and programmatic changes and his (2001) concepts of recommodification, cost containment and recalibration. These concepts have been particularly productive and useful in Hall's and Pierson's own analyses; however, on occasion it has proved difficult to put them to use in everyday applications. For one thing, there are examples when the distinctions between the levels and dimensions of change have become blurred (such as in van Kersbergen and Hemerijck, 1999); for another, the concepts fail to capture the possibility that path-breaking changes may take place through mechanisms other than 'increasing returns' (Pfau-Effinger, 2004b), for instance, by a series of small, incremental changes that may go almost unnoticed (Andersen, 2001; Hinrichs and Kangas, 2003).

In this volume, we make no pretence of having solved all the problems involved in conceptualising the changing face of welfare. The conceptualisations of change that are applied are thus tailored to the issues and problems raised in this book. The ambition of this volume is to analyse the changing face of welfare from a citizenship perspective. The concept of citizenship embraces an array of dimensions (Andersen and Jensen, 2002; Lister, 2002; Andersen, Chapter Five). Making citizenship the pivotal point of the study of change renders the following analytical levels relevant: discourses, rights and obligations, participation and the role perceptions of citizens themselves. In the same way, in this volume change will be analysed according to the following dimensions:

Discourses: New discourses serve as the precursors and successors of change in the welfare state. These discourses include new ideals about 'civicness' and new norms for appropriate and inappropriate civic behaviour. For example, the new discourse pertaining to activation is not merely a discourse about rebalancing the relationship between rights and obligations; rather, it contributes to the formulation of new civic virtues – a new role for the citizen – with its accompanying expectations for appropriate behaviour. Thus, new discourses call for a reinterpretation of the role of individuals as citizens. When they are analysed, however, there is a danger of confusing discourses with actual conditions of existence. Nevertheless, in order for discourses to materialise as actual change, they must become institutionalised, partly as change in the material and symbolic signals in the welfare state, partly as changes in citizens' schemes of perception.

The new discourses that have developed in European societies have often been related to neoliberal thinking and in part have had an impact on policy changes. Adrian Sinfield (Chapter Two) argues that social policy reforms, whether at national or intergovernmental levels such as the EU, the OECD and the World Bank, have mainly amounted to changes in discourses that have set off a process of 'policy closure'.

This process stems from the very ways problems have been formulated so as to restrict alternative means of handling them. Nonetheless, the extent and depth of change vary in a cross-national perspective within Europe.

Rights and obligations: With roots reaching back to Esping-Andersen (1990), an inherent aspect of the rights-obligations debate has been a tendency to focus on factors such as 'replacement rates' and 'duration of benefits', where it is simultaneously understood that, for example, 'long duration' is good, while 'short duration' is bad. However, on the basis of a citizenship perspective, there are no relations between rights and obligations that are 'right' or predetermined by nature. Instead, the focus must be aimed at so-called problem-solving capacities, such as that 'short duration' unemployment benefits may be adequate in combating marginalisation and exclusion in a situation with low unemployment, while 'long duration' may be necessary in periods of high and enduring unemployment. In other words, the relationship between rights and obligations ought to mirror the objective pressure of the problem, such as the size and structure of unemployment. Moreover, one must also consider the entire welfare architecture as a whole (Jensen, 1989; Esping-Andersen et al, 2002), as cutbacks in one programme may be compensated for by improvements in other programmes, thus rendering the overall situation unchanged. In other words, functionally equivalent results can be obtained by a variety of combinations of social programmes, social partners and firms. Furthermore, on account of factors such as implementation deficits (Schmid, 2003), it is not possible to draw conclusions regarding the actual conditions of existence for individuals on the basis of given rights and obligations. In sum, shifting relationships between rights and obligations must be evaluated as to whether they result in a loss of citizenship, epitomised as poverty, exclusion and marginalisation.

Participation: In keeping with the writings of T.H. Marshall (1950), full citizenship presupposes that the individual, as citizen, participates in all the various arenas, economic, social and political, of civic life. A lack of participation can thus be interpreted as a reflection of marginalisation and social isolation – or, in this case, a loss of citizenship. However, this does not merely have to do with observing degrees of participation in the arenas of civic life pointed out by T.H. Marshall. The welfare state is constantly developing new social technologies and the institutional production of welfare is constantly changing. Such changes are capable of generating new forms of participation and new arenas for participation. When it comes to activation, for example, it is standard practice in many countries for an individual action plan to be drafted prior to activation. An action plan makes it possible for individuals to have a say in the definition and solution of their own problems and can be interpreted as a new and advanced discipline technique. However, from a 'life political' perspective (Giddens, 1994), an action plan can also be interpreted in terms of an expansion of arenas of citizenship: it can provide freedom for individuals themselves to participate in the formation of their daily existence. To take this further, it might be possible to interpret an action plan as the crystallisation of an administrative citizenship.

Own role perception: A central dimension of citizenship deals with the manner in which citizens perceive themselves (for example, as inferior or as equals), and the manner in which the individual citizen is related to others (a meaningful life presupposes relations to others). This dimension of citizenship often plays a subdued role in the study of the new face of welfare, perhaps on account of problems pertaining to scientific method. For example, if one poses questions to homeless people living in a cardboard box about their situation and they respond, "This is my own choice and I am satisfied with my life", a statement of this nature would not be satisfactory in relation to a citizenship perspective. Consequently, when we analyse the way citizens perceive their own roles and their relations to others, we must utilise a combination of objective and subjective factors.

Finally, it is important to draw attention to the circumstance that changes relating to citizenship ought not be made the object of moralisation. Shifts in citizenship ought therefore to be analysed in relation to the historical and social conditions in which they are produced at a given moment in time. Or, to quote Durkheim, who is responsible for the landscape in which issues related to inclusion and exclusion are embedded, we must abandon "The habit, far too widespread ... of judging an institution, a practice or a moral maxim as if they are good or bad in or by themselves for all social types without distinction" (Durkheim, 1982, p 92).

Changes to the cultural and structural basis of citizenship

In all four dimensions outlined above – at the level of discourses, rights and obligations, participation and citizens' perceptions of their role – we can detect change in many respects that are based, according to our argument, on changes in underlying cultural values and ideal models of citizenship.

In industrial society, the concept of citizenship was previously based on a specific assumption concerning the role of the welfare state towards its citizens and the nature of citizenship itself. The citizen was constructed as a male employed citizen who, by virtue of his relatively strongly standardised employment biography on the basis of full-time employment, received social rights that were connected to the cultural concept of 'decommodification', that is, rights to maintain a reasonable standard of living during periods beyond employment such as unemployment, retirement and illness (Esping-Andersen, 1990; 1999). In the framework of the housewife marriage model that was the dominant family form in many countries, the citizenship of children and housewives was usually derived from the employment and citizenship status of the male breadwinner.

During the transition to a post-industrial service society, this basic cultural construction of citizenship has changed. We argue that this change can be characterised as a shift from a more passive cultural construction of citizenship towards an active one. The active citizen is expected to be autonomous and self-responsible, as well as flexible and extremely mobile (Sennett, 1998). Active citizens are expected to be able to create their biography individually and adapt it continuously to changing external conditions. Ulrich Beck (1986) speaks of a 'patchwork biography'. These citizens are also capable of engaging and organising themselves in relation to their own interests. In this context, the social rights of family members have been increasingly individualised, whereas derived social rights lose importance. Claiming responsibility for one's own life and well-being is, in this context, not merely an option: to a increasing degree it also represents an obligation.

This change was accompanied by a development towards an extended cultural construction of active citizenship based on a broader definition of the concept of work used in industrial society. The focus of social rights is no longer limited to waged work. Instead, the provision of care within the family or social networks has also increasingly constituted the basis of social citizenship, as reflected in the introduction of parental leave schemes, childcare allowances and new state schemes for paid informal elder care (Ungerson, 2000, 2003; Pfau-Effinger and Geissler, 2005). This new image of citizenship was introduced in the goals of welfare state policies in many welfare states, such as Great Britain, the Scandinavian countries and Germany. It is based on neoliberal as well as communitarian ideas (Pfau-Effinger, 2004c). It relates to different spheres of human life, the ways they are linked with the welfare state and the notions of citizenship connected with them:

- Active citizens as labour-market citizens. In this model social security entitlement is closely connected with labour-force participation and the extension of labour-force participation of women was promoted by many welfare states (Siim, Chapter Ten).
- Active citizens as consumers of social security. In this model citizens are increasingly expected to organise their social security themselves, such as by using schemes provided by the market.
- Active citizens as parents and caring relatives or friends. In this model informal family care was reconnected as an element of active citizenship. It was included in the cultural construction of citizenship and was connected with new social rights (Pfau-Effinger, Chapter Eleven).
- Active citizens who themselves engage in civil society for their own interests. In this model new forms of democratic participation were developed in civil society; and accordingly, new forms of governance structures were introduced in the welfare state.

New approaches to social policy and citizenship from a comparative perspective

The emergence of new ideas and new philosophies based on the notion of active citizenship has paved the way for changes in the institutional design of welfare states, namely, changes in the institutional production of welfare, which refer to the implementation, administration and governance of welfare programmes.

However, the development towards active citizenship in Europe is not uniform. The new cultural image of the 'active citizen' is interpreted differently in different welfare states (Halvorsen and Jensen, 2004, for the Scandinavian countries, Pfau-Effinger, 2004d, for Germany). Change is often ambiguous and path-dependent developments coexist in part with convergence in some policy fields.

The introduction of activation policies by European welfare states is an interesting example. The activation of social protection is one of the most important current transformations of social protection across Europe. However, there is disagreement over how it should be interpreted. Jean-Claude Barbier (Chapter Seven) analyses actual transformations and reforms that have occurred under the general banner of activation and their consequences on citizenship. The author argues that, in cross-national comparison, there is no such thing as a universal activation rationale: rather, a persisting diversity of solutions for activation exists from a cross-national perspective in both the broad and narrow senses. Even though social rights have been transformed considerably across Europe, Barbier shows that diverse forms of activation policies were developed by European welfare states, which in most cases fitted path-dependent processes in the restructuring of welfare state policies.

Jørgen Elm Larsen (Chapter Eight) introduces a critical view on the effects of activation policies by using the example of the impact of the activation policy on the integration of unemployed people in Denmark into the labour market. According to his findings, the effects of activation policies in terms of labour-market integration is very modest in most cases and, in the case of some activation measures, even negative. Within the framework of activation policies, however, empowering elements can also be strengthened in terms of the concept of the active citizen, as Asmund W. Born and Per H. Jensen demonstrate (Chapter Nine). They present an analysis of the implementation of the so-called individual action plan (IAP), which is yet another element of activation policies in the Danish welfare state. According to their argument, a new type of citizenship has emerged in this context, which is based on a new conception of the unemployed person as an active citizen. Born and Jensen then argue that the IAP represents the emergence of self-government or the formation of administrative citizenship. Accordingly, they argue, in the context of the late modern ad hoc society, administrative citizenship has, for all intents and purposes, become the proverbial ticket for admission to economic, social and political citizenship or a ticket for admission to the various arenas in society, as negotiations and self-presentation determine access to participation.

The degree to which the welfare state has supported the role of women as active citizen-workers in European welfare states is another example of the way that the convergent and path-dependent development of welfare state policies are interrelated. Birte Siim (Chapter Ten) argues that there is a tendency towards convergence towards an adult worker model with individualised social benefits in all the European welfare states, even though substantial differences remain in relation in the degree to which gender equality is promoted. While barriers to promoting women's role as 'active citizens' remain, particularly in neoliberal welfare states, Nordic welfare states have introduced new gender policies strongly supporting the new model of women as active citizens on the basis of the adult worker model with individualised social benefits. Birgit Pfau-Effinger (Chapter Eleven) argues that, in addition to conceptualisations of the active citizen that are based on full labour-market integration, there have also been new approaches towards the integration of family care in an extended cultural construction of the active citizen on the basis of new social rights for parents to provide care. The author shows that this model often coexists in welfare state policies with the "worker citizen model with state care". Social rights in relation to both models of the relationship between citizenship and care are most generous in social democratic welfare regimes. However, there is a trend towards an extension of social rights and services in relation to care in conservative welfare states as well.

Also, the consequences of welfare state policies for those who are excluded from active citizenship differ in a comparative perspective. As argued by Philip Taylor (Chapter Thirteen), early exit in the UK is primarily involuntary and, due to a minimum of social protection, causes the retirees economic hardship and low levels of self-esteem, such as the loss of citizenship. Early exit is also marked by (traditional) class-specific patterns in the dynamics and effects of early exit and early retirement. Historically, an alliance between employers, unions and government has excluded older workers in an attempt at rejuvenating the workforce. The UK experience thus indicates that a solution to new challenges or problems may be preconditioned by changes in actors and actor constellations. In contrast, the findings of an empirical study on the effects of the withdrawal of wage-earners from the labour market under early exit arrangements in relation to citizenship in Norway, Sweden, Finland and Denmark, reveal, as Laura Saurama (Chapter Twelve) argues, that the early exit situation does not correlate with a loss of social, economic and political integration for early retirees. Thus, the social democratic welfare state in the Nordic countries helps to uphold citizenship in the face of marginalisation and exclusion from the labour market.

The aims and central issues of this book

The purpose of this book is to improve, from a comparative perspective, our understanding of the causes and effects behind the changing relationships between social policy, marginalisation and citizenship. The causes of change are analysed at three levels simultaneously. At the macro level, analysis focuses on how the processes of societal change in different European countries, epitomised as a shift from fordism to post-fordism, pave the way for new directions in social policy and citizenship. At the institutional level, changes in social policy and citizenship may be perceived as a response to new challenges, for example, in terms of the flexibility of labour markets, the emergence of new family structures and changes in the life cycle, which bring about new patterns and features of economic, social and political marginalisation. At the level of social actors, changes in social policy and citizenship may be interpreted as an effect of changes in actor constellations. Thus, a multidimensional approach will be applied in order to explore the causes for amendments to welfare policy.

Amended welfare policies also produce new outcomes. Thus, new types of social policies can create new forms of social integration as well as new types of marginalisation and social conflict. New relationships between welfare states and their clients or consumers are emerging, thus, addressing the idea of active citizenship.

One of the specific characteristics of this book is its contribution to the further development of the theoretical and conceptual framework as to how to understand and interpret societal change. Cross-national analysis and national case studies provide new empirical insight into restructuring processes. The book differs from the existing literature in two ways: firstly, most publications within this field are based on static cross-national comparisons rather than applying a dynamic and change-oriented perspective. Secondly, the effects of policy changes are usually poorly understood in the welfare state literature.

The innovative approach of this book is made possible by the interdisciplinary cooperation of sociologists and political scientists. Moreover, the primary focus is on citizenship, which is unusual both in the policy literature and in the literature regarding change in social policy and marginalisation. The major questions raised are:

- First, what are the new developments in social policies and citizenship? What generates change and what is the character of change from a cross-national perspective? Do changes in social policy mirror changes in the character of social problems? How far is change an outcome of new actor constellations? How far is change generated by the emergence of new ideas and new philosophies: are policies 'new' and problems 'old'? Are welfare states undergoing profound changes: rapidly moving in qualitatively new directions? Or is change bounded: does ongoing welfare state reform remain within narrowly defined boundaries?
- Second, how do welfare states design policies in accordance with the concept of active citizenship, and how do such policies vary from an international comparative perspective? What are the philosophies behind these policies? What are the constellations of new actors?
- Third, what is the outcome of change and new policies directed at active citizenship? Does welfare policy reform create new patterns

of social marginalisation and social inequality? Are social rights weakened or are they merely adjusted to changes in society (recalibrated)? How does change affect citizenship, and what is citizenship? What are the implications of the shift in the cultural basis of citizenship towards the active citizen?

A multilevel approach is employed in order to respond to these questions. Thus, a central purpose of this book is to create speculation concerning conceptions of how the different dimensions of change are interlinked and to develop these conceptions further.

References

Andersen, J.G. (2001) 'Change without challenge? Welfare states, social construction of challenge and dynamics of path dependency', in J. Clasen (ed) *What future for social security? Debates and reforms in national and cross-national perspectives*, The Hague: Kluwer Law International, pp 121-38.

Andersen, J.G. and Jensen, P.H. (2002) 'Citizenship, changing labour markets and welfare policies: an introduction', in J.G. Andersen and P.H. Jensen (eds) *Changing labour markets, welfare policies and citizenship*, Bristol: The Policy Press, pp 1-13.

Barbier, J-C. (2004) 'Systems of social protection in Europe. Two contrasted paths to activation, and maybe a third', in J. Lind, H. Knudsen and H. Jørgensen (eds) *Labour and employment regulation in Europe*, Brussels: P.I.E.-Peter Lang, pp 233-53.

Beck, U. (1986) *Risikogesellschaft. Auf dem Weg in eine andere Moderne*, Frankfurt a.M.: Suhrkamp.

Durkheim, E. (1982) *The rules of sociological method and selected texts on sociology and its method*, S. Lukes (ed) London: Macmillan Press.

Esping-Andersen, G. (1990) *The three worlds of welfare capitalism*, Cambridge: Polity Press.

Esping-Andersen, G. (1999) *Social foundations of postindustrial economies*, Oxford: Oxford University Press.

Esping-Andersen, G., Gallie, D., Hemerijck, A. and Myles, J. (2002) *Why we need a new welfare state*, Oxford: Oxford University Press.

Ferrera, M. and Rhodes, M. (2000) 'Recasting European welfare states: an introduction', in M. Ferrera and M. Rhodes (eds) *Recasting European Welfare States. West European Politics*, Special issue, vol 23, no 2, pp 1-10.

Giddens, A. (1994) *Beyond left and right. The future of radical politics*, Cambridge: Polity Press.

Gilbert, N. (2002) *Transformation of the welfare state: The silent surrender of public responsibility*, Oxford: Oxford University Press.

Hall, P.A. (1993) 'Policy paradigms, social learning, and the state', *Comparative Politics*, vol 25, no 3, pp 275-96.

Halvorsen, R. and Jensen, P.H. (2004) 'Activation in Scandinavian welfare policy: Denmark and Norway in a comparative perspective', *European Societies*, vol 6, no 4, pp 461-83.

Hinrichs, K. (2001) 'Ageing and public pension reforms in western Europe and North America: patterns and politics', in J. Clasen (ed) *What future for social security? Debates and reforms in national and cross-national perspective*, The Hague: Kluwer Law International, pp 157-78.

Hinrichs, K. and Kangas, O. (2003) 'When a change is big enough to be a system shift: small system-shifting adjustments in pension policy in Finland and Germany', *Social Policy and Administration*, vol 37, no 6, pp 573-91.

Jensen, P.H. (1989) 'Employment and unemployment policies and the functioning of the labour market in a comparative perspective', *Acta Sociologica*, vol 32, no 4, pp 405-17.

Knijn, T. and Kremer, M. (1997) 'Gender and the caring dimension of welfare states: towards inclusive citizenship', *Social Politics*, vol 4, no 3, pp 328-61.

Lind, J. and Møller, I.H. (eds)(1999) *Inclusion and exclusion: Unemployment and non-standard employment in Europe*, Aldershot: Ashgate.

Lister, R. (2002) 'Citizenship and changing welfare states', in J.G. Andersen and P. Jensen (eds) *Changing labour markets, welfare policies and citizenship*, Bristol: The Policy Press, pp 39-58.

Maltby, T., de Vroom, B., Mirabile, M.L. and Øverbye, E. (eds) (2004) *Ageing and the transition to retirement: A comparative analysis of European welfare states*, Aldershot: Ashgate.

Marshall, T. (1950) 'Citizenship and social class', in T.H. Marshall and T. Bottomore (1992) *Citizenship and social class*, London: Pluto Press.

Naegele, G., Barkholdt, C., de Vroom, B., Andersen, J. Goul, and Krämer, K. (2003) *A new organisation of time over working life*, Dublin: European Foundation for the Improvement of Living and Working Conditions.

Pfau-Effinger, B. (2004a) *Development of culture, welfare states and women's employment in European societies*, Aldershot, Ashgate.

Pfau-Effinger, B. (2004b) 'Culture and path dependence of welfare state development', Paper presented at the European Network for Social Policy Analyses (ESPANET) Annual Conference 'European social policy: meeting the needs of a new Europe', University of Oxford, 9-11 September.

Pfau-Effinger, B. (2004c) *'Aktivierte, Citizens', Arbeitsgesellschaft und Globalisierung*, Discussion Paper Series. Centre for Globalisation and Governance, University of Hamburg.

Pfau-Effinger, B. (2004d) 'Culture and welfare state policies: reflections on a complex interrelation', *Journal of Social Policy*, vol 34, no 1, pp 3-20.

Pfau-Effinger, B. and Geissler, B. (eds) (2005) *Care and social integration in European societies*, Bristol: The Policy Press.

Pierson, P. (1994) *Dismantling the welfare state*, Cambridge: Cambridge University Press.

Pierson, P. (2001) 'Post-industrial pressures on the mature welfare states', in P. Pierson (ed) *The new politics of the welfare state*, Oxford: Oxford University Press, pp 80-106.

Scharpf, F.W. and Schmidt, V.A. (eds) (2000) *Welfare and work in the open economy*, vol 1-2, Oxford: Oxford University Press.

Schmid, G. (2003) 'Activating labour-market policy: "flexicurity" through transitional labour markets', in J.-P. Touffut (ed) *Institutions, innovation and growth*, Cheltenham, UK/Northampton, MA: Edward Elgar, pp 68-96.

Sennett, R. (1998) *The corrosion of character: Personal consequences of work in the new capitalism*, New York, NY: W.W. Norton.

Ungerson, C. (2000) 'Thinking about the production and consumption of long-term care in Britain: does gender still matter?', *Journal of Social Policy*, vol 29, no 4, pp 623-43.

Ungerson, C. (2003) 'Commodified care work in European labour markets', *European Societies*, vol 5, no 84, pp 377-96.

van Kersbergen, C.J. and Hemerijck, A. (1999) 'Negotiated policy change: towards a theory of institutional learning in tightly coupled welfare states', in D. Braun and A. Busch (eds) *Public policy and political ideas*, Cheltenham: Edward Elgar, pp 168-85.

TWO

The goals of social policy: context and change

Adrian Sinfield

In recent years changing labour markets accompanied by increased and persisting unemployment have been seen as requiring reforms in social security for those in the labour market. Across many countries there have been reductions in the duration and replacement rates of social security and restriction in its coverage (Clasen, 1999; Gallie and Paugam, 2000; ILO, 2000). Thus, "[i]ncreases in insecurity in society have been accompanied by decreases in the availability of social security" (Hill, 1999, p 89).

These declines in social protection have been driven by changing policy goals. There has been a narrowing and obscuring of objectives, which has had a considerable significance on people's social and economic security. Governments' concerns with present and future costs have risen and the imperative to do more for less has been promoted to a higher priority with much emphasis on the means and decreasing mention of the ends of social security. The original and primary goals of social security programmes have become insecure – 'precarious values', to use Burton Clark's phrase (1956). While these primary goals still receive occasional, almost ritual, acknowledgement, their connection to both general and specific day-to-day management has become obscured in many countries.

This chapter examines these policy changes and the reasons underlying them. This needs a broadly-based analysis which can make the links between "the personal troubles of milieu" and "the public issues of social structure" (Mills, 1959, p 9). Such a framework for analysis reveals the extent of change in policy thinking and the importance of 'policy closure' which occurs when the change in discourse – the presentation and discussion of an issue – shapes the policy agenda with effects that may be little recognised. It can "pre-empt the possibility of other ways of thinking and talking about the subject" and "invalidate the perceptions and devalue the experiences of those" who do not adopt this form of discourse (Veit-Wilson, 2000, pp 146-7). "Power in society is exercised partly through the privileging of particular modes of discourse, and the disqualifying of others; when subordinate groups speak, it is in a 'borrowed language'" (Gray, 1989, p 145).

'Policy closure' in the United Kingdom

What these general trends mean in different societies is often difficult to deduce from the international language that is used. The one country that I have studied in detail shows how marginalisation can be reinforced through policy change. Policy closure by Conservative governments in the UK after 1979 led to what was frequently claimed to be a change in the culture of the whole social security system. Much effort was devoted to decoupling the issue of the delivery of benefits from that of tackling poverty. The idea of a scientific concept of poverty was attacked and ridiculed (for example, the Department of Health and Social Security [DHSS], 1985; Moore, 1989, when he was responsible for social security as Secretary of State for Social Services). The establishment of a Benefits Agency to deliver benefits was used to remove the two central issues of adequacy and take-up from management concern. The benefits for people of working age were particularly targeted, with countless changes to controls.

Mass advertising and media campaigns against benefit fraud reinforced the negative image of both recipients and the system. In 1996, for example, Edinburgh buses carried full-length posters: "Spotlight on benefit cheats – the free ride on benefit fraud is about to stop – we are picking out the cheats in Edinburgh". The freefone service for social security advice and the out-of-hours emergency phoneline were replaced by a freefone to report cheats, and there were many other examples of taking what William Ryan (1971) identified as 'blaming the victim' to new heights of accusation (Cook, 1989 and 1997; Dean and Taylor-Gooby, 1992).

This was accompanied by and reinforced with much conflation and inflation of the official estimates of fraud. Future policy historians are likely to comment more forcefully than contemporary commentators have done on the government's use of evidence on fraud in ways that were themselves fraudulent. Figures for fraud, which at least one Secretary of State for Social Security went out of his way to publicise, included not only "confirmed fraud" but also the two highest levels of suspected fraud – "certain that a fraudulent situation has been discovered but insufficient information to establish the fraud" and "strong suspicion that fraud exists but no proof" (quoted in Sainsbury, 1996, p 18).

The systematic delegitimisation of both recipients and benefits weakened public support for both, making it easier to reduce, cut back and police benefits more harshly. Where independent research indicated poverty, the government saw the growth of an underclass and a culture of dependency. It was argued that the problems lay more with the poor, their lack of responsibility and their mismanagement of resources than with the levels of benefit. The broader goals of income maintenance or compensation, let alone of social integration and solidarity, became largely discarded. This successful policy closure also resulted in research closure. The shift of power in the labour market, strengthening the command of employers, was left unanalysed and relatively unnoticed.

Across the European Union and beyond

Discerning where the changes were greatest must not be allowed to dominate analysis across the European Union. However, "most member states are moving towards more flexible and less contributory schemes and towards greater individualisation of social security rights" (Commission of the European Communities [CEC], 2000c, p 21; see also CEC, 2000a and 2000b, p 6; "well-targeted protection is essential"). There has been little acknowledgement that greater use of means-testing or targeting – the CEC's main recommended instrument for achieving greater efficiency – tends to involve a shift away from certain goals such as compensation and the prevention of poverty. Concern with achieving greater efficiency has been presented as if it were only a matter of changing the means and little attention has been given to the impact on the intended goals and the shift in discourse and policy agenda which the goals of efficiency have brought about.

In 1999 four new key objectives for social protection were presented as part of the "modernisation of the European social model" (CEC, 2000a, p 3 and 2000b, p 2). Two of the "broad objectives to which social protection systems should respond" became "to make work pay and provide secure income" and "to promote social inclusion" (CEC, 2000a, p 3). "A guiding principle of the new Social Policy Agenda will be to strengthen the role of social policy as a productive factor" (CEC, 2000b, p 2).

The Commission's *Social protection in Europe 1999* gave particular attention to this change. A key chapter, 'Making social protection systems more employment-friendly', cited "the general consensus across the Union ... that social policy towards the unemployed as well as others not in work should shift away from *passive* income support towards *active* measures to help them into employment" (CEC, 2000a, p 94, emphasis added).

'Active' is used to denote training and employment measures helping people into work and 'passive' to refer to benefits encouraging inactivity. The use of these terms provides a particularly clear example of policy closure and the management of goals across many countries by the deliberate reshaping of discourse (see Schmidt, 2000, for a comparative analysis). The policy slogans, 'active' and 'passive', have become so well established that discussions of adequacy, take-up and compensation are disappearing off the policy agenda for those who are seen as having any potential labour-force attachment (Sinfield, 1997 and 2001a).

Although the 'active' theme appeared in Commission employment reports at the end of the 1980s, it was only after *The OECD jobs study* (1994a, 1994b) that the passive-to-active shift was made explicit. EU reports still showed a better awareness of the need for balance than most OECD or World Bank writing, explicitly recognising that so-called passive benefits "still need to provide an acceptable level of income" (CEC, 2000a, p 17).

The World Bank's proposals for people out of work were much tougher. A new policy discourse of 'social risk management', repackaging social protection, moved away from the concept of social insurance towards more targeted methods (Holzmann and Jørgensen, 2000). Governments should "reduce their direct involvement in risk mitigation"; act more as regulators of private insurance and private pensions; and "focus their involvement in coping on the incapacitated, very vulnerable, and crisis situations" (Holzmann and Jørgensen, 2000, p 26). Unemployed people were omitted altogether and support was only to be provided for "the critically poor". Only a footnote revealed who these were: "the poor, who could not provide for themselves even if employment opportunities did exist" (Holzmann and Jørgensen, 2000, p 10 and footnote 7). Public policy's direct responsibility was restricted to those seen as 'the deserving poor' in Victorian terms. Similarly, the World Bank's discussion of what has come to be called "optimal unemployment insurance design" argued that benefits should be cut as unemployment becomes longer and "premiums [should be] ... based on extensive experience rating" to avoid "adverse selection" or "moral hazard" (Karni, 1999, abstract). This ignored how experience-rating has been used to exclude marginal or "poor risks".

The dominant "active-over-passive" discourse has led to a failure to recognise that the conventional usage of these two terms is, in scientific terms, mistaken, misleading and politically loaded (Sinfield, 2001a). It is mistaken because there are many features of a benefits system which can assist and promote activity as well as elements of labour-market policies which can work against renewed employment activity and the best interests of the individual and the wider society. It is misleading because the routine use of these terms – especially the inclusion of 'active' in the phrase, 'active labour-market policies', and even more its abbreviation into ALMPs – discourages any systematic consideration of the form and extent of activity achieved. The assumption of action is built in, and any failure is transferred to those who are the object of the policy, rather than the policy itself. The unemployed are seen as failing the programmes. By contrast, connecting 'passive' to 'benefits' fosters a picture that those out of work are "resting on benefits", as one UK Conservative Minister of Employment put it (*Hansard*, 1994).

The usage is also politically loaded because of the way that the two terms resonate in public debate. No politician speaks in favour of 'passive' measures of supporting income when 'active' ones are available. "The notion of 'passive' has a pejorative connotation, whereas 'active' sounds virile, dynamic and positive" (Kosonen, 2000, p 421). In consequence, what is classified as 'passive' income support is condemned to lower priority, with second-class status and funding at best, and such 'support' to stigmatising dismissal, ever-tightening and humiliating conditions and continual cuts, if not abolition, at worst. This policy closure is well illustrated in the title of Murray Edelman's book: *Political language* and its subtitle, *Words that succeed and policies that fail* (Edelman, 1977). Successful activity is simply assumed of labour-market policies, while benefits are cast in a very different light – without necessarily good evidence for either viewpoint.

This reframing of the role of social security has a long history. "Because they derive from conflicting frames, the same body of evidence can be used to support quite different policy positions" (Rein and Schon, 1993, p 148). The context within which reframing occurs needs to be kept in mind instead of allowing policy and research discussions to become context-stripped (Andersen, 2001). This leads us to ask who is doing the reframing and from what position. We need to show more clearly how "discursive frameworks are connected with ways of governing" (Walters, 2000, p 148).

"What is the role played, for example, by government bureaucracies, or by inter-governmental organisations such as the OECD, which (without any formal competence) skilfully combines economic expertise, networking and backing by political power? Such issues should be addressed more critically than is often done" (Andersen, 2001, p 125). A comparative perspective can help to show how native discourses become overtaken by World Bankese, OECDese or Euroese each with their own particular and powerful reframing devices and policy closures. It is very unusual to find an instance of ILOese, and this in itself is an indication of the distribution of power across international organisations today.

The reforms have been accompanied by the merging and renaming of departments of social security in many countries under what Goodin has called the "perverse principles of welfare reform". This rebadging is not just cosmetic but "a genuine (and substantially successful) attempt to shift the function of protecting people against life's uncertainties away from the public sector and towards private sector institutions of market, family and community – institutions which ... are substantially not up to the task" (Goodin, 2003, p 203).

These changes, together with their reframing and policy closures, become one more reason for not accepting official definitions of social security or protection as setting the bounds for research and analysis (Berghman, 1997a and 1997b; Sinfield, 2001b). The myth of the welfare state, accompanied by the conventional notion of an excessive and 'premature' welfare state radically reversing inequalities, was exposed by Richard Titmuss nearly half a century ago (Titmuss, 1958, ch 2; also in Abel-Smith and Titmuss, 1987, ch 2 and Alcock et al, 2001, part II, 2). Many leading politicians and analysts since then have used what have since been labelled Thatcherite or Reaganite modes of discourse about how the welfare state weakens the family and destroys the moral fibre of society. Specifically linking the social division of welfare to the changing social division of labour, Titmuss drew attention to other forms of intervention in addition to public benefits and services which affected the welfare of the people – in particular, tax welfare and occupational welfare. These, he argues, contributed to and reinforced exclusion and marginalisation with "the demoralising effect of cumulative social rejection" (Titmuss in Alcock et al, 2001, p 145).

Today the case for not confining social policy to the welfare state is even stronger. With shifts in responsibility for providing, arranging and financing protection – and the consequent shifts in power – any analysis has to engage with non-state activities and take account of these functional alternatives to the welfare state. The much less visible and publicly accountable social protection of occupational welfare means that many established workers are much better protected against the usual range of risks than the rest. Governments have recognised the importance of these measures by supporting and encouraging them with tax reliefs which effectively cut the cost of labour to the employer and increase the value of the benefit to the employee. These hidden tax benefits now play an important policy role in many countries (Bryson, 1992).

Taxation, power and marginalisation

"The art of taxation consists in so plucking the goose as to obtain the largest amount of feathers with the least amount of hissing." Jean Baptiste Colbert, Finance Minister to the Sun King, Louis XIV of France, captures what we should be taking more account of – the rich variety of ways in which state redistributive processes, apart from those accounted for as public expenditure, are providing an invisible 'tax welfare state'. This encourages and subsidises support for many groups in society (generally the better-off) at the expense of many others (generally the poorer): it promotes a society in which the security of some is underwritten by the insecurity of others (Hill, 1999).

The combination of better state protection for the regular worker and the growth of functional alternatives leave those most vulnerable to changing labour markets significantly less protected. This is why some are less likely to become marginalised or excluded than others: for example, employers' severance payments to displaced workers are often tax exempt. In the UK the tax relief for these 'private' benefits to some redundant workers have for many years cost more than twice the contributory state benefit for the much greater number of unemployed workers.

One obvious – but surprisingly unremarked – effect of the increasing privatisation and individualisation of benefit systems at the time of increased turbulence in the labour market are poorer pensions for those without a full working career – and so a greater risk of poverty in retirement. With higher unemployment, far more people have multiple breaks in their working careers and generally lose much more with contribution breaks from private or occupational pensions than from state schemes. If the tax benefits for pensions are taken into account, the divisive effect becomes even clearer as private pensions are particularly privileged by tax relief. In most countries these tax benefits constitute the largest tax expenditure; often by far the largest (Sinfield, 2000). Private pension contributions are discounted for tax up to a generous limit, lump-sum payments are tax free up to a high ceiling and the fund profits are still basically exempt from tax.

In the UK tax benefits for non-state pensions cost the taxpayer almost one third more than all means-tested assistance for the poorest old people. While the government itself has made no estimate of the distribution of the pension tax benefit, there is a strongly regressive pattern with half the benefit of tax relief on pension contributions going to the top 10% of taxpayers, and a quarter to the top 2.5% alone (Agulnik and Le Grand, 1998, p 410).

Despite governments' continuing emphasis on the need for the better targeting of scarce resources to protect those in greatest need, this is generous redistribution upwards. These "upside-down" benefits (Surrey, 1973, p 37) have long provided most support to the most well-off, less to the average paid, and very little to the lower-paid and the poor – probably nothing at all to most low-paid who will not be receiving non-state pensions but are most vulnerable to poverty. This is a form of reverse targeting totally counter to social security reforms concentrating help on those most in need (Kvist and Sinfield, 1997).

This illustrates how changes in the labour market can combine with changes from social to private provision subsidised by the hidden tax welfare state to reinforce marginalisation in later life. This helps, for example, to explain how women, particularly those taking a break to raise children, lose out particularly badly in country after country. They have a very much greater risk of poverty in old age and are also forced into dependency on a usually better-paid male partner (Ginn et al, 2001).

These inequality-widening tax benefits are not revealed in public expenditure statistics and are not subject to the same parliamentary and public scrutiny and assessment that welfare state programmes are. If the World Bank – and even certain sections of the European Commission – are successful in shifting countries to placing a greater reliance on private provision, this problem will be very much greater (Ferge, 2002).

Another tax change deserving much closer attention is the shift from direct to indirect taxation in many countries (Joumard, 2002). The distributional implications of this move have received little attention as political and public debates in most countries focus on direct income tax. In the UK the incidence of total taxation has hitherto been spread fairly evenly across the whole population, but for the last decade the burden of taxation has fallen more heavily on the poorest groups in society. In 2001-02 the poorest fifth of households paid a fifth more of their income in taxes than the richest fifth – 42% compared with 34% (Lakin, 2003).

While the average share of income taken in taxes has been around 35-37% over the last quarter of a century, there has been a marked shift downward in the incidence of taxation. As inequalities have widened, people in poverty have had to contribute proportionately more than the rich for the cost of benefits and services. A major cause has been the shift from direct to indirect taxation as increasing income tax brings more 'hissing' from the tax geese than the less visible growth of indirect taxes, which fall much more heavily on lower incomes.

In these and many other ways the income tax system protects some people (the better-off) from the risk of poverty far more effectively than the social security system protects the majority of the population. Despite such evidence, there is little challenge to the belief of the well-off that they pay the taxes but others receive the benefits. In consequence taxation can reinforce and even widen inequalities, not only without public and parliamentary debate, but also while the dominant discourse frames debate in such a way that it closes off more egalitarian policies.

The value of a broadly defined measure of social policy

These brief examples of the neglected workings of the tax system illustrate the need to use a broad definition of social policy: "the underlying as well as the professed rationale by which social institutions and groups are used or brought into being to ensure social preservation or development" (Townsend, 1975, p 6).

If labour market changes are increasing insecurity at the same time as states are stepping back from the direct provision of social protection, those without regular employment in jobs where they can obtain occupational benefits subsidised by tax welfare become even more marginalised. The increased reliance on social assistance will, at best, bring the less secure in at the bottom. In policy debates choice is posed in terms of universal benefits to all, including those who do not need them, or more efficient, better-targeted selective benefit. In reality, means-tested conditionality for the poorer-off is generally accompanied by concealed public subsidies through the tax system which help the better-off to purchase their own protection. This closing off of universalistic and solidaristic policies is supported by reframing the concept of fairness – seen, no longer as the collective sharing of risks so that social costs do not fall unfairly, but as a fairness based on an individualistic calculus where you get out what you put in. Nothing becomes 'wasted' in redistribution or social protection in this 'individualisation of the social' (Ferge, 1997; Guillemard, 1986 and 2000).

The implications of widening inequalities

When inequalities are widening in many countries, the changing patterns of social security become all the more important. In the UK, for example, inequality grew faster at the end of the last century than at any other time for which we have reliable statistics. The poorest tenth of households experienced no boost to their income in real terms after 1979, while the richest fifth of households gained a 60 or 70% increase (against an average 50%). Exclusion from occupational welfare and tax benefits reinforced the insecurity of those on the margin.

The differing patterns and trends in inequality across similar countries are particularly important for policy. They reinforce the need for a broad, societal or structural policy approach. Differences in national redistributive policies are a key part of the explanation for the "differing experience across OECD countries with regard to inequality in disposable household income.... The driving force [of inequality] is social in origin, rather than trade or technology, [and this] means that there is more scope for political leadership" (Atkinson, 1999, pp 23 and 24). So policy matters.

The significance of patterns of inequality for the quantity of life, let alone its quality, is being brought out across many countries, both rich and poor. In the UK men in Glasgow City can expect to die 10 years sooner than men living in East Dorset or the Three Rivers area of Hertfordshire. "A growing body of new evidence ... shows that life expectancy in different countries is dramatically improved where income differences are smaller and societies are more socially cohesive" (Wilkinson, 1996, p 1).

These literally vital differences provide further evidence that inequality cannot be ignored in developing structural policies. Yet the significance of resource inequalities in policy analysis and making is largely overlooked (see Phillips, 1999, for a thought-provoking discussion of the different dimensions of equality and inequality). The work of Robert Coles raises issues which have not sufficiently informed the policy debate. The first volume of his *The children of crisis* (1964) analysed the lives of young children growing up in the deep south of the US in the first years of desegregation. The inferior views of themselves developed by southern black children, as opposed to white, were expressed in their drawings. By six or seven years of age, children portrayed scenes that revealed the considerable inequalities that were a part of their daily lives. This suggests that the unequal relationships give rise to or sustain the inferior self-images which they have already acquired at a very young age.

Black children's drawings of themselves and white classmates of the same size revealed very different perceptions. Black children drew themselves smaller and much more carelessly and sketchily, with the bodies generally 'less intact', such as lacking many facial features and fingers. The body was often not firmly located on the ground and the clothes were only partly drawn. They treated images of other black children in the same way (Coles, 1964, figures 1-12). When one black girl, Ruby, was eight and Coles had known her for two years, he

> asked her why she thought twice about how much brown she would give to a colored child ... she replied directly: "When I draw a white girl, I know she'll be okay, but with the colored it's not so okay. So I try to give the colored as even a chance as I can, even if that's not the way it will end up being". (Coles, 1964, p 50)

This much understanding at the age of eight! Other pictures revealed that the children, both black and white, had a very early understanding of the unequal world in which they grew up, especially one showing the different neighbourhoods of black and white children (Coles, 1964, figure 13).

So inequality matters – even for the world view which children are developing at such a young age. This must affect their hopes and plans, and therefore their own efforts as they grow up. I have seen no later exploration of these issues: what pictures would children on the margins – young Roma children, for example – draw for the Robert Coles of today? The work draws attention to the importance of preventing marginalisation from occurring in the first place; and, with policy reforms shifting from the social to the individual, the strategy of prevention has been much neglected.

Conclusions

"Today social and employment policy is characterized by its avoidance of questions about the wider system, in favour of a focus on the 'margins', and its downplaying of the involuntary dimension of unemployment while opting for a very subjective and personalized approach to the problem" (Walters, 2000, p 9). This analysis of labour-market policies and their development in one country, but over a whole century, catches the dominant international discourse.

Marginalisation and social insecurity cannot be successfully tackled by a focus on the margins alone without the structural analyses which link private troubles and public issues.

A broader view of social policy seeks to take account of all the different distributive mechanisms in society – not just the officially defined policies. As C. Wright Mills advised: "Do not allow public issues as they are officially formulated, or troubles as they are privately felt, to determine the problems that you take up for study" (Mills, 1959, p 226 – the final rule for what he called 'intellectual craftmanship'). This chapter has concentrated on some of the mechanisms, particularly social security and the tax system, but a full analysis would require more attention to others, including the regulation of the labour market and the extent to which this protects or constrains employers, employees, and the rest of society.

To use a discourse of health policy, there is a need to restore the balance between work 'upstream' on structural and preventive analyses and policies and the remedial and ameliorative 'downstream' policies with their more individualised focus on those so trapped into marginal positions that we call the people themselves 'marginal'. Upstream policies are needed to "tackle the causal chains which run back into and from the basic structure of society" to prevent exclusion and poverty from occurring in the first place (Acheson, 1998, pp 7-8).

While social policy research has been both improving and increasing, the welfare of many has got worse with widening inequality and increasing and deepening poverty in many countries. Yet much social science research gives little sense of the structural shifts in resources, status and power which have been occurring. "In social science there is no neutral act" (Ferge, 1979, p 15), but we have become caught up in debates set by others, and with insufficient awareness of this.

"Sociology's attention should, for a while at least, be focussed on the powerful and the consequences of their power on us all. For if it is not, then sociology will continue to be shaped by the powerful and will continue to obscure and mystify their power" (Bell, 1978, p 37). As with sociology, the balance in research on social policy has suffered. Much of this research has been on welfare states and much less on the welfare of the people – what Victorians called 'the condition of the people'. Insufficient attention has been given to identifying and studying the processes, whether public policies or not, which most affect people's welfare. What welfare states do is, of course, often discussed and examined, but such analysis is largely in terms of inputs and outputs – and much less in terms of outcomes for people and the wider society. There has been a neglect of issues of solidarity and social cohesion and a timidity about discussing any form of social vision (Ferge, 2001).

These omissions are significant because we can only make sense of the impact of changing labour markets and changing social protection – and the consequent power shifts – on citizenship by taking closer account of their impact on the condition of the people, and not simply, for example, the numbers in or out of work. In *States of denial: Knowing about atrocities and suffering* (2001), Stan Cohen analyses the personal, intellectual and political ways in which uncomfortable realities are avoided and even denied – but not confronted or tackled. There is a potential for applying this approach to poverty and marginalisation and the ways in which the rest of society, including social scientists, respond to them.

This raises what might be called the problem of 'passive' research. Social scientists researching the inequalities of health appear much less confined by official definitions of public issues and more active in trying to influence policy agenda, pursuing 'policy openings' as well as documenting 'policy closures' (Townsend et al, 1992). Without losing a critical, independent stance, they have identified alternative 'frames' to be considered, despite considerable political, commercial and other resistance both at country and international level. For many years the UK government would not consider discussion of health inequalities, and the tobacco and alcohol industries have long been vigorously challenging research on smoking and alcoholism.

This may be a particularly good time to take a more positive approach to reframing the research and policy agenda and relating policy trends to the structural issues of inequality in power, status and resources. Nationally and internationally, inside and outside governments, there are signs of growing concern with broader goals of welfare. In terms of the most limited objective, the Irish and UK governments, for example, have committed themselves to poverty reduction targets. European social scientists have been monitoring government commitments on poverty (Gordon and Townsend, 2000, with a statement signed by many hundred social scientists). EU indicators of social inclusion have been developed (Atkinson et al, 2001), and there have been increasing calls for the establishment of national and international minimum-income standards (Veit-Wilson, 1998).

Analyses of the 'social quality of Europe' are being developed by social scientists across Europe with a more positive focus than the eradication of negatives such as poverty (Beck et al, 1997, 2001; Walker, 2000). The ILO InFocus Programme on Socio-Economic Security has the theme, 'seeking distributive justice – basic security for all' (ILO, 1999, 2000).

However, many governments and influential international and supranational bodies have become increasingly concerned with narrowly defined and short-term cost-conscious objectives of efficiency which neglect the broader concerns of substantive justice. These individualise the causes of the problems as well as their solutions – and much social science research has slid 'downstream' with little challenge to the continuing 'individualisation of the social' (Ferge, 1997; Guillemard, 1986, 2000; Twine, 1994). This weakens attempts to promote broader, societal strategies of integration with their elements of risk-sharing, redistribution and compensation for social costs.

This chapter challenges those concerned about the impact of changes in labour markets and social protection on our societies to give greater priority to the advice of C. Wright Mills and to set analysis of all interventions in the labour market in a broad, structural context. A "frame-reflective discourse" (Rein and Schon, 1993, p 150) may also help to make a contribution to shaping and opening up policy and research agenda rather than allowing the closing of policy options to pass unnoticed. Making political and official reframings, their causes and consequences more visible and open to analysis may contribute to a better balance of both policy and research on upstream as well as downstream issues.

Note

I am very grateful to Jørgen Goul Andersen and, once again, to Dorothy Sinfield for their comments and advice.

References

Abel-Smith, B. and Titmuss, K. (eds) (1987) *The philosophy of welfare: Selected writings of Richard M. Titmuss*, London: Allen and Unwin.

Acheson, Sir D. (chair) (1998) *Independent inquiry into inequalities in health*, London: Stationery Office.

Agulnik, P. and Le Grand, J. (1998) 'Tax relief and partnership pensions', *Fiscal Studies*, vol 19, no 4, pp 403-28.

Alcock, P., Glennerster, H., Oakley, A. and Sinfield, A. (2001) *Welfare and well-being: Richard Titmuss's contribution to social policy*, Bristol: The Policy Press.

Andersen, J.G. (2001) 'Change without challenge? Welfare states, social construction of challenge and dynamics of path dependency', in J. Clasen (ed) *What future for social security? Debates and reforms in national and cross-national perspective*, The Hague: Kluwer, pp 121-38.

Atkinson, A.B. (1999) 'Is rising inequality inevitable? A critique of the transatlantic consensus', WIDER Annual Lectures 3, Helsinki: United Nations University World Institute for Development Economics Research (UNU/WIDER).

Atkinson, A.B., Cantillon, B., Marlier, E. and Nolan, B. (2001) *Indicators for social inclusion in the European Union*, Brussels: CEC, September.

Beck, W., van der Maesen, L. and Walker, A. (eds) (1997) *The social quality of Europe*, The Hague: Kluwer.

Beck, W., van der Maesen, L. and Walker, A. (eds) (2001) *The social quality: A vision for Europe*, The Hague: Kluwer.

Bell, C. (1978) 'Studying the locally powerful: personal reflections on a research career', in C. Bell and S. Encel (eds) *Inside the whale: Ten personal accounts of social research*, Rushcutters Bay: Pergamon Press, pp 14-40.

Berghman, J. (1997a) 'The social security concept and its operationalisation in a comparative context', in *Verfassung, Theorie und Praxis des Sozialstaats: Festschrift für Hans F. Zacher zum 70, Geburtstag*, Heidelberg: Müller Verlag, pp 15-33.

Berghman, J. (1997b) 'Redefining social security', in A. Robertson (ed) *Unemployment, Social Security and the Social Division of Welfare*, New Waverley Paper 13, Edinburgh: University of Edinburgh, pp 61-9.

Bryson, L. (1992) *Welfare and the state*, Basingstoke: Macmillan.

CEC (Commission of the European Communities) (2000a) *Report on social protection in Europe 1999*, Brussels: CEC, 21 March, COM (2000) 163 final.

CEC (2000b) *Communication from the Commission to the Council, the European Parliament, the Economic and Social Committee and the Committee of the Regions: Social policy agenda*, Brussels: CEC.

CEC (2000c) *MISSOC 1999: Social protection in the member states of the European Union, Brussels*: CEC Employment and Social Affairs.

Clark, B.R. (1956) 'Organisational adaptation and precarious values', *American Sociological Review*, vol 21, no 3, pp 327-36.

Clasen, J. (1999) 'Beyond social security: the economic value to giving money to unemployed people', *Journal of European Social Security*, vol 1, no 2, pp 151-80.

Cohen, S. (2001) *States of denial: Knowing about atrocities and suffering*, Cambridge: Polity Press.

Coles, R. (1964) *The children of crisis: volume I: A study of courage and fear*, Boston, MA: Little Brown.

Cook, D. (1989) *Rich law poor law*, Milton Keynes: Open University Press.

Cook, D. (1997) 'Social divisions of welfare: tax and social security fraud', in A. Robertson (ed), *Unemployment, social security and the social division of welfare*, New Waverley Paper 13, Edinburgh: University of Edinburgh, pp 17-29.

Dean, H. and Taylor-Gooby, P. (1992) *Dependency culture: The explosion of a myth*, Hemel Hempstead: Harvester Wheatsheaf.

DHSS – Department of Health and Social Security (1985) *Reform of Social Security*, Volume 3: Background Papers, Cmnd 9519, London: HMSO.

Edelman, M. (1977) *Political language: Words that succeed and policies that fail*, New York: Academic Press.

Ferge, Z. (1979) *A society in the making*, London: Penguin.

Ferge, Z. (1997) 'The changed welfare paradigm: the individualisation of the social', *Social Policy and Administration*, vol 31, no 1, pp 20-44.

Ferge, Z. (2001) Social Policy, *Blackwell Dictionary of Sociology*, Oxford: Blackwell.

Ferge, Z. (2002) 'European integration and the reform of social security in the accession countries', *European Journal of Social Quality*, vol 3, nos 1/2, pp 9-25.

Gallie, D. and Paugam, S. (eds) (2000) *Welfare regimes and the experience of unemployment in Europe*, Oxford: Oxford University Press.

Ginn, J., Street, D. and Arber, S. (eds) (2001) *Women, work and pensions: International issues and prospects*, Buckingham: Open University Press.

Goodin, R. (2003) 'Perverse principles of welfare reform', in D. Pieters (ed) *European social security and global policy: European Institute of Social Security Yearbook 2001*, The Hague: Kluwer Law International, pp 197-222.

Gordon, D. and Townsend, P. (eds) (2000) *Breadline Europe: The measurement of poverty*, Bristol: The Policy Press.

Gray, R. (1989) 'The language of factory reform in Britain, c.1830-1860', in P. Joyce (ed) *The historical meanings of work*, Cambridge: Cambridge University Press, pp 143-79.

Guillemard, A.-M. (1986) *Le déclin du social: formation et crise des politiques de la vieillesse*, Paris: Presses Universitaires de France.

Guillemard, A.-M. (2000) *Aging and the welfare-state crisis*, Newark: University of Delaware Press.

Hansard (1994) 28 June, column 677.

Hill, M. (1999) 'Insecurity and social security', in J. Vail, J. Wheelock and M. Hill, *Insecure times: Living with insecurity in contemporary society*, London: Routledge, pp 89-103.

Holzmann, R. and Jørgensen, S. (2000) *Social risk management: A new conceptual framework for social protection and beyond*, Washington DC: World Bank Social Protection Discussion paper no 0006, February.

ILO (International Labour Organization) (1999) *The ILO infocus programme on socioeconomic security: A medium-term workplan*, Geneva: ILO, October.

ILO (2000) *World labour report 2000: Income security and social protection in a changing world*, Geneva: ILO.

Joumard, I. (2002) 'Tax systems in European Union countries', *OECD Economic Studies*, 34, 2002/1, pp 91-151.

Karni, E. (1999) *Optimal unemployment insurance: A guide to the literature*, Washington DC: World Bank Social Protection Discussion Paper no 9906.

Kosonen, P. (2000) 'Activation, incentives and workfare in four Nordic countries', in *Comparing social welfare systems in Nordic Europe and France, vol 4*, Paris: Mire-drees, pp 419-43.

Kvist, J. and Sinfield, A. (1997) 'Comparing tax welfare states', in M. May, E. Brunsdon and G. Craig (eds) *Social policy review 9*, London: Social Policy Association, pp 249-75.

Lakin, C. (2003) 'The effects of taxes and benefits upon household income 2001-2002', *Economic Trends*, 594, May.

Mills, C. W. (1959) *The sociological imagination*, New York, NY: Oxford University Press.

Moore, J. (1989) *The end of the line for poverty*, London: Conservative Party Centre.

OECD (Organisation for Economic Co-operation and Development) (1994a) *The OECD jobs study: Facts analysis strategies*, Paris: OECD.

OECD (1994b) *The OECD jobs study: Evidence and explanations, Parts I and II*, Paris: OECD.

Phillips, A. (1999) *Which equalities matter?*, Cambridge: Polity Press.

Rein, M. and Schon, D. (1993) 'Reframing policy discourse', in F. Fischer and J. Forester (eds) *The argumentative turn in policy analysis and planning*, Durham, NC: Duke University Press, pp 145-66.

Ryan, W. (1971) *Blaming the victim*, London: Orbach and Chambers.

Sainsbury, R. (1996) 'Rooting out fraud: fraudulent until proved innocent', *Poverty*, no 93, pp 17-20.

Schmidt, V.A. (2000) 'Values and discourse in the politics of adjustment', in F.W. Scharpf and V.A. Schmidt (eds) *Welfare and work in the open economy: From vulnerability to competitiveness*, vol 1, Oxford: Oxford University Press, pp 229-309.

Sinfield, A. (1997) 'Blaming the benefit: the costs of the distinction between active and passive programmes', in J. Holmer and J. Ch. Karlsson (eds) *Work: quo vadis? Rethinking the question of work*, Aldershot: Ashgate, pp 79-100.

Sinfield, A. (2000) 'Tax benefits in non-state pensions', *European Journal of Social Security*, vol 2, no 2, pp 137-67.

Sinfield, A. (2001a) 'Benefits and research in the labour market', *European Journal of Social Security*, vol 3, no 3, pp 209-35.

Sinfield, A. (2001b) 'Managing social security for what?', in D. Pieters (ed) *Confidence and changes: Managing social protection in the new millennium*, The Hague: Kluwer, pp 143-61.

Surrey, S.S. (1973) *Pathways to tax reform: The concept of tax expenditures*, Cambridge, MA: Harvard University Press.

Titmuss, R.M. (1958) *Essays on 'the welfare state'*, London: Allen and Unwin.

Townsend, P. (1975) *Sociology and social policy*, London: Allen Lane.

Townsend, P., Davidson, N. and Whitehead, M. (1992) *Inequalities in health*, Harmondsworth: Penguin.

Twine, F. (1994) *Citizenship and social rights: The interdependence of self and society*, London: Sage.

Veit-Wilson, J. (1998) *Setting adequacy standards: How governments define minimum incomes*, Bristol: The Policy Press.

Veit-Wilson, J. (2000) 'Horses for discourses: poverty, purpose and closure in minimum income standards policy', in D. Gordon and P. Townsend (eds) *Breadline Europe: The measurement of poverty*, Bristol: The Policy Press, pp 141-64.

Walker, A. (2000) 'Social quality and the future of the European Union', *The European Journal of Social Quality*, vol 1, nos 1 and 2, pp 12-31.

Walters, W. (2000) *Unemployment and the social: Genealogies of the social*, Cambridge: Cambridge University Press.

Wilkinson, R. (1996) *Unhealthy societies: The afflictions of inequality*, London: Routledge.

THREE

Which way for the European social model: minimum standards or social quality?

Alan Walker

Overarching this chapter is a question that is of critical importance to the well-being of millions of Europeans and, indeed, to the character of the EU itself. In a nutshell, will the dominant social model (or models) promote exclusion or inclusion, or something in between? Will it aim for social justice for all, or only for the most needy or most deserving? Will it strive for an ambitious high-quality welfare horizon or settle for a minimum safety net? The importance of these questions is emphasised, as is the urgency of the answers they require, by the fact that, in some influential quarters, doubts have been cast on the European social model as well as it being potentially threatened by some policy developments.

This chapter catalogues briefly the key challenges to welfare in Europe. It then assesses the current stage of development of social policy at the European level, which is characterised as convergence towards the minima – the lowest common social minimum. The central argument here is that what we understand by the European social model is in jeopardy and, while there are some positive aspects of European social policies that could be built on in a progressive way, Europe lacks the common vision necessary to create a social model that maximises inclusion. Finally there is a summary of the progress of the social quality school of thought which is attempting to create a normative and empirical rationale for a Europe that aims for quality citizenship rather than minimum standards. There is no attempt at crystal ball-gazing here but, instead, an appraisal of the current direction of travel of the European social model and a contrast with the very different destination of social quality.

Before proceeding, at least one important question has been raised so far: is it possible or productive to speak about a single European social model? This is a controversial and frequently examined topic and there is not space to dwell on it here, beyond making three points. Firstly, the notion is often a crude, rhetorical overgeneralisation that is applied, willy-nilly, to Western Europe and, therefore, excludes Central and Eastern Europe. Secondly, it is essential when using the term to acknowledge the large variations between EU countries in the objective conditions of citizens, variations that in themselves cast doubt upon the very idea of a common social model. Thirdly, there are also significant institutional differences within that broad category – anything from two to four different welfare regimes, depending on which authority you consult (with four being the favoured number) and they are usually top-down scientific constructions.

Nonetheless there are sufficient similarities between the Western European countries to suggest that the label, 'European social model' has some validity. In terms of institutional characteristics, the comparison is usually made with the US or East Asia in terms of both the size of the state and the qualitative form of welfare institutions. As Gough notes:

> Summarizing drastically, the dominant European model of welfare is characterised by high levels of spending (especially on transfers), insurance-based social programmes, high intergenerational solidarity with modest to high vertical redistribution, in a majority of states a breadwinner model providing considerable employment protection and benefits for the core workforce, good social investment in human and social infrastructure capital and moderate to low levels of poverty and inequality. (Gough, 1997, p 80)

Thus we might characterise the main differences between the European and US social models as being that social protection payments and expectations in the US are low while both payments and expectations in most member states of the EU are high; while the proportion of GDP devoted to social protection in the EU is higher than that in the US. When we look at the results of different models we find that most Western European countries are markedly superior to the US in terms of the welfare of their citizens. For example Vobruba (2001) has compared Europe and the US according to two indices reflecting economic wealth (purchasing power priorities per capita) and human well-being (the human development index [HDI]). Most Western European countries show a high human development standard, coupled with relatively high economic performance, whereas the US combines higher economic success with a remarkably lower HDI standard. In fact, in HDI terms, the US ranks among countries with a much lower level of economic performance such as Portugal, Argentina and Slovenia. Incidentally, an important conclusion from this analysis is that "economic success is a necessary but not a sufficient precondition for human well-being" (Vobruba, 2001, p 254). Equally importantly, we should be reminded by this analysis that we live in some of the most advanced welfare systems in the world, a very privileged position in comparison with the south of the globe, particularly sub-Saharan Africa, where most of the world's deepest poverty and forms of social exclusion are concentrated. As we consider the present challenges to welfare we should remember that Europe is in a far better position to tackle them than other regions. Doing so is a function of the politics of welfare, rather than an absence of resources.

The new challenges to welfare

Based on the reports from the member states, the first Joint report on social inclusion (European Commission, 2002) lists four major structural changes that are occurring across the EU and may lead to new risks of poverty and social exclusion for "particularly vulnerable groups" (European Commission, 2002, p 21). First, there are transformational changes in the labour market and relations of employment which are said to result from "a period of very rapid economic change and globalisation" (European Commission, 2002, p 21). These include an increasing demand for new skills and higher levels of education and, at the same time, an expansion of low-skilled jobs in the service sector; new forms of employment and more part-time work and a decline in some primary and manufacturing industries. Each of these changes has the potential to create both new opportunities and new risks. For example, flexible forms of employment may enable people (mainly women) to balance home and work responsibilities but, at the same time, they can result in more insecurity. This is also the case with the second structural change: the very rapid growth of information and communication technologies (ICTs) and the knowledge-based society (Castells, 1996) that reinforce existing forms of exclusion for many while creating pathways to inclusion for others.

Third, there are demographic changes. In particular the historically unique combination of low fertility rates and increasing life expectancy has led to population ageing and, in particular, an expansion of numbers of the oldest people (most of whom are women). This change is taking place within a very short time frame and the oldest people are particularly vulnerable to exclusion. Population ageing challenges established welfare systems in three main ways. There is a need to provide adequate pensions, particularly for those (mainly women) who do not qualify for employment-related pensions or who qualify only partially. Then, although this is often overstated, there is a correlation between advanced old age and the need for social care and support and, finally, mechanisms must be developed to prevent or overcome exclusion and to promote participation (Walker and Maltby, 1997; Walker, 2002). Pressures on social protection funding are not primarily due to population ageing but its combination with the perverse trend towards early exit from the labour force (a trend encouraged by public policy in the EU) (Kohli et al, 1991; Walker, 1997). Another demographic change which has major implications for welfare systems in Europe is the growth in ethnic and cultural diversity. In the EU currently black and ethnic minority groups are some of the most socially excluded groups, mainly because of racial discrimination.

Fourth, there are changes in household structures and gender roles. Trends such as increasing marital break-ups, the destandardisation of family life, the impact of multiple role responsibilities borne by women in mid-life and the growth of one-parent households, present challenges to traditional welfare systems derived from a male breadwinner model. Incidentally, the common EU response to these challenges is to promote policies that enable parents to combine employment and home responsibilities. But, although such policies are needed, they do not solve the main problem. This is because it is women who are overwhelmingly caught in this position and who, as well as bearing the current pressures of multiple role occupation, will pay a price in the future in terms of inadequate pension entitlements (Evandrou and Glaser, 2004). Furthermore, one-parent households are overwhelmingly women (as are lone older people) and, outside Scandinavia, they are at an acute risk of poverty.

In addition to these four structural trends there is a familiar host of factors that increase the risks of poverty and social exclusion: long-term dependence on low incomes, long-term unemployment, insecure and low-paid employment, low levels of education and literacy, growing up in a chronically unstable or deprived family, disability, poor health, living in an area with multiple deprivation, precarious housing conditions and homelessness, being an immigrant and coming from an ethnic or racial minority and the concentration of poverty and exclusion in some communities.

There can hardly be any dispute about the importance of these factors for any strategy aimed at tackling social exclusion that has a hope of success. However the main challenge to welfare in the EU is not on this list and you will not find reference to it in any document from the Commission, because it is a political one. In brief it is the emergence of an economic ideology that is antithetical to the European social model. Of course, such ideologies have been around for at least two centuries, but what gives them special power nowadays is globalisation and the US domination of the global economic institutions. The result is that responses to globalisation have been framed within a narrow neoliberal ideology.

Neoliberal economic globalisation

Globalisation has many different dimensions but there is no doubt that the dominant one is economic. There is general agreement that the economic components of globalisation are:

- increasingly integrated financial markets, including markets for foreign exchange, equities and both long-term and short-term debt;
- the rapid growth of foreign direct investment and an increasing share of global production in the hands of transnational corporations;
- increases in world trade, which is both a cause and a consequence of policies to reduce barriers to trade;
- increasing transfers of technology through transnational forms, international licensing agreements and joint ventures;
- increases in international movement of people, both legal and illegal;
- rapid increases in the reach of new forms of communication (Walker and Deacon, 2003).

While this is relatively uncontentious, it is the international response to and encouragement of economic globalisation that has put pressure on Europe's welfare systems. Starting with the US and the Bretton Woods institutions (the Washington consensus) a form of neoliberal ideology has been embraced by some European governments, notably the UK and, under external pressure, some Central and Eastern European countries. This Transatlantic consensus supports free markets and trade liberalisation as the mechanisms to promote growth and improve living standards. Proponents of this position assume, like their national neoliberal forerunners such as Reagan and Thatcher, that global economic growth will 'raise all boats in the sea' as the benefits 'trickle down' to the poorest. There is no evidence for this theory in the national contexts to which it was applied but now it holds sway at a global level (Walker and Walker, 1997).

The Transatlantic consensus assumes that rising inequality is the inevitable result of technological change or the liberalisation of international trade and increased competition, or a combination of the two. Global competition means that taxation and social costs have to be minimised and that traditional public welfare states are not suited to a world in which flexibility and differentiation are the rule (Giddens, 1998). From this political perspective the nation state is powerless in the face of increasing market inequality and can intervene only to offset rising inequality in disposable income but, so the story goes, it must not go too far in this redistribution or it will endanger its own competitiveness. Stripped to its bare bones this is the case for minimal state intervention and a residual welfare state.

Contrary to the Transatlantic consensus, however, it is not inevitable that the response to globalisation has to be rampant trade liberalisation and an uncritical acceptance of the agenda of transnational corporations. There are other ways. In fact the non-English speaking member states of the EU have shown during the 1980s and 1990s that they can be both competitive in international trade and sustain the world's most generous public social-protection systems. Beyond Europe, too, there is significant opposition to the neoliberal hegemony of the Transatlantic consensus (Weiss, 1999; Yeates, 2001). Moreover the core economic assumption of the Transatlantic consensus – the negative relationship between taxation/social protection and labour costs and competitiveness – has been shown to be false (Atkinson, 1999). However, ideology is often impervious to reason and the political power of this argument is evident in policy developments in the EU that are threatening the existing compromise between flexibility and security. On the outcome of the present confrontation between the EU's social model and the prescriptions of neoliberal globalisation rest the socioeconomic security of millions of Europeans.

How has the Transatlantic consensus on globalisation manifested itself in EU policy making? The most obvious and striking example is the strategic goal for the EU set at the Lisbon Council in March 2000: "to become the most competitive and dynamic knowledge-based economy in the world capable of sustainable economic growth with more and better jobs and greater social cohesion" (European Council, 2000, p 2). I will come back later to the EU level of policy making. Among the member states the implementation of the Transatlantic consensus (not surprisingly, since it is primarily an Anglo-Saxon consensus), is most clearly evident in the UK in systemic reforms such as labour-market deregulation, privatisation, marketisation, the switch from universal social security provision to selective or means-tested benefits, the switch from universal services to a combination of self-help and user charges, and in the heavy emphasis on activation. At the same time there is a significant change in the engine of welfare policy from an emphasis on social justice to one on economic investment (the productive role of welfare). Although lagging behind the UK in welfare system reform, many other member states have instituted similar changes in the name of global competition (a curious justification, given that 80% of what is produced in the EU is for the internal market). The metaphors of change and reform are to be seen everywhere in the EU and the term 'modernisation' coined by the New Labour government in 1997 is the widely favoured currency. It has never been defined and, like motherhood and apple pie, no-one could possibly be against it. In practice it appears to mean a transformation of European welfare systems to reduce the role of the state in terms of provision and funding and to increase the roles of other sectors: from the welfare state to the welfare mix.

If we look at the world's leading welfare states (the Scandinavian ones), not only in terms of the proportion of GDP devoted to them, we find falling levels of social expenditure (as shown in Table 3.1). Except for the case of Finland the changes are not dramatic and I am not suggesting that we are witnessing the death of the classic welfare state. Indeed, per capita spending increased in the latter half of the last decade, and increased significantly in Denmark and Norway. However there has been a recent trend towards lower spending as a proportion of GDP and this is coupled with other trends, such as a move away from universalism in social security (based on residency) to an employment relation; a reduction in the tax financing of welfare; some privatisation and an increase in the contracting out of social services: in other words, what Abrahamson (2003, p 19) has called a "Europeanisation of the Scandinavian Welfare States".

In sum the EU's welfare systems are being restructured and there is a risk (my claim is no stronger than that) that in this process some of the key elements of the European social model will be downgraded

Table 3.1: Social expenditure as a percentage of GDP

	1995	2000	1995-2000
Denmark	32.2	28.7	−12.2
Finland	32.7	25.2	−29.8
Norway	27.4	25.3	−8.3
Sweden	35.8	32.3	−10.8
EU 15	28.3	27.6 (1999)	−2.5

Source: Abrahamson (2003, p 22)

or lost altogether. This is contested terrain, even with the European Commission and the signs of concern are visible in the afterthought at the end of the EU's Lisbon commitment, in the inclusion of social cohesion in the EU's social agenda and in the Sixth Framework Research Programme. Clearly there is an awareness within the Commission of the potential risks of modernisation.

The development of European social policy

Turning to the role that the EU itself is performing in the social policy field, and the question of whether or not it helps or hinders the process of addressing the challenges, the development of social policy competencies at the European level may be grouped crudely into three phases. At the start it was nearly stillborn, occupying a very minor role with only 12 of the 248 articles of the Treaty of Rome being devoted to social policy. There was then a belief that economic growth would lead automatically to social development. In fact, social policy only entered the Treaty as a mechanism to prevent market distortions and, specifically, to facilitate the mobility of labour. In other words, social policy was subordinated to economic policy and so it has remained ever since. During the 1970s and 1980s subsidiarity was a powerful doctrine but convergence and harmonisation were mentioned now and then. These notions were banned in the early 1990s but nonetheless Europe embarked on a phase of social policy expansion, which included the formation of observatories (to encourage coordination) on the family, older people and poverty and social exclusion, which culminated in the Amsterdam Treaty. The third and current phase is already the most active and interesting. It might be characterised as representing a shift from coordination to convergence, but 'harmonisation' is still a forbidden term (European Commission, 2000, p 8).

In 2000 the EU published its first *Social policy agenda*, which emphasised the dynamic interaction between economic policy, employment policy and social policy (Figure 3.1). It also included a commitment to social quality, which amazed those responsible for this perspective. I will come back to this issue later but, for now, it is worth noting the following statement: "A key message is that growth is not an end in itself but essentially a means to achieving a better standard of living for all" (European Commission, 2000, p 14). This runs counter to 45 years of European thinking on social policy and is very close to a social quality formulation of the relationship between economic and social policy. Indeed, the previous Commissioner,

Figure 3.1: The EU policy triangle

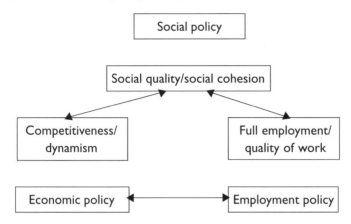

The policy mixes to be established to create a virtuous circle of economic and social progress should reflect the inter-dependence of these policies and aim to maximise their mutual positive reinforcement.
Source: European Commission (2000)

Diamantopoulou, publicly acknowledged the influential role of the social quality thesis on the development of the social policy agenda (Diamantopoulou, 2001). In a similar vein the Agenda acknowledges that employment is not the answer to every aspect of social exclusion (European Commission, 2000). Nonetheless the document as a whole and the five-year agenda it contains reflects the long-standing subordination of social to economic policy. Titmuss's (1974) old handmaiden model of social policy is remodelled to "social policy as a productive factor" ... "a guiding principle of the new Social Policy Agenda will be to strengthen the role of *social policy as a productive factor*" (European Commission, 2000, p 7, italics in original). This aim was reaffirmed in the mid-term review of the Agenda (European Commission, 2003). This is not at all surprising in view of the history of European social policy on the one hand and, on the other, the Lisbon Council's commitment to "become the most competitive and dynamic knowledge-based economy" (2000, p 2).

As well as this overarching commitment, the Lisbon Council in 2000 agreed to extend the new instrument for policy coordination – the open method of coordination – to the field of poverty and social exclusion. This should be seen, in my view, as a clever mechanism to encourage policy convergence. Member states share national action plans (NAPs) and report annually (every two years for the NAPs incl) on progress towards them, with the Commission analysing the results.

This instrument was first applied in 1988 to employment policies. At the Laeken Council in December 2001 a first set of 18 statistical indicators was approved, covering four dimensions of social inclusion and exclusion: financial poverty, employment, health and education. There are ten primary indicators referring to the most important aspects of social exclusion and eight secondary ones to cover other dimensions. The report of Atkinson et al (2002) on social inclusion indicators has been influential in this work.

Now, in adopting a critical perspective on this latest important development in European social policy, I acknowledge the considerable advances represented by its commitment to tackle social exclusion, the mechanism put in place to encourage knowledge sharing and policy convergence and the endeavour to standardise indicators. The importance of information for democracy should not be underestimated. But these measures should be constructively criticised on two main fronts. Firstly, the strategy against social exclusion is limited. It focuses overwhelmingly on employment: "Participation in employment is emphasised by most member states as the best safeguard against poverty and social exclusion " (European Commission, 2002, p 12). This is as far as the member states are prepared to go, but remember the comment in the *Social policy agenda* about the limitations of this strategy. As for the Commission, "this reflects adequately the emphasis laid on employment by the European Council at Nice" (European Commission, 2002, p 72). What about those for whom employment is not a viable option, such as very elderly people? Furthermore, although it is important to tackle extreme forms of exclusion, why stop there? Doing so makes it clear that we are confronted with a minimalist approach to the European social model: one concerned to reduce poverty and hardship and to preserve social cohesion, but not one that focuses on higher standards for all. Although the First Joint Report uses the term 'social inclusion', its emphasis is on combating exclusion.

Second, reflecting the restricted nature of the strategy, the proposed indicators reinforce the conclusion that is concerned with minimum standards. A much more fundamental criticism of the indicators used and the whole school from which they are derived is the absence of any theoretical or conceptual basis for the indicators selected. The answer to the question, 'why this one or that one?' cannot be answered scientifically and usually boils down to what is available. For example, why are relationships, neighbourhoods and families absent from the EU indicators of social exclusion? Without a defensible theoretical perspective it is not possible to say anything general about states of inclusion or exclusion in the EU and how different dimensions interact, only that there are more people at risk of poverty in country A than B, or more or less at risk now than previously. This is an important step in itself and is one entirely consistent with a minimal view of social policy, which brings me to the final section.

An alternative to minimum standards: social quality

The concept of social quality is specifically intended to provide a vision of what the European social model could consist of and it is designed to alter radically the unequal relationship between social policy and economic policy by making them both subordinate to the pursuit of social quality. The origins of the concept go back to the early 1990s when a series of meetings was held aimed at pooling knowledge from two of the Commission's Observatories. The major conclusion reached was that the main sources of the recent crises in European social policy were the unequal relationship between economic policy and social policy, together with the increasing tendency for economic policy to define the content and scope of social policy ever more narrowly. In short, the social dimension appeared to be viewed increasingly as being in conflict with an economic or monetary one and, as a consequence, risked serious downgrading. It seemed that this process was taking on an air of inevitability and that, therefore, the European social model itself was in jeopardy.

What was required to address the unequal relationship between economic and social policy was a new conceptualisation: one which would help to establish a balance between economic and social development in Europe by re-examining the foundations and goals of social policy. The search for a concept that both represented what the European model had sought to embody and focused attention on the goals of social policy – recast from its narrow administrative form to a broader societal one – led rapidly to the invention of the term 'social quality'. This was appealing because it conveyed the achievement of the EU member states in creating a unique blend of economic success and social development not found in either the US or East Asia. It also suggests a mission that is unfinished: a reminder of what the EU should be striving for and a guiding star for plotting the required direction of change. In other words, the European model is characterised by elements of social quality, but this focus has not been articulated in this way before.

Conceptualisation of 'social quality'

'Social quality' was originally proposed as a standard by which to measure the extent to which the quality of the daily lives of citizens have attained an acceptable European level. To measure this social quality requires a broad multidimensional standard, broader than more familiar social indicators like poverty and social exclusion. Moreover, social quality is a feature of societies and their institutions, even though it is assessed with reference to its impact on citizens. The concept of human needs did not capture what was needed in this notion. Also, given the highly developed nature of the EU, it would have been inappropriate to employ a concept such as 'basic needs'. It also had to incorporate a mixture of structural factors and individual-level ones, in order to represent properly the delicate balance in Europe between collective and individual responsibility. Standard 'quality of life' scales were not adequate for the purposes outlined above because of their lack of theoretical coherence (Walker and van der Maesen, 2004).

In the light of all these considerations, social quality was defined as: "the extent to which people are able to participate in the social and economic life of their communities under conditions which enhance their well-being and individual potential" (Beck et al, 1997 p 7). That is, the extent to which the quality of social relations promotes both participation and personal development. In order to achieve an acceptable level of social quality it is hypothesised that four conditions have to be fulfilled.

First, people need access to *socioeconomic security* – whether from employment or social security – in order to protect them from poverty and other forms of material deprivation. Socio-economic security in the EU requires good-quality paid employment and social protection to guarantee living standards and access to resources: income, education, health care, social services, environment, public health, personal safety and so on.

Second, they have to experience *social inclusion* in, or minimum levels of social exclusion from, key social and economic institutions such as the labour market. Social inclusion concerns citizenship. This may be a wide and all-embracing national or European citizenship, or an exclusive one, with large numbers of outcasts and quasi-citizens (who are denied citizenship completely or partially by means of discrimination). Room (1995) has argued that exclusion is the denial or non-realisation of social rights.

Third, they should be able to live in communities and societies characterised by *social cohesion*. Social cohesion refers to the glue which holds together communities and societies. It is vital for both social development and individual self-realisation. The contemporary discussion of cohesion often centres on the narrow concept of social capital but its legacy stretches back, via Durkheim, to solidarity, shared norms and values.

Fourth, they must, to some extent, be autonomous and socially empowered in order to be able to participate fully in the face of rapid socioeconomic change. Social empowerment means enabling citizens to control their own lives and to take advantage of opportunities. It means increasing the range of human choice. Empowerment therefore goes far beyond participation in the political system to focus on the individual's potential capacity (knowledge, skills, experience and so on) and how far these are being realised.

These four components may be represented diagramatically in a two-dimensional model (Figure 3.2). On the one hand there is the distinction between the macro and micro levels – between structure and agency in sociological terms, while, on the other, there is a horizontal relationship between the formal and the informal, between institutions, organisations and communities, groups and individuals. Thus the vertical axis represents the tension between societal development and biographical development while the horizontal axis represents the tension between institutional processes and individual actions (between, in Lockwood's terms, system integration and social integration or, in Habermas's terms, between the system and the lifeworld). Each cell in the quadrangle is itself represented by a continuum: socioeconomic security/insecurity; social cohesion/fragmentation; social inclusion/exclusion and empowerment/dependency. The underlying assumption is that each of these components may be operationalised and, thereby, the model, or a more refined version of it, could become a practical tool for policy makers and policy analysts.

Social quality as policy

Remarkably, before the ink was dry on the first formulation of social quality in 1997, it had been translated into policy when the Netherlands Ministry of Welfare and Sport employed it as a guiding principle in evaluating the impact of its policies. Gradually, over the last few years, European policy makers have been seeing potential in the term – as an embodiment of European ideals and a touchstone for the European model. Thus the *Social policy agenda* of the European Commission includes references to social quality and 'quality' has been adopted as

Figure 3.2: The social quality quadrangle

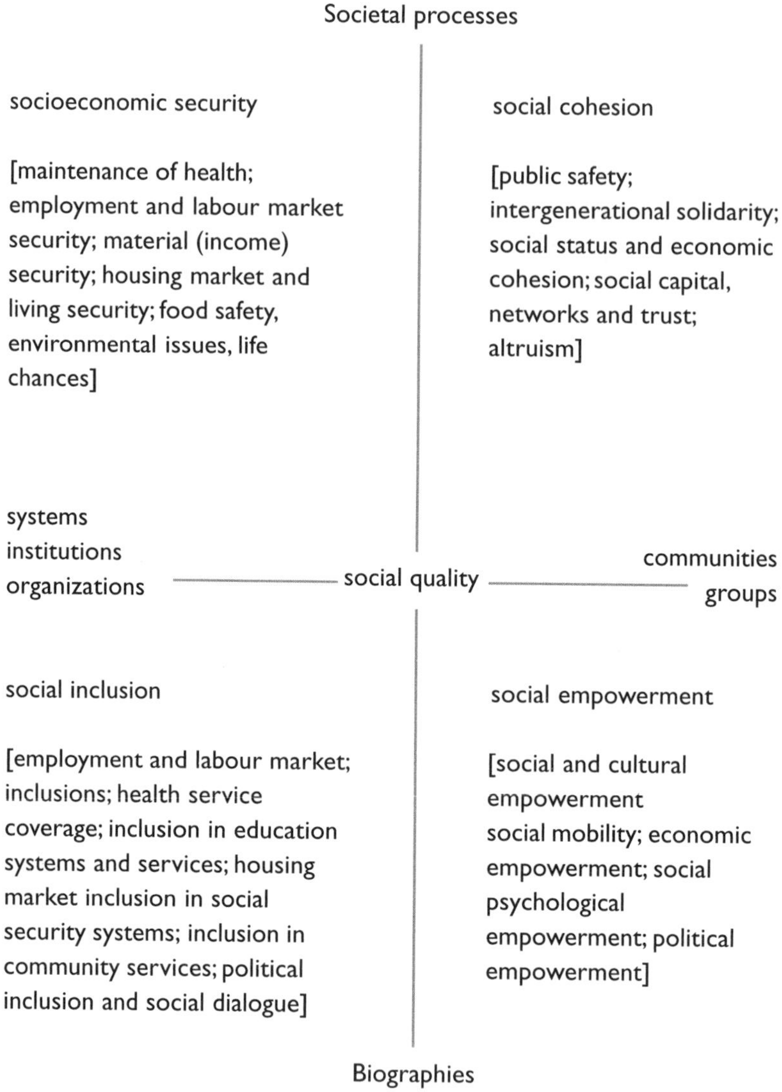

Societal processes

socioeconomic security

[maintenance of health;
employment and labour market
security; material (income)
security; housing market and
living security; food safety,
environmental issues, life
chances]

social cohesion

[public safety;
intergenerational solidarity;
social status and economic
cohesion; social capital,
networks and trust;
altruism]

systems
institutions
organizations ———————— social quality ———————— communities
groups

social inclusion

[employment and labour market;
inclusions; health service
coverage; inclusion in education
systems and services; housing
market inclusion in social
security systems; inclusion in
community services; political
inclusion and social dialogue]

social empowerment

[social and cultural
empowerment
social mobility; economic
empowerment; social
psychological
empowerment; political
empowerment]

Biographies

Source: Beck et al (2001)

one of the key themes of European social policy (European
Commission, 2000, p 13). However, in the formulation used in the
Social policy agenda, the integrative potential of social quality has been
lost and it is placed confusingly alongside social cohesion.

Theorising social quality

One of the early criticisms of the concept of social quality is that it lacked a theoretical foundation and, therefore, could be mistaken for a purely instrumental idea, like other terms in the quality domain, such as total quality management (TQM). A theoretical journey into the philosophical foundations of social quality led to the realisation that the search for a rationale for social policy was too restricting and, instead, what was required was a scientific framework which establishes whether the *social* component of social quality was an authentic entity in its own right and, if it was, would that enable us to develop conclusions about its quality. It was the failure to pursue this endeavour that has left social policy trapped in the limited domain defined by economists as non-economic (Donzelot, 1979; Walker, 1984). Classical economists defined society's problems as 'social' rather than 'economic' and social policy has been working within that straightjacket ever since.

The heart of what is 'social', it is argued, is the self-realisation of individuals, as social beings, in the context of the formation of collective identities (Beck et al, 2001). Thus the "social" is the outcome of constantly changing processes through which individuals realise themselves as interacting social beings. Rather than being an atomised economic agent, a person's self-realisation depends on social recognition (Honneth, 1994). The processes whereby we all achieve self-realisation, to a greater or lesser extent, are partly historically and, therefore structurally determined and partly shaped by the agents themselves.

According to this theory as previously stated, the social world is realised in the interaction between (and interdependence on) the self-realisation of individuals as social beings and the formation of collective identities. This is called the *construction* of the social. Second, four basic conditions determine the opportunities in which social relations can develop in the direction of social quality (Figure 3.2). People must have the capability to interact (they must be empowered); the institutional and structural context must be accessible to them (they must be included); they must have access to the necessary material and other resources that facilitate interaction (they need socioeconomic security); and the necessary collectively accepted values and norms that enable community building must be in place (there must be cohesion). This refers to the *opportunities* or conditions for social quality and there may be substantial variations between individuals on one or all of these conditions. Third, therefore, the actual nature, content and structure of what is the social component of human relations is a function of the relationship between two axes. In Figure 3.3 the horizontal axis represents the tension between systems, institutions and organisations, on the one hand, and communities and groups on the other. The vertical axis mirrors the tension between social processes and biographical ones. These twin tensions create the dynamic which influences both self-realisation and the formation of collective identities and which transforms social actors into ones capable of realising social quality (Figure 3.3). This refers to the constitution of competence for social quality.

Given that the two sets of tensions are in permanent confrontation, social quality is realised by the dynamic between the world of systems and the world of human praxis in the context of the relationship between the two axes. On the horizontal axis we see the contrast between rationality and subjectivity, between demos on the left and ethnos on the right. On the left side we are concerned with the relationship between the individual and the world of systems and institutions, in short, with social recognition. On the right side there are relations between individuals and social groups and communities in the negotiation of everyday life. Access and belonging in these relationships concern social recognition and appreciation but also the individual's capacity to participate. The vertical axis represents the worlds of societal and biographical developments, and within them are embedded values, norms, principles, rights, conventions and so on. The left-hand side of the axis concerns the rule of law and social justice while the right-hand side indicates social responsiveness. These four constitutional factors are derived normatively from the social quality approach (Beck et al, 2001).

Figure 3.3: The constitution of competence for social quality

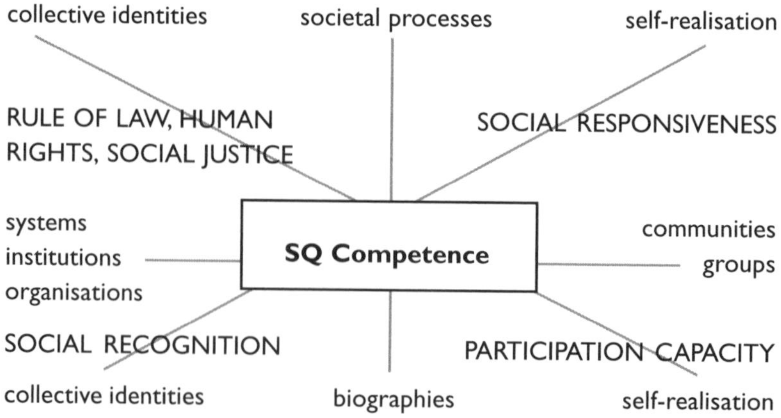

It is obvious that the outcome of this set of processes that produce the quality of the social world may be positive or negative. Self-realisation may mean autonomy or egocentrism, while collective identities may be open and liberating or closed and authoritarian. Ethical guidelines are therefore required to distinguish between acceptable and unacceptable outcomes. This means that social quality must have an ideological dimension. As previously noted, from the beginning there were two engines – scientific and political – behind the social quality initiative and the two have been brought together in the campaign for human dignity in Europe. This is centred on the Amsterdam Declaration on Social Quality in 1997 that calls, above all, for respect for fundamental human dignity (Walker, 1998). The four components of the social quality quadrangle also reflect this perspective: socioeconomic security points to social justice; inclusion refers to the social rights of citizens; cohesion implies an interdependent moral contract and solidarity and empowerment means equity in life chances. Social quality concerns the dignity of individuals as social beings.

Having conceptualised what was unique about the term 'social' in such a way that we may be able to develop conclusions about its quality, the final unresolved issue was, what do we mean by 'quality'? The answer comes in six parts. First, because the heart of the social world concerns the self-realisation of individuals as social beings, the main point of reference for quality must be the circumstances of daily life. Second, therefore, quality is a function of permanently changing interactions among actors in everyday life and cannot be reduced to processes between systems and communities and groups. Third, quality does not have a one-dimensional nature. There are no quality standards independent of the dynamic historical and situational circumstances in which the social world is manufactured. Fourth, it is not an option to interpret European quality in terms of minimum standards for everybody. In Therborn's (2001) terms, social quality implies an 'open horizon' rather than a 'social floor'. Fifth, quality depends on capacity. In other words, quality is realised if people are enabled to develop communicative capacities in ever more complex circumstances. Finally, quality is not a question only of outcomes but of processes as well. The nature of interventions, the choice of strategies for action, and the type of organisation have an important bearing on the quality of the process.

With regard to its practical application in the social policy sphere, this conceptualisation of social quality has the potential to provide guidelines for policy makers in the development and implementation of policies. It can do so because it provides the essential connection between needs, policy actors and policies. Thus, for example, it can transform the abstract relationship between economic policy, social policy and employment policy in the EU policy triangle (Figure 3.1) into a concrete and practical one by providing the connections between them. In other words, the notion of social quality has an integrative role. This means, first, that it encompasses all policies (economic, social, cultural and so on). Second, it covers all phases of policy making, from design to evaluation. Third, success in the interrelationships between needs, actors and policies depends on the existence of basic conditions (such as public forums, public ethics and systems for communication and understanding). Fourth, the appropriate method to develop policies promoting social quality is an iterative one that depends on communication and dialogue. Fifth, policies have to be integrative in order to produce social quality (which implies, at the very least, mechanisms for coordination). Finally, the definition of problems has to be adequate – both in legal and functional terms (which depends on consensus with regard to the notion of justice). Operationalised in this way, it is argued that social quality has the potential to make policies more rational and effective and policy processes more democratic.

Conclusion

The argument of this chapter is a simple one: on its current course those responsible for the maintenance and reproduction of the European social model aspire, at best, to minimum social standards. The only way that higher standards can be aimed for is if the vision behind policy is quite different from the currently dominant, economistic one. The quest for social quality is to find the methodological foundations to provide a practical democratic alternative; one in which the European social model will be encouraged to grow and develop, to enlarge citizenship rights and to maximise inclusion.

Thus Europe is faced with a choice. In one direction lies a version of the neoliberal-inspired Transatlantic consensus in which economic, and especially financial, interests determine the shape of social policy; while in the other lies the ideal of universal social quality. At the moment the EU seems to be torn between these two alternatives – seeking a compromise in the form of the 'productive role of welfare' or the sustainability of pension systems (as agreed at Laeken). But the evidence so far suggests the absence of the vision necessary to build on the European model and turn it into one of inclusive citizenship.

Moreover the choice facing Europe has become much more complicated since 1 May 2004, because the enlargement of the EU embraces several countries that were forced to follow the 'advice' of the World Bank and privatise their social protection systems, particularly their public pension schemes. In addition, as Ferge's (2002, p 15) analysis of the accession reports from ten Central and Eastern European countries shows, the European Commission at the time itself actively encouraged privatisation.

The major challenge to welfare in Europe, therefore, is the present threat to the European social model. It is emphatically not a technical matter of social protection system design, but a question of what welfare and, ultimately, social life means for millions of people: what kinds and levels of socioeconomic security? What form of citizenship? Inclusion or exclusion? There is no question that the model needs reform in all sorts of ways, but it is the current direction of reform that poses the question: minimum standards or social quality?

References

Abrahamson, P. (2003) 'The end of the Scandinavian model? Welfare reform in the Nordic countries', *Journal of Societal and Social Policy*, vol 2, no 2, pp 19-36.

Atkinson, A. (1999) *Is rising inequality inevitable?*, WIDER Annual Lectures 3, World Institute for Development Economics Research.

Atkinson, T., Cantillon, B., Marker, E. and Nolan, B. (2002) *Social indicators*, Oxford: OUP.

Beck, W., van der Maesen, L. and Walker, A. (eds) (1997) *The social quality of Europe*, The Hague: Kluwer International.

Beck, W., van der Maesen, L., Thomése, F. and Walker, A. (eds) (2001) *Social quality, a vision of Europe*, The Hague: Kluwer International.

Castells, M. (1996) *The rise of the network society*, Oxford: Blackwell.

Diamantopoulou, A. (2001) 'Foreword', in W. Beck, L. van der Maesen, F. Thomése and A. Walker (eds) *Social quality, a vision for Europe*, The Hague: Kluwer International, p xv.

Donzelot, J. (1979) *The policing of families*, London: Hutchinson.

European Commission (2000) *The social policy agenda*, Brussels: EC.

European Commission (2002) *Joint report on social inclusion*, Brussels: EC.

European Commission (2003) *Mid-term review of the social policy agenda*, Brussels: EC.

European Council (2000) 'Presidency conclusions', Press Release SN 100/00 EN, Lisbon, 20 March.

Evandrou, M. and Glaser, K. (2004) 'Family, work and quality of life: changing economic and social roles through the lifecourse', *Ageing and Society*, vol 24, no 5, pp 771-92.

Ferge, Z. (2002) 'European integration and the reform of social security in the accession countries', *European journal of social quality*, vol 3, issue 1/2, pp 9-25.

Giddens, A. (1998) *The third way*, Oxford: Polity Press.

Gough, I. (1997) 'Social aspects of the European model and its economic consequences', in W. Beck, L. van der Maesen and A. Walker (eds) *The social quality of Europe*, The Hague: Kluwer International, pp 89-108.

Honneth, A. (1994) 'Die Soziale Dynamik von Missachtung', *Leviathan*, vol 1, pp 80-95.

Kohli, M., Rein, M., Guillemard, A.-M. and Gunsteren, H. (1991) *Time for retirement*, Cambridge: Cambridge University Press.

Room, G. (ed) (1995) *Beyond the threshold*, Bristol: The Policy Press.

Therborn, G. (2001) 'On the politics and policy of social quality', in W. Beck, L. van der Maesen, F. Thomése and A. Walker (eds) *Social quality, a vision of Europe*, The Hague: Kluwer International, pp 19-30.

Titmuss, R. (1974) *Social policy*, London: Unwin.

Voruba, G. (2001) 'Coping with drastic social change, Europe and the US in comparison', in W. Beck, L. van der Maesen, F. Thomése and A. Walker (eds) *Social quality, a vision of Europe*, The Hague: Kluwer International, pp 251-70.

Walker, A. (1984) *Social planning*, Oxford: Blackwell.

Walker, A. (1997) *Combating age barriers in employment*, Luxembourg: Office for Official Publications of the European Communities.

Walker, A. (1998) 'The Amsterdam Declaration on the social quality of Europe', *European Journal of Social Work*, vol 1, no 1, pp 109-11.

Walker, A. (2002) 'A strategy for active ageing', *International Social Security Review*, vol 55, no 1, pp 121-39.

Walker, A. and Deacon, B. (2003) 'Economic globalisation and policies on ageing', *Journal of societal and social policy*, vol 2, no 2, pp 1-18.

Walker, A. and Maltby, T. (1997) *Ageing Europe*, Buckingham: Open University Press.

Walker, A. and van der Maesen, L. (2004) 'Social quality and quality of life', in W. Glatzer, S. von Below and H. Stoffregen (eds) *Challenges for quality of life in the contemporary world*, The Hague: Kluwer International, pp 13-31.

Walker, A. and Walker, C. (eds) (1997) *Britain divided*, London: CPAG.

Weiss, L. (1999) 'Managed openness: beyond neoliberal globalism', *New Left Review*, no 238, pp 126-40.

Yeates, N. (2001) *Globalisation and social policy*, London: Sage Publications.

FOUR

The advent of a flexible life course and the reconfigurations of welfare

Anne-Marie Guillemard

This chapter is intended to shed light on the heuristic value of a life-course perspective for analysing welfare policy changes and their impact on individuals and their social protection, integration and citizenship. The concept of the life course helps us link a macrosociological analysis of this institution to a microsociology of the biographical trajectories of individuals. In this respect, it is a fundamental conceptual tool for analysing and understanding rearrangements in the changing relation between labour markets and welfare policies.

This chapter's starting point is the assumption that every societal model interconnects three spheres: the labour market, the welfare state and a life-course regime. Castel (1995) has shown that industrial wage-earning societies have relied on a strong connection between the dependent economic status of wage-earners and an extensive system of protection against risks. My aim is to show that a third dimension has to be added to this key pair in industrial society. This third dimension is the life course and the way it has been socially organised. Studies have shown how the advent of industrial society was closely tied to the tripartate social organisation of the life course, which was gradually institutionalised as the status of wage-earner developed along with a welfare state based on social rights and citizenship (Riley et al, 1972; Kohli, 1987; Guillemard and van Gunsteren, 1991; Guillemard, 2000). The convulsions now occurring with the advent of a new, knowledge-based society affect these three major dimensions of work, welfare and life course organisation.

After recalling the key role welfare states have had in organising the tripartite life course in industrial society (education during youth, work during adulthood and retirement during old age), this chapter will examine how, given changes in the world of work, this tight correlation between the spheres of employment, welfare and the life course is now coming undone. Changes in the workplace, as fordism is declining and an information society is emerging, are desynchronising the ages of life. A new, more flexible life course in a knowledge-based society is offering individuals a variety of career possibilities but, too, chaotic, unforeseeable biographical trajectories with, as a consequence, new uncovered risks, as we shall see. Our rigid welfare institutions are increasingly unable to satisfy the needs for security that are thus arising. The last section of this chapter will raise questions about how the welfare state might be reconfigured so as to guarantee security for individuals in a new, flexible organisation of time over the whole life course.

1. Welfare policies: the main instrument for shaping the life course

Social policies have played a key part in organising and institutionalising the threefold life course pattern. Increasingly strict laws have been passed about the age of compulsory schooling and the ages for work (specifically for regulating child labour and, more recently, setting the retirement age). They have divided the life span into three distinct ages, each with its own function: childhood for education, adulthood for work and old age for inactivity and rest from work. The state has regulated these ages through increasing interventions in the economy and society (Guillemard, 2001). By 'policing ages' (Percheron, 1991), it has played the leading role in constructing the life course. In particular, it has distributed social rights, duties and activities by organising the triangular relations between family, work and school into an orderly succession of stages (Smelser and Halpern, 1978). Each age in the life course has been assigned a distinct activity that endows it with meaning and identity. This tripartite organisation has become an institution as the welfare state has expanded and as age norms have been enacted in law.

Welfare entitlements tend to individualise and organise the life course in a life-long biographical pattern, since they define clear-cut situations and accentuate the cleavages between work and the periods before and after it: "In the welfare state, the continuous flow of life is transformed into a series of situations all of which have a clear formal definition.... Periodization of life and proliferation of sharp transitions which derive from the social insurance system combine into a life-long biographical pattern" (Mayer and Schoepflin, 1989, p 198). Owing to its own rules, formulated in terms of the chronological age for benefits, the welfare state has standardised life events and gradually institutionalised the life course by defining the following: the number of successive ages, their social content, the timing for making transitions from one age to another, the (more or less ritualised) nature of these transitions, the milestones for marking thresholds and, not to be forgotten, forms of solidarity or competition between age groups or generations. This life course institution conditions individuals' trajectories throughout life, sets the timing and determines plans as a function of 'temporal horizons'. Together with Sue, we can say that "social times" are "big categories of blocks of time that a society grants itself and conceives in order to designate, articulate, give a rhythm to, and coordinate the principal social activities to which it attributes special importance" (Sue, 1995, p 29).

The invention and generalisation of retirement pensions, in particular, have been decisive in constructing and consolidating this 'tripartition' of the life course (Kohli, 1987) in four principal ways.

- Pension systems have been a major factor in determining the order and hierarchy between the three principal ages of life with work, as the social content of adulthood, at the centre. They have staked out a life course where the adult's contribution to the world of work conditions the right to rest at the end of life.
- Pension systems, along with other social policies (such as education), have relied heavily on chronological criteria in order to form the thresholds between stages in the life course. Old-age pensions have chronologised the life course.
- This division into three chronological stages has standardised the life course. At the same age, everyone moves quite predictably from one phase to the next. Entering the world of work occurs at the same age for nearly everyone with an equivalent level of education and the retirement age sets the date when everyone will stop working.
- Retirement pensions have also fostered new ways of making plans for the future. Pensions, along with a much longer life expectancy, have helped individualise and temporalise the life course by endowing the individual with prospects.

2. The advent of a flexible life course: destandardised, uncertain trajectories

Industrial society's tripartite organisation of the life course is coming undone

In industrial society, time was homogeneous and unified around an opposition between the dominant pole of the time spent working (a segment measurable by the clock) and the pole of the time for inactivity (defined as the reverse side of work). The status of wage-earner, implying as it does subordination to an employer, contributed to the predominance of work time. This central stage of work served as the basis for indexing all other time segments in the life span. It imprinted its quantitative, linear and segmentary qualities on the whole life course.

The predominance of the time spent working over other periods accounts for the synchronised timing of personal biographies with occupational careers. For men, entry in adulthood corresponded to stable access to the labour market and the founding of a family via marriage with, shortly thereafter, the birth of the first child. The threefold life-course model laid down a standard trajectory for men, to whom were assigned the roles of head of family and breadwinner. Time was organised quite differently and less rigidly for women. Turned towards the domestic sphere and care-giving, women lingered for a long time on the margins of the wage-earning workforce. Their jobs provided what was considered to be a supplementary income. Nonetheless, the predominant tripartite organisation of time affected them too, but to a lesser extent and in an indirect way through their eligibility for welfare benefits, thanks to their wage-earning husband's entitlement.

This arrangement of work, welfare and the life course under fordist industrial society is coming apart. Work and welfare are coming out of phase while the life course – less and less an orderly, linear succession of stages – is becoming more flexible (Best, 1981).

The concept of a continuous career is disintegrating. Life-long occupations are becoming scarcer. The time spent working is less uniform and continuous: active life is interspersed with periods of training and inactivity. These facts signal that what has been called industrial society's 'regime of temporality' is coming undone.

The structure of welfare systems, solidly grounded in the tripartite distribution of ages and activities over the life course, has also been shaken. New, intermediate and usually ad hoc social programmes are being implemented in order to cope with job problems and new forms of precariousness. From the fringes of welfare systems, programmes for integrating young people in the world of work, early exit schemes for older employees or contracts for helping the jobless return to employment offer benefits that are tied less to a person's occupation. This thoroughly modifies the nature of universal welfare state entitlements (Guillemard, 1997) and might even break the linkage between wage-earning status and entitlements.

Finally, the orderly tripartite organisation of a foreseeable life course is coming apart. This affects the aforementioned hierarchisation, chronologisation, standardisation and individualisation of stages in the life course, as well as the possibility of fitting individuals into a highly foreseeable long-term structure, running up to and including old age.

Deinstitutionalisation and destandardisation of the life course

Most sociologists who adopt the life-course perspective agree that industrial society's tripartite life-course model is in the throes of deep change and that individuals' biographical trajectories no longer follow the pattern of three successive, distinct, well-ordered stages.

Beyond this widely shared diagnosis, the literature on this subject proposes differing interpretations of the changes under way. Authors such as Beck (1992) have referred to an increasing 'destandardisation' of the life course that comes along with the destandardisation of work and the generalisation of occupational insecurity. In his comparative analyses, Heinz (2001) has drawn up a balance sheet that charts the life course as ever more contingent. According to him, the uncertainty introduced in the restructured life course can mainly be set down to the haphazard alternation of periods of employment and unemployment throughout careers. The timing and succession of these periods are closely linked to policies for restructuring industry and to a country's welfare regime (Heinz, 2001). In his study of network societies, Castells (1996, pp 376-7) has reached similar conclusions about "social temporalities" and the life course. According to him, simultaneity in the flow of information dissolves time. The life course is now characterised by the disintegration of the tripartite model and by a "social arrhythmia". Having focused on rearrangements in periods of time and their consequences on the life course, Bessin (1993) has also observed a 'deinstitutionalisation' of this threefold organisation. Accordingly, the life course is no longer a linear succession of irreversible stages. It no longer divides into three successive segments organised around the predominance of the time devoted to work.

Changes in the world of work and the family are major factors producing a new mixture of socially defined periods of time. The linear, measurable regime of temporality that assigned adults to work no longer plays the central role it did under the tripartite model. After a period of 'monochrony', 'polychrony' prevails. Bessin (1993, p 234) has proposed a new paradigm, *kairos* (a Greek word meaning the right moment), of a temporality whereby regulation by norms yields to a regulation by the actors themselves, who choose the right moment for carrying out an action.

In line with the lessons drawn from this review of the literature, let us try to clarify the terminology by distinguishing two levels of analysis. This distinction rests on the concept of the life course and its macro- and microsociological dimensions, whereby a society's basic institutions are connected to individuals' biographies. As an institution, the life course is a model with systems of rules and norms for the purposes of socialisation and regulation. It provides for an orderly movement of individuals over the life span through positions conferring statuses and roles. It shapes their prospects and views. It has a symbolic function since it organises time and sets the timing for their actions. The de-institutionalisation of the life course refers to changes in this normative framework, which shape personal biographies. This is the level where age thresholds are gradually being levelled and the ages of life blurred. At the individual level, biographical trajectories are being destandardised. They are diversifying and becoming less certain and more contingent, given the crisis in the normative framework of the life course. Individuals no longer fit as tightly into an orderly sequence of positions. They now have a broader range of choices. In Beck's words, biographical trajectories are becoming "auto-reflexive" (1992, p 290). What used to be socially formatted is now a personal configuration.

All these sociologists agree on the importance of the following change: the rise of an 'individual sovereignty' over time, which is diversifying biographical trajectories and turning them into a matter of negotiation.

The advent of a flexible life course: empirical evidence

European data might provide evidence of the changes under way at three points in the ideal life course for men in industrial society. These comments on cross-sectional data are intended to make a small contribution to a vast research project that has not yet been systematically undertaken. As Heinz (2001) has rightly pointed out, such a project would call for a rigorous strategy associating a quantitative, longitudinal analysis based on panels with qualitative studies of individual biographies. This is the only strategy that will shed light on the relations between macrostructural trends, institutional changes in welfare systems and modifications in individuals' trajectories. The data presented here are intended to provide us with an idea of the nature of the changes affecting the tripartite life-course model.

Fragmenting and individualising work time

The first changes to take into account are those related to work time. Over the past century, we have witnessed a spectacular reduction in the amount of time devoted to work during a year (Maddison, 1995). In Europe, this reduction has continued since 1960 at varying rates, depending on the country. From 1983 to 1995, the length of the workweek decreased from 40 to 38.5 hours (Bosch, 1999). Besides these major quantitative trends, the most important changes tend to be qualitative. Socially defined periods of time have fragmented and now overlap each age category. A continual movement back and forth between training, work and economic inactivity (unemployment, but also time for one's self and one's family) punctuate individuals' trajectories.

The stages of life devoted to economic activity or inactivity have broken up into a multiplicity of distinct, unstable periods scattered throughout the life course. Biographical trajectories now combine these periods in a random, destandardised way. Entering and exiting the labour force follow each other, with transitional (or even chronic) periods of joblessness (with or without unemployment compensation) in between, or phases of part-time or short-term employment, or employment with more than one employer. It is thus hard to detect patterns in this new tangle of socially defined times.

Nonetheless, a diversification of socially defined periods of time and of work schedules can be detected in many countries, as well as an increasing differentiation of the length of time spent working in each country. This fragmentation of work time is to be understood in relation to the disintegration of the model of industrial production with its organisation of time. Wage-earning labour, with the implications of a stable, lasting subordination to an employer and of full-time employment with precise tasks to be performed and a life-long career plan is being eroded. The principle of a standard, normative organisation of time has come under question. There is much evidence of this, including the extreme diversification of work schedules and conditions. The number of wage-earners with the same daily schedule and the same number of workdays per week is decreasing rapidly. In the UK, where the law does not regulate work time, only 10% of wage-earners put in 40 hours a week. Additional evidence for these changes is that the new forms for organising work tend towards flexible rhythms and schedules (just-in-time organisation, 'de-hierarchisation' and the development of horizontal, autonomous units and networks). Furthermore, new forms of atypical employment are spreading: employment contracts of limited duration, temporary jobs, freelance work and jobs with several employers at the same time.

As evidence of these qualitative changes in work time, attention must be drawn to the rapid rise in the number of flexible jobs. As Table 4.1 shows, flexible employment increased significantly in the EU between 1985 and 1995. Given a base of 100 in 1985, the indicator in the EU's 15 member states rose to 115 in 1995. Spain turned out to be the champion of flexible employment (from 121 to 174), with the Netherlands not far behind (from 106 to 162), although part-time jobs were more frequent than temporary ones there (De Grip et al, 1997). Denmark, which had average flexible employment for the EU in 1995, along with Greece, were the only countries where this trend had tapered off from 126 to 114.

Table 4.1: Growth of flexible employment[a] in the European Union (1985-95)

(EU = 100 in 1985)	1985	1995
Austria	–	86
Belgium	85	93
Denmark	126	114
Finland	88	115
France	76	107
Germany [West Germany only]	87	98
Greece	168	132
Ireland	95	116
Italy	92	103
Luxembourg	58	57
Netherlands	106	162
Portugal	126	117
Spain [1987 instead of 1985]	121	174
Sweden [1987 instead of 1985]	126	134
United Kingdom	107	119
European Union	100	115

Note: [a] Flexible employment refers to self-employment, part-time jobs and wage-earners on temporary contracts.

Source: Eurostat quoted in De Grip et al, 1997, p 5, Table1.

Blurring the ages of life

Besides the fragmentation of work time, the specific functions assigned to each of the three stages of the life course now coexist during each stage. We are witnessing a despecialisation of the ages of life. Industrial society's synchronisation of stages in the life course with its orderly succession of ages is imperilled. The binary opposition between work and nonwork no longer shapes an orderly life course.

Nowadays, biographical trajectories are becoming flexible and individualised in line with increasing flexibility and individualisation in the world of work. Work and free time are now very much mixed up during each age of life. Free time is no longer lodged at the two ends of life; it punctuates the period devoted to work. The success, everywhere in Europe, of parental leaves for raising children, the development of sabbaticals and of life-long learning, the multiplication of leaves for training or of 'time savings account' (for depositing unused vacation time, unpaid overtime, and so on), is all evidence of how entangled the socially defined periods of time have become.

Various indicators provide evidence of this desynchronisation as the ages of life have lost their specialisation. For example, the economic inactivity rate is rising in all age-groups (Table 4.2). This increase in the time that is neither employment nor unemployment is not limited to the two ends of life, since it now also affects the middle-aged. The inactivity rate of men 35-44 years old has risen significantly since 1985 and now tends towards or above 6% in European countries such as Denmark, Finland, Belgium, Germany, Sweden and the UK (see Table 4.2). There are three possible explanations: more of these individuals are undergoing training, or have stopped looking for work or have temporarily left the labour market. The Netherlands, unlike other EU countries, has experienced a decrease in the inactivity rate for the young and middle-aged, and a stabilisation for individuals over the age of 55; but this exception might be attributed to the growth of part-time employment there.

Another example of the blurred stages of life is that training and education no longer concern the young alone. Periods of training and job conversion increasingly interrupt time spent in the labour force. Table 4.3 provides data about life-long education, which is becoming significant in Denmark, Finland and Austria. Approximately 30% of the 25-34 age-group and 15-20% of the 35-59 group are in education or training.

Table 4.2: Changes in men's inactivity rates by age group (1970-2000)

Men 15-24 years old	1970[a]	1975	1980[b]	1985	1990	1995	2000[c]
Belgium	–	–	54.0*	56.8	63.0	64.0	61.3
Denmark	–	–	31.7*	21.2	23.5	23.0	24.8
Finland	35.9	42.6	42.9	45.0	41.9	57.0	50.3**
France	39.7	44.4	48.0	51.9	60.4	67.2	67.9
Germany	24.5	34.1	38.2	39.3	37.5	45.4	44.3
Italy	47.9	55.2	50.6	52.7	53.9	54.0	54.9**
Netherlands	34.7*	45.3	50.6	49.5	38.2	34.5	31.1*
Portugal	–	21.2	21.6	27.2	33.5	50.7	48.8**
Spain	26.4**	28.1	29.8	34.9	38.3	47.5	47.3**
Sweden	33.0	27.6	27.7	33.2	30.7	47.3	48.6*
United Kingdom	–	–	–	17.2	16.5	25.6	26.8**
EU (15 members)	–	–	–	–	–	49.6	49.0

Men 35-44 years old	1970	1975	1980	1985	1990	1995	2000
Belgium	–	–	3.5*	3.6	5.2	5.7	5.7
Denmark	–	–	4.4*	5.1	4.1	7.7	7.0
Finland	4.5	5.2	5.2	4.1	5.3	7.2	7.2
France	2.2	2.1	2.1	2.4	3.0	3.6	3.9
Germany	1.1	2.2	2.1	2.7	3.0	3.7	4.1
Italy	–	–	–	–	–	–	–
Netherlands	3.1*	4.0	4.8	6.0	4.7	5.2	4.9*
Portugal	-	3.8	3.9	4.0	3.5	4.1	5.3**
Spain	2.4**	2.1	3.2	3.8	3.8	4.9	5.1**
Sweden	3.6	3.3	3.3	3.3	3.8	6.8	8.5**
United Kingdom	–	–	–	3.4	4.3	6.2	6.7
EU (15 members)	–	–	–	–	–	4.6	4.9

Men 45-54 years old	1970	1975	1980	1985	1990	1995	2000
Belgium	–	–	9.7*	11.3	15.7	12.7	14.1
Denmark	–	–	8.1*	9.7	6.6	10.2	10.8
Finland	9.4	12.8	12.9	11.4	11.0	12.6	12.1
France	4.8	5.1	5.3	6.5	6.9	6.6	7.0
Germany	4.0	5.3	5.7	5.0	5.3	7.0	7.4
Italy	–	–	–	–	–	–	–
Netherlands	6.2*	9.0	11.4	14.2	11.7	10.3	9.2*
Portugal	-	3.8	9.3	10.4	9.7	9.2	9.1**
Spain	4.1**	4.6	7.2	8.9	8.3	4.9	9.3**
Sweden	5.2	5.9	5.3	5.1	5.5	7.5	9.2**
United Kingdom	–	–	–	7.1	8.0	10.2	11.9
EU (15 members)	–	–	–	–	–	9.6	9.7

Men 55-64 years old	1970	1975	1980	1985	1990	1995	2000
Belgium	–	–	49.4*	54.9	64.6	64.1	63.7
Denmark	–	–	32.8*	34.2	30.8	32.1	35.5
Finland	25.1	34.4	43.1	48.3	52.9	55.4	54.6
France	24.6	31.0	31.4	49.9	54.2	58.5	57.4**
Germany	19.8	30.2	32.7	41.2	41.7	45.5	47.5
Italy	–	–	–	–	–	–	–
Netherlands	19.4*	27.8	36.8	53.0	54.3	57.7	53.1*
Portugal	-	21.8	25.4	33.7	33.5	39.3	35.4**
Spain	15.8**	20.2	23.9	32.8	37.6	45.1	42.2**
Sweden	14.6	18.0	21.3	24.1	24.7	29.3	27.7**
United Kingdom	–	–	–	31.0	31.9	37.6	36.5**
EU (15 members)	–	–	–	–	–	48.9	48.5

Notes:

The inactivity rate, the opposite of the activity rate, is the proportion of the age-group's economically inactive population (those who are neither active nor unemployed) to its total population.

[a] In the 1970 column, * indicates data from 1971; ** data from 1972.

[b] In the 1980 column, * indicates data from 1983.

[c] In the 2000 column, * indicates data from 1998; ** data from 1999.

Source: OECD (2000) Labour force statistics and Eurostat

Table 4.3: Proportion of 15- to 59-year-olds in education or training in the European Union (1998)

	15-24			25-34			35-59		
	Total	M	W	Total	M	W	Total	M	W
Austria	47.5	49.5	45.3	36.8	39.0	34.1	15.6	14.7	16.7
Belgium	62.8	61.6	64.1	7.2	7.9	6.5	3.8	4.3	3.2
Denmark	71.9	71.8	72.0	29.0	27.7	30.3	17.9	15.4	20.4
Finland	72.0	69.2	74.7	25.1	26.7	23.4	14.6	12.7	16.6
France	69.0	69.0	69.0	6.1	6.0	6.3	1.5	1.3	1.7
Germany	68.4	68.8	68.0	12.7	14.7	10.5	3.1	3.2	2.9
Greece	55.1	55.2	55.0	3.0	3.0	2.9	0.3	0.3	0.4
Italy	54.4	52.3	56.5	10.7	10.8	10.6	2.7	2.9	2.5
Luxembourg	62.8	64.0	61.6	8.5	8.7	8.2	4.1	4.5	3.7
Netherlands	69.6	71.3	67.9	21.4	24.4	18.2	9.9	10.2	9.7
Portugal	52.9	50.3	55.4	7.6	7.7	7.4	1.3	1.0	1.6
Spain	59.0	54.5	63.7	10.6	9.6	11.7	1.7	1.4	2.0
Sweden	67.4	63.9	71.1	20.4	17.6	23.3	9.1	7.0	11.2
United Kingdom	47.3	47.5	47.2	17.0	17.0	16.9	11.6	11.1	12.2

Note: M = Men; W = Women.

Source: Eurostat, Labour force survey (1998)

Figure 4.1: Percentage of employed 25- to 64-year-olds having received occupational training during the last four weeks by age group (1999)

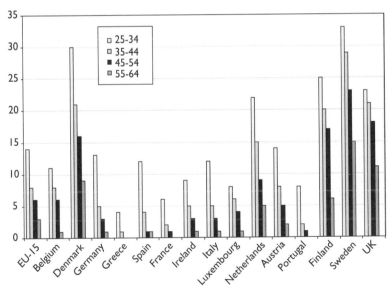

Source: Eurostat (1999)

In the UK, 25% of new enrolments in higher education in 1994 were at least 30 years old. In Denmark and Sweden, this age-group represented a high proportion (18%) of first-year students. On-the-job training is being offered more often to all age-groups in Scandinavia and, to a lesser extent, the UK and the Netherlands, where large numbers from the 35-44, 45-54 and even 55-64 age-groups have received training (Figure 4.1). 'Life-long learning' is already a reality. For all EU member states, however, access to occupational training during employment is clearly restricted after the age of 45.

Levelling age thresholds

The blurring of the ages of life has wrought disorder in the hierarchy of life-course stages, each assigned a specific social function. The principle of a clear-cut transition from one age to the next is thus coming into question, along with the role of age thresholds as chronological markers of the passage from one stable status to another. As Roussel notes in his study on the 'uncertain family' and the upheaval in traditional biographies:

> The thresholds used to have a twofold function: in the present, they made one situation incompatible with the others; and over time, they marked points of irreversibility. The person passing over a threshold thus entered a new, distinct and, in a way, definitive situation. We are now witnessing the gradual levelling of these thresholds. (Roussel, 1989, p 224).

This levelling of age thresholds has come along with the reversibility of transitions and itineraries. Partial, reversible transitions are made toward uncertain statuses. For instance, entry into the world of work is increasingly characterised by longer periods of formal education and the difficulty young people have finding steady employment. It is marked with alternating periods of employment, training and joblessness. Getting a job and founding a family no longer signal irreversible entry into adulthood. Furthermore, these events are often desynchronised. Not only can this passage be reversed, it is also being deinstitutionalised. At the other end, definitive exit from the labour market, given end-of-career precariousness, involves disorderly alternations between periods of unemployment, training and odd jobs before entitlement to retirement.

Given this levelling of thresholds, crossing them is more often than not reversible. Biographical trajectories are ever more contingent (Heinz, 2001) with partial, reversible transitions toward uncertain statuses. New families are founded at the age of 40 or 50. Late parenthood is becoming more common. At the age of 40, persons undergo training for new jobs or enter the ranks of the long-term unemployed. Others, experiencing unemployment at the age of 35, go back home to live with their parents. Repeated entries into and exits from the labour market follow each other in disorder: for young people, odd jobs fill the gap and for older wage-earners, what Doeringer (1990) has called 'bridge jobs' – usually atypical jobs on a secondary labour market while waiting for a pension – are sought. As we see, the major transitions towards and away from economic activity (which used to mark the three principal ages of life) are becoming indistinct.

Similarly, rites of passage from one age of life to the next, such as communion, the draft, marriage or ceremonies for departure on retirement, are no longer being observed. This evidence of the levelling of age thresholds provides us with a glimpse of the slack in a collective regulation of the life course.

As a consequence of this blurring of the ages of life and levelling of age thresholds, biographical trajectories are becoming complex and uncertain for everyone. They are being destandardised and differ from person to person. This situation has led to a crisis of norms and life plans.

First, the life course's normative framework is losing relevance. Welfare system regulations still follow principles based on linear biographical trajectories and a compartmentalisation between life's stages. They are still grounded in uniform, universal categories (such as chronological age) even though personal trajectories have been destandardised. The gap between old norms and new situations spawns uncertainty. It also leads to inadequate coverage for new social risks and unfairness in the administration of welfare programmes.

Second, life plans are in crisis. Unable to foresee their new trajectories and confronted with a desynchronised life course, people experience the future as being socially insecure. Faced with deep uncertainty, they cannot make plans. This crisis of life plans coincides with the crisis of the fordist welfare state, since this uncertainty undermines the insurance model, based as it is on a probabilistic future.

3. Reconfiguring welfare in conformity with a flexible life-course regime

Welfare and security must be redesigned so as to take into account this new organisation of time over the life course. Relatively rigid fordist welfare states are no longer capable of adjusting to new risk profiles. New forms of work and the greater temporal flexibility of the life course have no counterpart in the changes made in welfare systems. The current structure of welfare, with its lists of insured risks and corresponding entitlements and benefits, is still tightly linked to the triple organisation of the life course. It cannot, therefore, provide coverage for new risk profiles. The gap is widening between rigid welfare instruments and new needs for coping with insecurity. Linked to the new flexibility of the life course is a need for protection so as to cope with the rapid obsolescence of knowledge and skills, which entails increased mobility and more frequent job conversions. There is also a need for coverage during the periods of inactivity that affect all age-groups since, as we have seen, inactivity no longer characterises the end of the working life alone.

As we know, the industrial model of labour relations entailed the wage-earner's subordination to the employer as a counterpart for a secure job and broad coverage for various risks (Castel, 1995; Supiot, 2001). This dependent employment status was paired with an extensive welfare system, which was fully instituted following World War II. This model clearly corresponded to the needs of big industry and its wage-earners. Nowadays, a large number of employment situations do not fit into this model. The subordination/protection pair is out of phase with firms' current needs and their management of human resources. Less emphasis is being given to dependence but more to employee autonomy and responsibility (Menger, 2002) and to project management or the setting and meeting of objectives (Boltanski and Chiapello, 1999). Human resource management is ready to grant employees more freedom, but with more responsibility and less security.

Given all this, we must redesign security so that it reaches 'beyond employment' in Supiot's words (2001). The problem is no longer to protect individuals from foreseeable social risks but to provide people with the concrete means for assuming their new responsibilities and autonomy. The notions of welfare and security have to be reconfigured for a flexible life course.

In the coming era, security will be the central paradigm in social protection, as compared to the notions of responsibility and fault that prevailed during the 19th century, or the principles of solidarity and risk-coverage that underlay 20th-century welfare states (Ewald, 1992). The major objective will not be to compensate for major risks (by socialising liability) and to provide stable jobs. Instead, it will be to improve the security of individualised, mobile, uncertain life-course trajectories. Actively providing support for continuity in flexible biographical trajectories can achieve this. Various proposals in recent years seek to reconfigure welfare by combining security with flexibility. Whether referring to "social investments" (Esping-Andersen, 1996), "social drawing rights" (an extension of the aforementioned time savings account, see Supiot, 1999), "asset-based welfare" or "transitional labour markets" (Schmid, 2002), these proposals all aim at redefining the paradigms underlying welfare systems inherited from the industrial era so as to provide the "optimal management of uncertainty" (Ewald, 1992, p 21). These solutions resolutely turn their backs on partial reforms or mere adjustments to the business cycle. They all address the problem of the very architecture of welfare itself (Esping-Andersen, 2002).

From this perspective, income replacement is but one function of welfare among others. Welfare states must now support and promote the autonomy of individuals by providing continuity despite their alternations between periods of economic activity and inactivity. Maintaining occupational capacities and employability is a key issue necessitating a new welfare architecture. This is the very meaning of the phrase 'social investments' as worked out by Esping-Andersen. For him, the objective of equal opportunities now implies measures different from the usual arrangements for redistributing income. These new measures should develop human capital and provide access to education and vocational training. They might be reinforced for the underprivileged. This formulation in terms of a 'social investment' is still not very clear. It tells us nothing about how to combine and coordinate actions between the main pillars in the welfare state, namely, the state, the marketplace, firms, individuals and the family.

Proposals for reconfiguring welfare differ in the degrees of socialisation of the new risks to be covered (see Guillemard, 2003, for a fuller discussion of these proposals). Depending on how broad or how narrow the conception underlying them is, they might refer to either liberal, social democratic or continental approaches. In line with Barbier's remarks (Chapter Seven herein) about the two distinct types of 'activation of social protection' in Europe, we can point to two different ways of reconfiguring welfare as a function of the weight carried by the welfare state's main pillars. Formulas for an asset-based welfare defend the principle of a patrimonial social state that intervenes preventively upstream from the marketplace so as to help individuals acquire various sorts of capital – financial, real estate but also human (education, training) and social – with the aim of requalifying people for a return to the marketplace. This capital would be accumulated in individual accounts, replenished directly by the state and indirectly by various public (in particular fiscal) incentives for individuals to save or for firms to pay into their employees' accounts. The advocates of this approach insist on its capacity for increasing the independence, autonomy and choices of individuals, thus allowing them to shape their own future and become the 'entrepreneurs' of their own careers and lives. In brief, this approach would help empower them. This formula assigns a key role to the individual in line with the 'welfare-to-work' conception. It seeks to provide security by reintegrating people in the labour market as it exists. In contrast, formulas based on 'social drawing rights' and proposals referring to 'transitional labour markets' emphasise collective regulations and their coordination by the main actors, especially the state. In this model, individuals would not be left to themselves in the labour market and a network of actors and programmes would be the key to making personal trajectories more secure.

Whereas the asset-based welfare model centres around the free, responsible individual, the transitional market one emphasises the 'social rights' of the actively employed and the regulations that shape and guide their mobility between the many states of activity and inactivity that now mark careers. Its focus on the systematic and negotiated rearrangements of the passageways between these states accounts for the name 'transitional markets'. Its underlying principle is to remunerate these transitions, and not just employment itself. To this end, the labour market and welfare should be reformed so as to provide continuity and security, despite discontinuous career paths, with countless back and forth movements between changing statuses and alternations of periods of activity and inactivity. Unemployment compensation insurance would thus become an 'employability insurance' that, instead of simply trying to maintain a level of income, would enhance the person's income-earning potential. A second reform would be to create a 'mobility insurance' so as to provide security for a change of job or activity status. Supiot's (2001) proposals for social drawing rights of various sorts fit into this line of thought; the intention being to work out new instruments whereby rights are associated with the person, rather than the latter's occupation or employment status. These rights would no longer be conditioned by the individual's past or present employment status and would no longer represent the only counterpart to a risk. Thus separated from employment, they would represent a credit that has been built up and can be transported from one employer to another. The decision to use these credits would be freely made by the titleholder instead of being tied to the occurrence of a risk. All these proposals for reconfiguring welfare have a similar objective; namely, create a more flexible, optional security that provides for continuity in biographical trajectories in a world where career pathways have become more and more uncertain and where life trajectories, no longer linear, do not have regulated points of transition. But as we see, the solutions being proposed are different.

In the case of asset-based welfare, each individual would become a stakeholder thanks to public funding, but would alone bear the responsibility for using these benefits to build up their own personal security. The danger here is that individuals are left to themselves when making choices and drawing up life plans: what Osterman (1999) has called a 'pack-your-own-parachute strategy'. On the contrary, the solutions related to transitional labour markets or social drawing rights are based on both the institutionalised financing of individualised entitlements and a shared responsibility for using them. In this case, however, the coordination exercised via a super-organisation comprising all actors in the labour market and in welfare might turn out to be overly complicated and any shortcoming in coordination might open a breach in the provision of active security throughout life.

As we see, the reconfiguration of welfare is still in an experimental state. It raises problems, and the proposed solutions have not yet been fully worked out. However, the aims of any reconfigured welfare state arising from these proposals will be more preventive than curative; and the welfare state itself will be based on life-course policies more than on programmes segmented by age. Given this perspective, such policies are becoming a major challenge for the future development of a social Europe.

References

Beck, U. (1992) [German edition 1986] *Risk society*, Newbury Park: Sage.

Bessin, M. (1993) 'Les seuils d'âge à l'épreuve de la flexibilité temporelle' in *Chaire Quételet: Le temps et la démographie*, Louvain: Département de Démographie de Louvain-La-Neuve.

Best, F. (1981) *Flexible life-scheduling: Breaking the education-work-retirement lockstep*, New York: Praeger Special Studies.

Boltanski, L. and Chiapello, E. (1999) *Le nouvel esprit du capitalisme*, Paris: Gallimard.

Bosch, G. (1999) 'Le temps de travail: tendances et nouvelles problématiques', *Revue internationale du travail*, vol 138, no 2, pp 141-62.

Castel, R. (1995) *Les métamorphoses de la question sociale. Une chronique du salariat*, Paris: Fayard.

Castells, M. (1996) *The rise of the network society*, Cambridge: Blackwell.

De Grip, A., Hoevenberg J. and Willems, E. (eds) (1997) 'L'emploi atypique dans l'Union Européenne', *Revue internationale du travail*, vol 136, no 1, pp 5-78.

Doeringer, P. (ed) (1990) *Bridges to retirement: Older workers in a changing labor market*, Ithaca, NY: Industrial and Labor Relations Press.

Esping-Andersen, G. (1996) 'Positive-sum solutions in a world of trade-offs', in G. Esping-Andersen (ed) *Welfare states in transition*, London: Sage, pp 256-67.

Esping-Andersen, G. (2002) *Why do we need a new welfare state?*, Oxford: Oxford University Press.

Ewald, F. (1992) 'Responsabilité, solidarité, sécurité. La crise de la responsabilité en France à la fin du 20ème siècle', *Risques*, 10, pp 9-24.

Guillemard, A.-M. (1997) 'Rewriting social policy and changes in the life-course organization: a European perspective', *Canadian journal on aging*, vol 16, no 3, pp 441-64.

Guillemard, A.-M. (2000) *Aging and the welfare state crisis*, Cranbury, NJ: Delaware University Press.

Guillemard, A.-M. (2001) 'Age policy', in N. Smelser (ed) *International encyclopedia of the social and behavioral sciences*, vol 3, no 15, article 6, The Hague: Elsevier.

Guillemard, A.-M. (2003) *L'âge de l'emploi. Les sociétés à l'épreuve du vieillissement*, Paris: Armand Colin.

Guillemard, A.-M. and van Gunsteren, H. (1991) 'Pathways and their prospects: a comparative interpretation of the meaning of early exit', in M. Kohli, M. Rein, A.-M. Guillemard and H. van Gunsteren (eds) *Time for retirement: Comparative studies of early exit from the labor force*, Cambridge: Cambridge University Press, pp 362-88.

Heinz, W.R. (2001) 'Work and the life course: a cosmopolitan-local perspective', in V. Marshall, W. Heinz, H. Krüger and A. Werma (eds) *Restructuring work and the life course*, Toronto: University of Toronto Press, pp 3-22.

Kohli, M. (1987) 'Retirement and the moral economy: an historical interpretation of the German case', *Journal of Aging Studies*, vol 1, no 2, pp 125-44.

Maddison, A. (1995) *L'économie mondiale 1820-1992: Analyse et statistiques*, Paris: Organisation for Economic Co-operation and Development.

Mayer, K.U. and Schoepflin, U. (1989) 'The state and the life course', *Annual review of sociology*, vol 15, pp 187-209.

Menger, P.M. (2002) *Portrait de l'artiste en travailleur, métamorphoses du capitalisme. La république des idées*, Paris: Seuil.

Osterman, P. (1999) *Securing prosperity*, Princeton, NJ: Princeton University Press.

Percheron, A. (1991) 'Police et gestion des âges', in A. Percheron and R. Remond (eds) *Âge et politique*, Paris: Economica, pp 111-39.

Riley, M., Johnson, M. and Foner, A. (1972) *Aging and society: A sociology of age stratification*, New York, NY: Russell Sage Foundation.

Roussel, L. (1989) *La famille incertaine*, Paris: Odile Jacob.

Schmid, G. (2002) 'Towards a new employment compact', in G. Schmid and B. Gazier (eds) *The dynamics of full employment*, Cheltenham: Edward Elgar.

Smelser, N. and Halpern, S. (1978) 'The historical triangulation of family, economy and education', *American Journal of Sociology*, vol 84, Special issue, pp 288-315.

Sue, R. (1995) *Temps et ordre social*, Paris: Presses Universitaires de France.

Supiot, A. (2001) *Beyond employment: Changes in work and the future of labour law in Europe*, Oxford: Oxford University Press.

FIVE

Citizenship, unemployment and welfare policy

Jørgen Goul Andersen

Citizenship has become a key concept in many fields of social science, from the analysis of social rights to normative political theory and empirical research on political participation and political culture (Andersen and Hoff, 2001). With such a broad scope of applications a variety of meanings[1] inevitably follows (van Gunsteren, 1998). This problem is aggravated by the fact that precise definitions are often missing in the literature. Definitions tend to be replaced by vague notions that citizenship is about rights and duties – or about equality and empowerment, eligibility and entitlements, membership and participation, integration and civicness and so on. These are certainly some of the keywords, but they need to be arranged and spelled out more clearly. Furthermore, analytical and normative aspects of the concept often tend to be conflated. This chapter seeks to elaborate and clarify the concept of citizenship, to specify how it may be used in various fields of welfare research, and to discuss some of the advantages of phrasing research questions in the language of citizenship. Finally, it comments briefly on the notion of 'active citizenship'.

Citizenship and what is it about

Unlike much research on citizenship, we do not conceive of citizenship as only a set of rights and duties. Of course, rights and duties are central aspects of any notion of citizenship. But we prefer to emphasise the dimension of practices. More specifically, practices include two further aspects: participation and orientations (sometimes labelled identities). This tripartition is in line with a Scandinavian tradition of democracy studies (Petersson et al, 1989; Andersen et al, 1993; Andersen and Hoff, 2001), but can be identified also in feminist research (Lister, 1997; Siim, 2000) as well as in research on social exclusion (Room, 1990, 1995; Berghman, 1995; Vleminckx and Berghman, 2001). It may be appropriate, however, to introduce yet another aspect: social conditions (material situation and psychological well-being), which may be conceived as an intervening variable between rights and participation.

Whereas rights and duties refer to institutions, social conditions, participation and orientations refer to outcomes. Thus, we speak of social rights not only as the embodiment of full citizenship, but also – and even more – as a determinant of full citizenship. In the final analysis, what matters most, is not social rights, but their effects. We may define citizenship as de facto full membership of society as citizens. This definition needs elaboration, however, including a specification of what is meant by the terms, 'full membership' (empowerment and participation) and 'citizens' (equal status and civicness).

In the following, we treat citizenship both as a perspective and as a benchmark, focusing on analytical rather than on normative aspects, and we distinguish clearly between the dimensions of rights, social conditions, participation and orientations. In doing so, we elaborate on the seminal work of T. H. Marshall (1950), *Citizenship and social class*, where citizenship was introduced as a sociological concept by presenting social rights as a core aspect of citizens' rights and as a precondition of de facto status as equal citizens. Social rights imply (more) equal social conditions. But the actual fulfilment of this formally equal status as citizens also requires equal access to participation in social and political life (Room, 1990; Lister 1997). The lack of such a de facto equal status, on the other hand, implies that society is divided between first-class and second-class citizens (Roche, 1992, p 55). Extrapolating somewhat from Marshall, but in line with his thinking, we suggest including empowerment (or high access to participation) as an aspect of the participation dimension. Finally, to the dimensions of rights, social conditions and participation, we suggest adding civic orientations as a separate dimension of practices, answering the question of how people orient themselves as citizens to their fellow citizens and to the community. This latter aspect was also hinted at by Marshall (1950, p 56) who emphasised that true citizenship requested, "a direct sense of community membership based on loyalty to a civilisation which is common possession".

Such discussions used to be centred around social class. To what extent could the ideal of equal citizenship be realised in a society characterised by class inequality? What contributed to keeping the discussion alive in the 1980s and 1990s, however, was gender more than class. Women enjoy the same legal status as men, but it is questionable whether they also enjoy full and equal citizenship.[2] In addition to the gender issue, a number of new challenges have been added. A core challenge is immigration. Whether they are formally state citizens or not, do immigrants become second-class citizens in the societies where they live? Another issue is Europeanisation; that is, the development of rights, participation and orientation as citizens at a European level. Furthermore, the developed welfare state has added yet another dimension to the discussion about citizenship; the question of the 'empowerment' of users and clients vis-à-vis authorities and service providers. Rather than just speaking of 'equal citizenship', we prefer to speak of 'full and equal citizenship' in order to underline the fact that citizenship is both a question of empowerment and a question of equality.

The issue of unemployment and unemployment policy is also frequently addressed as a new challenge to citizenship. Does long-term unemployment lead to a new division of society between insiders and outsiders, perhaps even to the development of a distinct underclass at the bottom of society? Do the unemployed enjoy equal social rights, are they treated "with equal concern and respect" (Dworkin, 1997, p 275), and do they have full access to participation in social and political life?

For analytical purposes, then, citizenship becomes a benchmark against which one can measure the actual fulfilment of this ideal in society. In addition to the traditional challenge of social class, there are a number of new challenges to the ideal of full and equal citizenship in society: gender, immigration, long-term unemployment and multilevel governance. In this chapter, we focus mainly on the challenge of unemployment.

Unemployment as a challenge to citizenship

To Marshall, the core problem was the tension between class inequality and the position of individuals as equal citizens. This tension was unavoidable in a capitalist society – occasionally, Marshall even spoke of a war between class and citizenship – but according to him, it could (and would) be limited by the extension of social rights, enabling society to approach the ideal of full citizenship for all its members, even under capitalism.

In Marshall's world, this was preconditioned by full employment. Employment is indeed a fundamental source of empowerment and equality, and to prevent unemployment has always been a priority goal of the labour movement. However, the question is what happens to citizenship when this goal is not attained. The classical answer which has legitimised generous social security for the unemployed is that such welfare arrangements could at least alleviate the consequences of unemployment for citizenship.

However, critics have claimed that social protection is ineffective or even counterproductive as an instrument of citizenship and that unemployment inevitably entails powerlessness, loss of autonomy and social marginalisation, regardless of economic compensation. Sometimes it is even claimed that generous welfare arrangements make things worse. In the first place, labour-market economists have argued that generous social protection and labour-market regulation gives the unemployed too little incentive to work and keeps 'reservation wages' at a level where the market cannot provide a sufficient number of jobs for the less skilled. As a consequence, many less skilled people become entrapped in long-term unemployment. Thus, it was frequently argued in the 1990s that advanced welfare states face a trade-off between equality (including social rights) and employment (OECD, 1994, 1997).

Secondly, some sociologists have added an emphasis on identities and on the relationship between rights and duties or responsibilities. Unemployment may lead to welfare dependency and welfare dependency turns citizens into – sometimes demanding – clients. Many such discussions (including discussions about the underclass and dependency culture) were initiated by the 'New Right' (Murray, 1984) but have to some extent been endorsed also by other sociologists (Gilbert, 1995; Giddens, 1998). Such considerations have remained largely speculative as empirical evidence for them is weak. But it raises the question about what should be measured in order to test such hypotheses.

The discussion earlier serves to illustrate that citizenship is not only about social rights and social conditions, but also about participation and civic orientation, and the benchmark is not only equality, but also empowerment. In Scandinavia, the so-called 'Stockholm school', which has been a leading force in the discussion about social citizenship, has sometimes seemed to conceive of citizenship and equality as nearly the same phenomenon (but see Korpi, 2002). This was developed and modified, however, by Esping-Andersen (1990) who defined the essence of 'decommodification' not as equality but rather as citizenship in the Marshallean sense of the word. Others, like Rothstein, (1998) have even more explicitly underlined the empowerment aspect by claiming that the core of citizenship is that everybody has the same possibility to make autonomous choices. We shall not discuss here the characteristic tension between a classical social democratic tradition emphasising equality and more social liberal or republican traditions emphasising empowerment. For our purposes, it is important to note, however, that the benchmark of citizenship is both equality and empowerment and that some scholars claim a trade-off, rather than a mutually reinforcing relationship, between these two aspects. This is also one of the starting points for the notions of 'active citizenship' discussed towards the end of the chapter.

Specification of citizenship: rights, social conditions, participation and orientations

To sum up so far, citizenship is a multidimensional phenomenon where we distinguish between four aspects: rights and duties; social and economic conditions (economic situation and well-being); participation (social and political) and civic orientations, or identities in the broadest sense.

The dimension of rights includes both civil, political and social rights. In relation to the problem of unemployment, the social rights of unemployed people is the important aspect. Rights can be understood simply as a legal status and effective citizenship as the actual fulfilment of such rights. We propose, however, a broader, sociological conception of rights which includes not only formal rights but also institutionalised practices, not least in order to take account of the implementation side and informal norms. Rights enable action, and this holds not only for legal rights but also for other institutionalised opportunities. When we speak of the social rights of the unemployed, it is not only their formal rights and duties that are of interest but also institutionalised patterns such as the actual administration of the work test and of activation. This also means that social rights can change even without the law being changed; for instance, by changes in the implementation and administration of the formal rules.

In relation to unemployment, classical parameters include formal criteria like the criteria of eligibility (such as contributions or state citizenship and residence); the criteria of entitlement (means-test, flat-rate or earnings-related); forms of governance (whether centralised or decentralised, state-administered or corporatist); duration, adequacy and replacement levels (Korpi, 2002).[3] To take account of the increasing emphasis on duties, one may choose to replace eligibility with the broader notion of 'eligibility and conditionality' (Dwyer, 2000). Needless to say, the actual ratio between the number of persons receiving unemployment benefits and social assistance is also a key indicator when we speak of rights.

However, measures of social rights should also include information about patterns of implementation,[4] such as the practising of the works test and the implementation of activation. It is important to know, to take a Danish example, that people who are receiving unemployment benefits are required to accept any kind of job, or to accept a daily commuting time of four hours, but it is even more important to know whether such requirements are ever made in practice. By the same token, it is important to know whether activation plans are negotiated between the unemployed person and the job officer, or whether they are de facto imposed on the unemployed as some disciplinary device. This is also the subject of political battle, sometimes as much as the formal rules are.

In short, what we need to know is to what extent welfare institutions are designed and function to strengthen the status of people as full and equal citizens. At the level of welfare regimes, 'decommodification' (Esping-Andersen, 1990) is a relevant indicator, but it is difficult to measure; and at any rate, we need more detailed information at a more concrete level. Whereas citizenship or equality was the leitmotif of most welfare reforms until the 1980s, later reforms of social protection have been more concerned with retrenchment or with incentives. Not infrequently, however, such changes have also been justified for their positive effects on citizenship as they empower people by making them able to provide for themselves. Even the idea of 'workfare' (Lødemel and Trickey, 2001) claims legitimacy on such grounds, and so do ideas of a 'social investment state' (Giddens, 1998), or of an 'enabling state' (Gilbert and Gilbert, 1989; Gilbert, 1995, 2002). Needless to say, this holds even more true for Scandinavian activation policies. We comment briefly on such notions later on.

From a classical citizenship perspective, on the other hand, "activating citizens" is exactly what generous (so-called "passive") welfare arrangements do by providing them with the necessary resources to participate in society (Loftager, 2002). In this perspective, most of the changes heralded as enabling or activating should be characterised as 'recommodification', 'de-universalisation', 'targeting' or 'residualisation'; in short, as changes that undermine equality and citizens' rights and, not least, the common treatment of all citizens as equal vis-à-vis the state (Andersen, 1999; Kuhnle and Kildal, 2002; Clasen and van Oorschot, 2002). However, evaluating the rules and actual administrative practices (Barbier, Chapter Seven), and examining empirically the consequences for social conditions, participation and identities could help us to assess which interpretation is the most appropriate.

The dimension of social conditions refers to objective and subjective aspects of welfare; including poverty, deprivation in relation to objective living conditions (like housing and health), economic hardship (difficulties to make ends meet, economic insecurity) and subjective well-being (including well-being, overall life satisfaction, psychological distress and self-esteem).

These are the kinds of variables usually included in studies of multidimensional deprivation which frequently forms the core operationalisation of social exclusion (Kieselbach, 2002). Like the dimensions of participation and orientation, these social conditions are partly the outcomes of social rights and partly the effects of the market system (class and other stratification mechanisms in society). The leading question here is to what extent welfare arrangements (social rights) can modify the consequences of the market forces operating in the labour market.

The dimension of participation includes any form of participation in social life, that is, both social and political participation. Social participation refers to integration in primary and secondary groups as well as to participation in associations and other tertiary groups (as in Gallie and Paugam, 2000), and even leisure activities. Being a citizen means being effectively a 'member of society', and this means participating – and, in particular, not being excluded from participation. In the broad sense, this also includes participation in the prevailing ways and standards of life. From a democratic perspective, political participation is of particular interest. Thus, this dimension includes integration in primary and secondary groups – family and friends (versus isolation); participation in associations and other tertiary groups; participation in leisure activities and political participation of all sorts.[5]

Traditionally, unemployment has been linked to a notion of social isolation and withdrawal from social and political life – both for economic and psychological reasons (Jahoda, 1982). A core question is to what extent this is an inevitable effect of unemployment, and to what extent it can be alleviated by social rights (see also Schlozman and Verba, 1979). If the withdrawal from public life, the deterioration of social networks and vicious circles of social isolation are intrinsically linked to unemployment, regardless of compensation, this dictates a different trade-off between employment and equality than if economic inequality is the key factor underlying such a deterioration of citizenship.

As empowerment and the non-exclusion of citizens are the main concerns from a citizenship perspective (full and equal citizenship being a somewhat imprecise benchmark), the participation dimension should include not only participation in the narrow sense, but also individuals' capabilities to participate and exert influence (Sen, 1992), both in society at large, and in everyday life at the workplace, or as user of public service institutions ('small-scale democracy' in Petersson et al, 1989). To use a standard phrase of the political participation literature originally launched by the American election studies in the early 1950s (Campbell et al, 1954), *efficacy* becomes a central concern. This includes, in turn, two subdimensions – competence (internal efficacy) and the responsiveness of those who makes the decisions (external efficacy). These concepts may be applied both to politics at large and to small-scale democracy in everyday life: being a citizen is a matter of having some degree of control in both contexts.

The dimension of orientations or identities (largely corresponding with the notion of 'civicness') includes nearly all aspects of citizens' orientations and attitudes qua citizens. This involves at least three subdimensions: orientations towards the community (including the political system); citizens' orientations towards each other and one's own role perceptions, including one's perceptions of one's duties. The normative concept of civic virtues – what it takes to be a 'good citizen' – cuts across all these three subdimensions.

Orientations towards the authorities and the political system – sometimes referred to as 'vertical citizenship' – roughly corresponds with the concept of 'political culture' in the political culture tradition (Almond and Verba, 1963). Elaborating on this, one could list the following aspects: (diffuse) support for the political system and political trust; orientations towards collective problems and common interests and own orientation towards the role of the self in politics as an active citizen.[6]

Taking unemployment as an issue, important questions are to what extent and under what conditions people who have been unemployed for a long time become integrated into the political regime or alienated from authorities; whether they assume an active or passive orientation to society and to what extent employed and unemployed people are able to maintain orientations towards collective problems and common interests (including fighting unemployment and the social protection of the unemployed). If unemployed people are neglected or blamed for their own situation by those in employment this indicates a loss of citizenship.

Citizens' orientations towards each other – so-called horizontal citizenship – includes the following aspects: solidarity, stigmatisation, social trust (or generalised norms of reciprocity; see Putnam, 2000) and social and political tolerance.

Again, the questions in relation to unemployment are fairly obvious:

to what extent and under what conditions do employed people maintain solidarity with unemployed people and regard them as equals and does long-term unemployment lead to a decline of social trust and tolerance (perhaps even a search for scapegoats)? In short, what does long-term unemployment mean for civicness, and to what extent does this depend on welfare arrangements?

Own role perceptions. This is a somewhat less well-elaborated theoretical category that refers to the discussion about welfare dependency. This category would include at least norms of self-responsibility (being able to provide for oneself and to act autonomously); norms of social responsibility (from the workplace or community to the society at large) and norms of compliance with the law.

As can be noted, these are some of the critical variables from a dependency culture or underclass perspective: do long-term unemployed people become clients, unable to take responsibility for their own situation? Does generous social protection contribute to, prevent or catalyse such tendencies? What are the effects of such unemployment on individuals' work ethics? Does long-term unemployment have any effect on an individual's norms of family responsibility, responsibility towards the community and law-abidingness – and how does this depend on the social protection of the unemployed?

The conceptual scheme mentioned earlier does not amount to a theory, nor should it do so. It serves to point out relevant variables as seen from a citizenship perspective and it indicates how citizenship can be operationalised. The illustrations are drawn from the field of unemployment, but an equivalent conceptual scheme can be applied to questions like class and ethnic inequality and even to the issue of multilevel governance (Andersen, 2002, 2004).

Citizenship, poverty and social exclusion

This brings us to the issue of whether it is worthwhile analysing threats of marginalisation from a citizenship perspective, rather than taking our point of departure in somewhat more mainstream concepts like poverty, new poverty, marginalisation or social exclusion. To some extent, this is simply a matter of terminology. Different terms are applied to the same concept and much literature about new poverty or social exclusion even take their point of departure from the concept of citizenship in Marshall and the post-Marshall tradition. All the same, the operationalisation of the concepts tends to differ, and this typically reflects the roots of the vocabulary in different theoretical frames of reference.

The concept of poverty is the classical concept in the social policy literature. Its disadvantage is that it either refers narrowly to economic distribution or tends to become all-embracing, just like concepts such as living conditions or welfare. There are few theoretical guidelines for making priorities. The concept of new poverty (Room, 1990) for example, serves to underline the differences between class inequality and new inequalities between the employed and the chronically unemployed, but basically, this means a narrowing of the scope of independent variables.

Another alternative is the concept of marginalisation (or marginality – we don't distinguish here). This is a concept which has been given an enormous variety of meanings. Sometimes it has been used as a purely operational measure referring to average degree of unemployment over a certain period, for instance three years. In the absence of any theoretical definition, however, it often tends to be interpreted as a proxy for social marginalisation (Born and Jensen, 2002). Needless to say, this is not scientifically legitimate. The relationship between labour-market marginalisation and social marginalisation is exactly one of the core issues in the debate about the capacity of the welfare state to ensure full citizenship – an issue to be examined, rather than taken for granted.

As such, marginality is a theoretically empty concept. At most, it may be defined as involuntary absence of full participation (Svedberg, 1995). But it has meaning only if it is specified in relation to some particular arena, such as the labour market. Further, the concept of marginalisation is not per se attached to any particular theoretical perspective but achieves various meanings, depending on the theoretical perspective being used such as citizenship or social exclusion. The concept is useful, but it does not represent any theoretical perspective of its own.

The concept of social exclusion is also slippery. It was invented in France in the early 1970s and formed part of a national political discourse of French governments in the 1980s. However, when the concept was adopted by the European Commission and referred to in the preamble of the European Social Charter in 1989 (Littlewood and Herkommer, 1999; Vleminckx and Berghman, 2001), it immediately spread to most of Europe where it combined with the British tradition of poverty research (Room, 1995). Against this background, the ambiguity of the concept is hardly surprising

(Halvorsen, 2000). At least three different meanings can be distilled from it.

The first is found mainly in official documents where social exclusion is often equated with labour-market exclusion (Levitas, 1998) and connotes a deviance that should be corrected (Born and Jensen, 2002). Another meaning of social exclusion is found in sociological analyses where the concept most often refers to a process of cumulative deprivation in several areas (Berghman, 1995; Room, 1995; Littlewood and Herkommer, 1999). This may also include the notion of spatial segregation. Finally, a variant equates social exclusion with the formation of an underclass as a group outside society with its own norms and culture – in line with American New Right analyses (Murray 1984). Unlike the 'New Right' interpretation, however, a social exclusion perspective sees the underclass as an effect of deprivation, not as a cause of it (Littlewood and Herkommer, 1999).

Citizenship and social inclusion – different frames of reference

Obviously, there is much similarity between loss of citizenship and social exclusion, understood as multiple deprivation or as the formation of an underclass (Roche, 1992). However, the frames of reference are different. Typically, the notion of social exclusion is rooted in a sociological problem complex of social integration. The concept of citizenship, on the other hand, originates from a problem of democracy: the contradiction between democracy and class inequality. Finally, the concept of poverty stems from a (sociologically oriented) problem complex of economic distribution. It may be useful to locate the concepts in a field between a sociological, economic and a democratic (political) perspective (see Figure 5.1).

An economic perspective on labour-market marginalisation will, by its very nature, emphasise work and economic distribution. These are simply the tools available for an economic approach. For a sociological perspective, it is perfectly natural to put social integration – and its negation: social exclusion – at the core of the analysis, as this is more or less the basic problem of sociology. Finally, a democratic perspective is intrinsically concerned with empowerment, equal status and equal worth as citizens, equal participation, and – as the equivalent of civic orientations – with political integration. The concept and perspective of citizenship comes closest to the democratic (political) corner in the triangle in Figure 5.1. The concept and the discussion of social exclusion comes closer to the sociological pole. The concepts

Figure 5.1: Location of competing concepts of inclusion in the field between an economic, a sociological and a democratic perspective

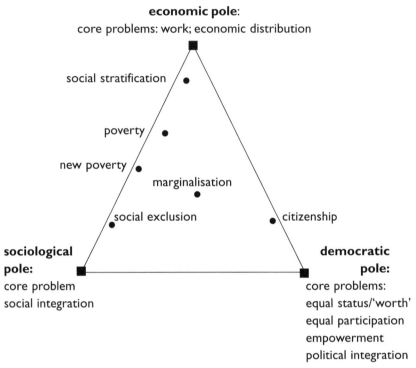

of stratification, poverty and new poverty can be conceived of as located close to the axis between a sociological perspective and an economic one.

This may serve to clarify why these perspectives and concepts differ in focus. To illustrate, nonvoting and lack of contact with family and friends could serve as operational components of both social exclusion and the loss of citizenship. But nonvoting would come quite close to the core of a citizenship concern, and whereas the deterioration of social networks could be a central indicator of certain concepts of social exclusion nonvoting, on the other hand, would rarely be thought of as an operationalisation of social exclusion. Another difference between a social exclusion perspective and a citizenship perspective is that a citizenship perspective does not imply any kind of cumulativity. The relationship between labour-market marginalisation and marginalisation in other arenas (which is tantamount to a loss of citizenship) is exactly the question that is to be examined. The classical social security paradigm predicts that adequate social protection may alleviate or even prevent such spill-over effects from the labour market to other arenas.

A note on 'active citizenship'

As the notion of active citizenship is a key issue of this book, it is natural to ask how this notion would be addressed from the perspectives and the conceptual map sketched earlier. Only three connected aspects are commented upon here. Perhaps we may distinguish between 'active citizenship' as a perspective and ideal of citizenship, as a way of summarising current changes in social rights and duties and as a set of hypotheses about the effects of citizenship rights. To begin with the ideal and the perspective, the notion of active citizenship is not too different from the ideal and perspective that is presented here. The notion of citizenship in this chapter implies precisely that the existence of empowered and active citizens is the benchmark against which the actual state of citizenship can be measured and participation is explicitly spelled out as the key dimension of this benchmark. Further, the notion of orientations also includes some of the ideals of civicness implied by the notion of active citizenship. But the ideal and perspective spelled out here also maintains equality as the central criterion of citizenship. This immediately leads to the question whether there is some conflict between the two ideals in the way that social rights and duties are formulated and implemented. Basically, this is a question that must be answered empirically. We return to it below.

As a way of summarising current changes in social rights and duties, the notion of active citizenship is perhaps even more compatible with the perspective sketched here. Indeed, this seems to be a highly promising way of summarising these changes, as it avoids both the pitfalls of seeing only retrenchments and potential blindness to the trade-off between rights and duties. Indeed, there are many instances when social rights are strengthened, but they are often accompanied by a strengthening of duties – which may be a perfectly natural adaptation to a society with more resourceful, skilled and individualistic citizens. Whether or not new rights and duties are balanced – and equally balanced across social groups – is, once again, basically an empirical matter than can be judged from an assessment of outcomes. Once again, of course, the perspective sketched here would be particularly alert to the issue of equality: in practice, does active citizenship mean the expansion of rights for the strong and the tightening of obligations for the weak?

This brings us to the question of the underlying hypotheses in the various notions of active citizenship. To start with, this itself is an open question. But the perspective sketched here would potentially be at odds with some of the (tacit or explicit) assumptions in notions of active citizenship. In particular, a Marshallean perspective would hypothesise that usually social protection is anything but passive: on the contrary, generous social security is assumed to be 'activating' by itself as it strengthens the resources of the individual. Further, a Marshallean perspective would reject any mechanical assumptions about spill-over effects from labour-market marginalisation to social marginalisation. This is assumed to be conditional on social rights. But basically, these are competing hypotheses that may be tested empirically using the criterion of outcomes. It must be acknowledged that in practice, things are not always that simple. Empirical analyses are always conducted within a theoretical perspective and the notion of active citizenship will to some extent affect the criteria by which outcomes are evaluated. Still, the fact that the notion of active citizenship makes it imperative to consider the broader context does not exclude the fact that the underlying assumptions can be confirmed or falsified. The key message of this chapter is precisely that they should be tested.

Conclusion: citizenship, and what it is about

This chapter has tried to develop, firstly, a relatively precise definition of citizenship, its component aspects and, not least, its potential operationalisation. Clearer distinctions need to be made between the dimensions of rights, social conditions, social and political participation and civic orientations. These dimensions may be analysed separately, as in studies of social law, studies of living conditions, studies of political participation and studies of political culture. Here, the notion of citizenship provides a particular perspective, a benchmark and dimensions for measurement.

Secondly, the notion of citizenship contributes to point out the most important social and democratic challenges of contemporary societies, and the definition above may also serve to bridge some of its different uses. With small modifications, the indicators earlier may be applied to different fields of research such as studies of the impact of unemployment and unemployment policies, immigration and immigration policies, or even multilevel governance. The important question is whether such societal changes tend to produce new divisions between first-class and second-class citizens and whether social policies contribute to alleviating or aggravating such divisions.

This is also more generally the case when analysing social policies. From a citizenship perspective, the two key issues are whether social policies (in actual practice) contribute to equality among citizens and whether they contribute to producing active and efficacious citizens, both in relation to their influence on society and their control over their own situation. This implies that we should look for the actual outcomes of social policies, not only for institutional change.

Finally, the chapter has emphasised the analytical aspects of citizenship. However, as indicated by the brief discussion about active citizenship, the normative theoretical discussions that we have largely by-passed in this article are important also from an analytical perspective, as they provide a debate about what should serve as benchmarks and standards of measurement.

Notes

[1] The confusion starts with the fact that in English there is only one word for the two different concepts of formal 'state citizenship' and 'full membership of society as a citizen'. In French, citizenship connotes both formal state citizenship and the broader set of rules defining citizens' rights (in the context of a specific republican tradition). In German and in the Scandinavian languages, there are two different words for '*Staatsbürgerschaft*' and '*Mitbürgerschaft*', but in Sweden, the latter term is often used to mean state citizenship. In Danish and Norwegian, the words previously did, in fact, cover the distinction between state citizenship and full membership of society as citizens (*Ordbog over det danske sprog* [*Dictionary of the Danish Language*]), but the latter meaning was lost and its rediscovery is spreading, but only slowly, from academic to ordinary language.

[2] Even more so, feminist research has been occupied with gendered citizenship and criticism of the gender-blindness of previous analyses of citizenship (Siim, Chapter Ten).

[3] Korpi (2002) uses the criteria of eligibility, benefit levels and governance for a classification at the level of individual policy areas (see also Korpi and Palme, 1998) into five institutional types: targeted, voluntary state subsidised, corporatist, basic security and encompassing models. This serves as an alternative to Esping-Andersen's (1990) classification of welfare regimes at a more aggregate and abstract level. However, in Korpi's analysis, replacement levels and adequacy are dependent variables, whereas for our purposes these are part of the independent variable. What matters most in relation to analysing effects on effective citizenship, is variables such as minimum levels and replacement ratios.

[4] To put this differently, Korpi's notion of governing the social insurance programme should be replaced by a broader notion of governance, in order to take into account implementation.

[5] A citizenship approach to empirical studies of political participation and political culture was introduced by Petersson et al (1989) and elaborated in Andersen et al (1993).

[6] At this point, Almond and Verba (1963) distinguish between parochial, subject or participant orientations.

References

Almond, G.A. and Verba, S. (1963) *The civic culture*, Princeton, NJ: Princeton University Press.

Andersen, J., Christensen, A-D., Siim, B. and Torpe, L. (1993) *Medborgerskab. Demokrati og politisk deltagelse*, Herning: Systime.

Andersen, J.G. (1999) 'Den universelle velfærdsstat er under pres: men hvad er universalisme?', *GRUS*, no 56-57, pp 40-62.

Andersen, J.G. (2002) 'Danskerne, Europa og det "demokratiske underskud". Den stille revolution i danskernes forhold til EU', in T. Pedersen (ed) *Europa for Folket? EU og det danske demokrati*, Aarhus: Aarhus University Press, pp 32-67.

Andersen, J.G. (2004) *Et ganske levende demokrati*, Aarhus: Aarhus University Press.

Andersen, J.G. and Hoff, J. (2001) *Democracy and citizenship in the Scandinavian welfare states*, Houndsmill: Palgrave.

Berghman, J. (1995) 'Social exclusion in Europe: policy context and analytical framework', in G.J. Room (ed) *Beyond the threshold: the measurement and analysis of social exclusion*, Bristol: The Policy Press, pp 10-28.

Born, A. and Jensen, P.H. (2002) 'A second order reflection on the concepts of inclusion and exclusion', in J.G. Andersen and P.H. Jensen (eds) *Changing labour markets, welfare policies and citizenship*, Bristol: The Policy Press, pp 257-80.

Campbell, A., Gurin, G. and Miller, W.E. (1954) *The voter decides*, Evanston, IL: Row & Peterson.

Clasen, J. and Oorschot, W. van (2002) 'Changing principles in European social security', *European Journal of Social Security*, vol 4, no 2, pp 89-116.

Dworkin, R. (1977) *Taking rights seriously*, London: Duckworth.

Dwyer, P. (2000) *Welfare rights and responsibilities. Contesting social citizenship*, Bristol: The Policy Press.

Esping-Andersen, G. (1990) *The three worlds of welfare capitalism*, Princeton, NJ: Princeton University Press.

Gallie, D. and Paugam, S. (eds) (2000) *Welfare regimes and the experience of unemployment in Europe*, Oxford: Oxford University Press.

Giddens, A. (1998) *The third way. The renewal of social democracy*, London: Polity Press.

Gilbert, N. (1995) *Welfare justice. Restoring social equity*, New Haven, CT: Yale University Press.

Gilbert, N. (2002) *Transformation of the welfare state. The silent surrender of public responsibility*, Oxford: Oxford University Press.

Gilbert, N. and Gilbert, B. (1989) *The enabling state. Modern welfare capitalism in America*, New York: Oxford University Press.

Halvorsen, K. (2000) 'Sosial eksklusion som problem. En kritisk vurdering av begrepet sosial eksklusion med spesiell referanse til dagens Norge', *Tidsskrift for velferdsforskning*, vol 3, no 3, pp 157-71.

Jahoda, H. (1982) *Employment and unemployment: A social-psychological analysis*, Cambridge: Cambridge University Press.

Kieselbach, T. (2002) *Youth unemployment and social exclusion. A comparison of six European countries*, Opladen: Leske and Budrich.

Korpi, W. (2002) *Medborgerskab, magt og velfærdsstat*, Aarhus: Magtudredningen.

Korpi, W. and Palme, J. (1998) 'The strategy of equality and the paradox of redistribution', *American Sociological Review*, vol 63, no 5, pp 661-87.

Kuhnle, S. and Kildal, N. (2002) 'The principle of universalism: tracing a key concept in the Scandanavian welfare model', Paper presented at BIEN 9th Bi-annual Congress, 12-14 September, International Labour Office, Geneva.

Levitas, R. (1998) *The inclusive society? Social exclusion and New Labour*, Basingstoke: Macmillan.

Lister, R. (1997) *Citizenship: feminist perspectives*, London: Macmillan.

Littlewood, P. and Herkommer, S. (1999) 'Identifying social exclusion: some problems of meaning', in P. Littlewood, I. Glorieux, S. Herkommer and I. Jönsson (eds) *Social exclusion in Europe*, Aldershot: Ashgate, pp 1-22.

Lødemel, I. and Trickey, H. (2001) 'A new contract for social assistance', in I. Lødemel and H. Trickey (eds) *'An offer you can't refuse'. Workfare in international perspective*, Bristol: The Policy Press, pp 1-39.

Loftager, J. (2002) 'Aktivering som ny velfærdspolitisk tredjevej', *Politica*, vol 34, no 3, pp 296-312.

Marshall, T.H.(1950) *Citizenship and social class and other essays*, Cambridge: Cambridge University Press.

Murray, C. (1984) *Losing ground. American social policy 1950-1980*, New York: Basic Books.

OECD (1994) *The OECD Jobs Study*,1-2, Paris: OECD.

OECD (1997) *Implementing the OECD Jobs Strategy*, Paris: OECD.

Ordbog over, det danske sprog (1981) 4th edn, Copenhagen: Gyldendal.

Petersson, O., Westholm, A. and Blomberg, G. (1989) *Medborgarnas Makt*, Stockholm: Carlssons.

Putnam, R.D. (2000) *Bowling alone. The collapse and revival of American Community*, New York: Simon & Schuster.

Roche, M. (1992) *Rethinking citizenship. Welfare, ideology and change in modern society*, London: Polity Press.

Room, G. J. (1990) *New poverty in the European Community*, London: Macmillan Press.

Room, G.J. (1995) 'Poverty and social exclusion: the European agenda for policy and research', in G.J. Room (ed) *Beyond the threshold: The measurement and analysis of social exclusion*, Bristol: The Policy Press, pp 1-9.

Rothstein, B. (1998) *Just institutions matter,* Cambridge: Cambridge University Press.

Schlozman, K.L. and Verba, S. (1979) *Injury to insult. Unemployment, class and political response*, Cambridge, MA: Harvard University Press.

Sen, A. (1992) *Inequality reexamined*, Cambridge, MA: Harvard University Press.

Siim, B. (2000) *Gender and citizenship. Politics and agency in France, Britain and Denmark*, Cambridge: Cambridge University Press.

Svedberg, L. (1995) *Marginalitet*, Lund: Studentlitteratur.

van Gunsteren, H.R. (1998) *A theory of citizenship: Organizing plurality in contemporary democracies*, Boulder, CO: Westview Press.

Vleminckx, K. and Berghman, J. (2001) 'Social exclusion and the welfare state: an overview of conceptual issues and implications', in D.G. Mayes, J. Berghman and R. Salais (eds) *Social exclusion and European Policy*, Cheltenham: Edward Elgar, pp 27-46.

SIX

Paradoxes of democracy: the dialectic of inclusion and exclusion

Marina Calloni

The aim of this chapter is to challenge the concept of citizenship in the light of the main paradox of politics and democracy, consisting of the dialectic of inclusion and exclusion within a delimited territory. A reconstruction of the recent debate on social citizenship, multiculturalism and cosmopolitanism – which refers to the transformation of the welfare state, the process of European unification and the effects of globalisation – allows for the reconceptualising of the notions of marginalisation and social policy within a more complex international scenario. This factor should permit one to extend and, at the same time, to restrict the political/cultural boundaries of the nation/welfare state. Indeed, the main challenge consists of rethinking the normative basis and meaning of a 'cross-borders' democracy, social justice and global governance, starting from local experiences.

The cohesive/exclusive power of culture in the political domain

In contemporary western liberal states the idea and practice of social policy is a constitutive principle of the self-interpretation of legitimate political institutions, oriented towards the well-being of all citizens, a fair government and the respect for human rights. But in a nation state, social policies are mainly addressed to individuals who belong to a specific territory and who hold the right to vote. Social policies are, thus, strictly connected to domestic laws as well as local cultures and political traditions. This factor is cohesive for the inhabitants but selective for the 'others'.

The dialectic of culture (Berger and Luckmann, 1967; Eder, 1992), as a form of exclusion and inclusion, is a constitutive but ambivalent issue characterising politics and democracy, as the ancient history of the polis and the modern tradition of the nation state indicate. For this reason, in order to reframe the idea and practices of social policy, this section focuses on reconstructing the overlapping and contradictory connections between the constitution of a community, the limits of culture and the notion of marginalisation within a specific territory.

In Greek philosophy politics was associated with the image of a polis that is protected by walls and where freedom and citizenship were granted to male individuals only, who acquired it by being born of parents in the city. Yet, Greek mythology stresses that the constitution of the polis was the violent result of the extermination of pre-existing populations, wars for the control of the territory and even conflicts within the same ethnic group or family, as Sophocles's tragedy *Antigone* shows. The power that became a key concept for politics meant, on the one hand, the coercive manipulation of other individuals, and on the other hand, was a legitimate mandate issued by citizens in democratic communities. The political history of the West initiated thus a dialectic between violence and interest in reaching peaceful forms of government based on rules agreed by the community.

Yet the ancient political paradigm differs from the modern one in terms of its foundation. According to Aristotle's *Politics* and *Nicomachean ethics*, individuals live together and constitute political societies, fulfilling a 'natural' predisposition. In the modern age, the idea of the contract – a concept derived from private law – became the basis of a political agreement among individuals, who decide to found a political society, stressing a break with the past. Between the 16th and 18th centuries, theories of the foundation of the state (by Hobbes, Locke and Rousseau, albeit with different assumptions and conclusions) thus refer to the regulative idea of an initial social contract among consenting individuals.

The ancient conceptualisation of democracy related to the polis therefore came into conflict with the modern notion, referred to as the state, because of the different basis of political foundation and legitimation in each period. That said, they have various points in common, despite crucial differences: in antiquity as well as in modernity, citizenship relates to individuals who belong to a specific community on the basis of the *ius sanguinis* (that is, their cultural origin, as in Athens) or of the *jus soli* (that is, the place where citizens are resident, as promoted by the French Revolution). Citizens live in a territory delimited by boundaries, with specific rules and laws, which everyone, including resident noncitizens, are bound to respect. The concept of the city as well of the state can be thus pictured as a delimited space which defines who are the members and excludes those who are not, that is, those who are the foreigners, the strangers. The marginal is the other, the alien.

This dynamic also characterised the nation state in the construction of a national identity, which later became the ideological basis for nationalism. This historical process, however, was also due to the transformation of the previous notion of sovereignty, based on the theocratic idea of the king's investiture by God. The king was sovereign over the territory (considered as a part of his possessions) as well as over the life of subjects. After the French Revolution and the secularisation of political power, people became a collective sovereign subject, on whose will was founded the legitimacy of the state. The power of law and the reference to a common culture become the basis of the constitutional pact.

Even though in the ambivalent French revolutionary model the state was meant as a cohesive nation that promulgated and defended human rights alongside the rights of citizenship, nevertheless the perspective of a national culture became central for the identification and homogenisation of citizens. Indeed, the nation state had to refer to a restricted notion of culture and tradition in the construction of the ideology of 'fatherland' or 'mother-country' (gendering political institutions), which consequently affected the 'constitutive elements' of citizenship. Culture was a common basis intended both to empower struggles of national liberation and to foster the construction of a collective identity of those who belonged, by virtue of having the same 'origin', language, history, culture and religion. Starting from the 19th century, the radicalisation of this background became the basis of forms of aggressive nationalism and ethnical wars. However, struggles for recognition have reinforced practices of inclusion (Bobbio, 1999), where 'newcomers' must observe the Constitution in the form of 'constitutional patriotism' in a democratic state (Habermas, 1992). Culture is thus a dialectical process of exclusion and inclusion of marginal people – both citizens and noncitizens – within given political borders.

This dialectic is also visible in the 20th century, when democratic, mainly European, welfare states – with different historical backgrounds and motivations – employed new political strategies in order to confront the conflicts and social inequalities created by industrialism and capitalism. On the one hand, welfare states were designed to improve the well-being and the quality of life of citizens (Calloni, 2001) through labour policies that would be able to defuse class struggles. On the other hand, they were interested in including the struggles for recognition of social actors excluded from the political representation and public arena. The transformation of the state (Marshall, 1992) has been thus associated with the social actions of pressure groups claiming an extension of the traditional rights of citizenship, from civic and political to socioeconomic rights. The practice of citizenship was thus transformed in relation to the participation of social actors and movements, who sought the integration of excluded/not recognised issues and individuals/human groups in the political arena and institutional framework. Citizenship rights were diversified to encompass the cultural rights of indigenous peoples as well. But human rights and the rights of citizenship remain distinct: citizenship is, in fact, recognised on the basis of the political right to vote, while human rights are addressed to all human beings as such.

Since the end of the 20th century the tension between human rights and citizenship has become evident in western societies due to different factors: the structural and economic crisis of the welfare system, which has induced the state to develop a more protective attitude in terms of social provisions; the affirmation of multiculturalism connected to the worldwide phenomenon of migration, which requests differentiated forms of inclusion of 'foreigners' and the increasing processes of financial globalisation that mark out the limits of the nation state; the reinforcement of the EU as a supranational political organism through enlargement towards the east. In this new scenario, what does marginalisation, social exclusion and deprivation mean (Geddes, 2000)? Is it possible to reframe the traditional notion of citizenship within this context? What kind of social policies can be conceptualised in order to increase the well-being of people in a wider political space?

Challenging liberal states: egalitarianism and multiculturalism

Reconceptualising citizenship implies rethinking the meaning and role of the state. Such redefinition requires one to consider how to define the state at the beginning of the new millennium. It can no longer be thought of as a homogeneous nation state because it includes cultural differences, that is groups of people with different backgrounds. Nor can it be understood as a perfectly functioning welfare state, due to the internal restructuring of industrial societies and the change of the domestic and international labour market. Indeed, the political form that the state has acquired in western societies in the last two centuries has been deeply challenged by radical internal, as well as external, transformations over the last decade.

The geopolitical effects of the change of the world order have thus become evident both at the local and international levels. The processes of decolonialisation in Africa and Asia, together with the consequences of the fall of communist regimes in eastern Europe, have induced, on the one hand, the constitution of a new free market in terms of movement of goods and workers (or, in the worst case, of trafficking in human beings). On the other hand, such processes have been catalysts for the development of bloody conflicts, civil wars and genocides that are started, among other reasons, in order to redefine the borders of collapsed geopolitical systems and to precipitate the reconstruction of space for new collective identities.

Culture (Benhabib, 2002) and territory are here brought to a crossroads of tension: on the one hand, there are constructions of invented ethnicities and 'imagined communities' (Anderson, 1991) through the manipulation of tradition (as in the case of the former Yugoslavia) in the form of excluding the 'others'. On the other hand, there are the escalation of struggles for recognition, by neglected cultures within the borders of liberal democracies (such as in Europe and in the US). While in the former the redefinition of the belonging is based on a violent redefinition of the idea of the *jus sanguinis*, in the latter the presence of 'foreign' cultures questions the very possibility of the coexistence under the same laws of various populations with different daily practices and costumes.

Yet both cases indicate the limits of the traditional concept of citizenship, which is based mainly on political rights. While there is a claim that cultural origin and political membership should coincide, thereby excluding whoever is 'different', there is also, on the other side, the necessity to reframe the political approach to citizenship. In fact, whoever is not allowed to participate in elections (that is, to elect and to stand for election) may not take part in political decision making or designate representatives because such a person does not have political rights, even though he or she is resident in and works in the nation state. The voices and interests of 'foreigners' may be reported only indirectly in institutional political contexts by elected members. 'Aliens' and migrants have a delimited set of rights: they cannot vote but, as workers they are guaranteed socioeconomic rights (including social protection, pensions and so on) and as human beings have basic liberties (such as the freedom to organise associations and participate in differentiated sectors of the public sphere).

The key issue of multiculturalism thus radically questions the institutions and the self-comprehension of the liberal state.

Between the 1970s and the 1980s, the international public debate was focused on the discussion about the possibility of founding a theory of justice (following Rawls's thematisation) in liberal societies, where the issue of distribution was deduced by the principles of equal liberty and difference. The experience of western welfare states was at the core of a form of self-reflection upon a capitalist society based on industrial labour, class struggles and economic competition, which produced social exclusion and marginalisation. Rawls's *A theory of justice* (1971) was thus an attempt to conceptualise (and operationalise) a normative theory of distributive justice from the point of view of a democratic nation/welfare state. The implicit question advanced by Rawls was: can a liberal society be fair? Is it in principle able to found universal criteria to determine the fair distribution of common resources and goods?

In this context, marginalisation was understood as the social exclusion of social actors, who lived at the margins, without having the benefits and the opportunities that people at the centre enjoyed. The image of marginalisation indicated thus the centrifugal force of a capitalistic society, which simultaneously creates wealth and poverty, expelling 'weak subjects' and creating vulnerable groups. The history of the welfare state in Europe indicates – in both the 'individualistic' Nordic and 'familistic' Mediterranean variants (Calloni, 1997) – the attempt to confront poverty, by employing different instruments ranging from the subsidence approach to the interest in creating new labour strategies right up to the development of social policies addressed to target groups through forms of 'selective universalism' (Pennacchi, 1997). The counterface of the European models of the welfare state was the communist regime with its different approach to labour policy, social/ gender equality and class conflicts, through the centrality of the party. The fall of communism has cancelled the challenge between the welfare state and the socialist system, leading to the development of processes of 'Europeanisation' in eastern countries.

The present nation/welfare state, compared with its predecessors, has become poorer in material resources while richer in human capital and cultural 'differences'. Yet this richness could imply a social impoverishment in job opportunities, the creation of new class divide and the difficulty of applying the principle of fair distribution to all inhabitants, citizens and foreigners alike. A theory of distributive justice should be thus reframed in order to understand and face new forms of poverty both at the domestic and international level.

Indeed, Rawls's approach to social justice has been questioned over the years from many different perspectives, mainly from the point of view of restricted communities and non-western countries. The traditional role of the welfare state – as paternalistic/maternalistic 'protector' of its citizens – was questioned regarding the conditions necessary for a fair distribution of societal goods and the limits of intervention in the life of people.

Communitarian theorists such as Sandel (1982) and Macintyre (1988) criticised the Rawlsian formalistic approach because it denied the importance of values and the specific content of the good in circumscribed communities. Moreover, values and goods cannot be the same for all individuals.

Amartya Sen (Sen, 1992) put a broader question to Rawls. He referred to developing countries and the idea of development in general (Fukuda-Parr, 2003): when we talk about equality, we must be clear as to the precise meaning of equality, 'equality of what?'. By this question Sen wanted to stress the diversity of opportunities in life and starting points that citizens have in a nation state. Sen argued that social justice should be conceived as a matter that primarily concerns the development of human capabilities and then material goods. Poverty – as experienced by developing countries – prevents the functioning of these capabilities and a respect for basic freedoms (Sen, 1999, 2000). Socio-economic development in such situations cannot take place without a respect for human rights and the establishment of democratic governments (UNDP, 2000). Distribution on its own seems to be an insufficient criterion for creating a fair society. Avishai Margalit (Margalit, 1996) argued that if a state is able to provide a welfare system for its inhabitants but at the same time humiliates them, then the state cannot be defined as a 'just' institution. The objective is to construct a decent society, where justice also has to do with moral sentiments.

From these critiques of Rawls's paradigm, it is possible to deduce that the idea of a fair distribution of resources – even though allocated differently in various societal spheres (Walzer, 1985; Miller and Walzer, 1995) – is simply not enough for rethinking the goals of a fair and democratic state, whose tasks were changed and enlarged over the years due to increased systemic complexity, the changing cultural composition of the inhabitants and the affirmation of a new international horizon.

Multiculturalism has thus put the self-representation of liberal countries into a state of crisis. Do foreigners and citizens have the same basic freedoms? Or does freedom for foreigners have boundaries? And, in particular, to what extent can they practise traditional customs which may be at variance with the positive law in force in their country of residence? How can the state intervene in cases of conflicts with minorities, taking into account the fact that the cultural rights and the rights of peoples are constitutionally recognised and protected by international charters?

Some theorists think that a theory of justice should be based on 'the politics of difference' (Young, 1990, 2000), while others see scope for a possible coexistence between liberal rights and the rights of cultural minorities (Kymlicka, 1995, 2000). In general, however, the blindness of liberal theorists towards cultural diversity is criticised (Taylor, 1991; Parekh, 2000) because this prevents the state from defending liberty and affirming equal treatment for all individuals and not just citizens. This issue has also been summarised in the guise of struggles for 'recognition' versus struggles for redistribution (Fraser and Honneth, 2003), stressing the changing scenario of cultural-political conflicts and the different composition of social actors in the public arena: from activists in black, worker and women's movements to the action of cultural minorities. 'Marginal' groups and 'moral minorities' thereby claim a socio-political centrality. But in the case of minorities the recognition of the existence of neglected groups implies the admission of specific space for cultural autonomy or 'separateness' and the debate consists of defining the extent of liberty that to allows for specific practices.

Thus, culture may contain the potential for discrimination which a democratic state should deny. This is the case in gender issues. The debate on multiculturalism has in fact raised questions related to the private sphere and intimacy. Can the state intervene in the private life of people when the main liberal principles underscore the dichotomy between the public and the private, the defence of privacy and the concept of liberty both of the space for free agency and, indeed, from state intervention in the private life of individuals, distinguishing liberalism from the Soviet model (Berlin, 1969)?

But different 'generations' of rights could clash (Bobbio, 1990). In fact, liberal rights seem to collide with the rights of cultural groups, as indicated by gender issues. In many western countries there has been public debate on topics such as polygamy, forced marriage, the wearing of a veil, and genital mutilation, which refer the life condition of women. In this case, do individual rights take precedence over cultural rights or vice versa? Liberal feminists have argued that "multiculturalism is bad for women" (Moller Okin, 1998; Cohen et al, 1999) because it observes traditions and religions based on patriarchy and the subjection of women both in the family and society. In many countries women are not recognised as persons (Nussbaum and Glover 1995; Nussbaum, 2003) and live in situations of deprivation and subjection. Therefore, pluralism is a constituent ingredient of political liberalism, where differences should be respected. Yet some authors think that the state should maintain an egalitarian position towards all individuals, thanks to a common framework of laws and educational programmes (Barry, 2000).

In sum, due to the transformation of a nation state based on a monolithic 'patriotic' view and the change of the welfare state related to an industrial society, the traditional idea of political citizenship has become an issue of much debate. Due to the increasing presence of a more diversified population over recent decades western states have had to develop new forms of intervention and negotiation, including a more articulated set of social policies and provisions addressed not only to marginalised citizens but to 'noncitizens'. Moreover, they have had to employ new labour strategies because of the intersectionality and overlapping kinds of marginalisation on the basis of gender, age, community, ethnicity, nationality, disability and so on, and not only because of unemployment. Poverty has acquired different faces for all inhabitants, both citizens and foreigners and the term does not refer only to exclusion from the labour market.

This new trend implies a different approach to social policy, services and social work, where the development of human capabilities, the valorisation and appreciation of human and social capital and the improvement of intellectual resources become central. A theory of global justice (Pogge, 2001) – considered from the viewpoint of a transformed nation state and welfare state – must take into account these new challenges and perspectives.

Marginalisation and social policies: a shift from the welfare state to the EU

The perspective of a more inclusive idea of social (Lemke, 2001; Magnusson and Strath, 2004) or negotiated citizenship in Europe (Calloni and Lutz, 2000) was advanced to oppose the inordinately narrow conception of political citizenship which is related to the 'boundaries' of a nation state. Yet citizenship is a guarantee of social protection and rights. Indeed, citizenship can be conceptualised as a series of concentric circles referring to different areas of institutional belonging (from the municipality, province and region, up to the nation), where citizens have an opportunity to express their political preferences through the vote.

In the last decade, this principle became extended for citizens belonging to some European states, members of the European Union (EU). Article 8 of the Maastricht Treaty (1993) asserts, "Citizenship of the Union is hereby established. Every person holding the nationality of a Member state shall be a citizen of the Union". Citizenship means here the extension of previous political rights for some European citizens, who acquire a new 'political identity'. But this process implies the construction of new boundaries for non-EU citizens. The construction of a cohesive European identity can thus become culturally restrictive towards 'new foreigners'. As a corollary, how could it be possible to recognise or to 'include the others' (Habermas, 1996) in our identity? How could one avoid the possibility of erecting the EU as a protective fortress?

Putting this aside, the acquisition of a new political identity is a complex sociocultural process. Is the EU's citizenship complementary to member state nationality or can it become a factor of conflict? In case of divergence, which would take precedence: EU institutions or the nation state?

The question about the compatibility or opposition between nation states and the EU lies at the basis of the ongoing debate on the draft of the European Constitution, the definition of shared values and the meaning of common political institutions and policies. One of the main questions is: should the EU be a confederation of states or should it ultimately constitute a new kind of state? It is difficult to answer this question because the EU is not a de facto super-state due to the openness of the political process, which has become more complex with the recent enlargement towards the east. Eight former communist/socialist countries, which were part of the former Soviet Union or under its influence, have become members of the EU in the hope of building a democratic common political institution. The question is how these different historical backgrounds on the role of the state and the organisation of the social system could be re-elaborated in the perspective of common EU policies. The EU is more diverse than ever before, in terms of cultures, political ideologies, economic standards and institutional traditions. Could this diversity be utilised as a resource, in an attempt to find agreements based on common values, political strategies and social policies? Or will diversity become a new reason for social exclusion?

In the EU there are different traditions of political institutions and social provisions in a postnational constellation and a postcommunist scenario of states that are now unified by common interests. How could this framework be employed for increasing bottom-up experiences of deliberative democracy in order to build up a social Europe? To what extent are EU citizens or a European public sphere able to influence political decision making with the aim of avoiding disparity among (also foreign) citizens and populations?

Many public debates (including disputes on the Internet) have been developed on this topic, underlying the possibility of employing new forms of participation and increased civic discussions among citizens about issues of common relevance. In a legitimate democracy, citizens, as stakeholders, should be the ultimate, antecedent, subjects, who decide the forms of citizenship and the constitutional pact they want to have. Policy makers and politicians cannot assume the deliberative role that citizens must have. Yet it is not clear what political form the EU could assume after the promulgation of a common Constitution.

The Union itself is the result of a complex process started in the post-war era. The unification of European states was, in fact, initiated after World War II on the basis of political ideals (Spinelli, 1988, 1996) as well as to foster the promotion of economic interests through the establishment of cooperation among sovereign states. After the constitution of a common market (Maastricht Treaty, 1993) and monetary unification for some states, the most important advances concerned the political constitution of a unified Europe, based on the declaration of the fundamental rights that would serve as the basis of a new political society. Until the Amsterdam Treaty (1997), fundamental rights did not have a specific relevance in the Community Treaties (started with the Treaty of Rome, 1957) because the main interest at the earlier time was functionalist.

The Charter of Fundamental Rights of the Union, signed in Nice in 2000 and now included in Part II of the draft of the European Constitution, asserts the importance of common values for EU citizens. Therefore, the preamble declares:

> Conscious of its spiritual and moral heritage, the Union is founded on the indivisible, universal values of human dignity, freedom, equality and solidarity; it is based on the principles of democracy and the rule of law. It places the individual at the heart of its activities, by establishing the citizenship of the Union and by creating an area of freedom, security and justice. The Union contributes to the preservation and to the development of these common values while respecting the diversity of the cultures and traditions of the peoples of Europe as well as the national identities of the Member states and the organisation of their public authorities at national, regional and local levels; it seeks to promote balanced and sustainable development and ensures free movement of persons, goods, services and

capital, and the freedom of establishment (European Union, 2004, C310/41).

The preamble indicates the search for communalities and the respect for diversity alongside principles of solidarity and subsidiarity. In particular, the principle of autonomy for local public authorities and the interest in a balanced development are clearly acknowledged. The struggle against social exclusion thus becomes a key issue for the construction of a European identity (Liebert, 2004). Article II. 94 is in fact devoted to social security and social assistance. It reads:

> 1. The Union recognises and respects the entitlement to social security benefits and social services providing protection in cases such as maternity, illness, industrial accidents, dependency or old age, and in the case of loss of employment, in accordance with the rules laid down by Community law and national laws and practices. 2. Everyone residing and moving legally within the EU is entitled to social security benefits and social advantages in accordance with Community law and national laws and practices. 3. In order to combat social exclusion and poverty, the Union recognises and respects the right to social and housing assistance so as to ensure a decent existence for all those who lack sufficient resources, in accordance with the rules laid down by Community law and national laws and practices (European Union, 2004, C310/48.49).

Yet these commitments were usually undertaken at the level of the nation/welfare state, while now they are recognised as a main task for the EU. Is it possible to harmonise the role of the EU with traditional provisions of the welfare state? In the final analysis, who is the main institution in charge of social policies and the perspective of social inclusion? It is evident that the role and the space for action for nation/welfare states has been restricted because the necessity for domestic parliaments to make legitimate decisions is not compatible with the legislation and directives issued by different organisms of the EU, which are supranational in origin.

In sum, European citizenship – which implies a self-restriction of the autonomy by each member state – is a challenge that underlines both the limits of the nation state and the crisis of the welfare state, while maintaining the solidaristic tradition it has developed. Social policies against marginalisation should thus be redefined in the reconfiguration of the role of domestic institutions, which maintain administrative responsibilities and governmental duties over a restricted territory in the respect of the needs of people. Yet this process is not at all an easy one, because of the possibility of creating or reinforcing social inequalities in the crisis of "traditional mechanisms of social cohesion" and "the fragmentation of social life" (Giddens and Diamond, 2005) on the one hand, and increasing disparities between the richest and poorest countries and regions on the other. The political government of communities should be thus confronted with the idea of governance.

Globalisation, governance and cosmopolitanism

The priority of the sovereignty of independent states over the role of supernational institutions and vice versa is at the core of ongoing discussions about national cultures, European identity, global governance and cosmopolitanism (Held, 1996). Processes of globalisation (Held and McGrew, 2003; Held, 2004a) have either produced or, at least, accelerated, recent problems in relation to the creation of new communalities among peoples. Therefore, specific cross-borders questions could be considered specifically in a global way.

One of these issues concerns the debate on the idea of a global citizenship and an overlapping global civil society (Anheier et al, 2003), where the state has cosmopolitan features (Archibugi et al, 1998). This idea finds its philosophical origin in the Kantian's perspective of a *perpetual peace* among nation states and the creation of a cosmopolitan law, which overcomes the limits of traditional international law. Citizenship will no longer be based on the restrictive principle of political belonging but on the fact of 'humanity', which includes all individuals. In this case, the world will become a political space open to all subjects, individuated as global citizens.

Despite the possibly utopian features of this perspective, it is important to consider its normative content in relation to the ongoing debate on globalisation, cultural identities and conflicts and also in relation to the possibility of developing common social policies that are diversified according to the different needs of the targeted populations. Equality and diversity (Benhabib, 1996) become the two milestones of the debate on the meaning of redistribution of wealth and respect for human beings in a global era.

This is the case of the discussion about the role of the EU in international conflicts. The aim of constructing a common identity and political destiny should help to avert the construction of eurocentrism and instead to influence the constitution of a new approach to international law. In this case, the EU, as a form of government apart from the nation state should collaborate with supernational organisms (starting with the UN) for the attainment of peace and the well-being of human beings. "The will of the majority should not repress the voices of defeated minorities" (Habermas and Derrida, 2003).

Yet in this case the notion of governance seems to be crucial for overcoming the paradoxes of citizenship and political rights and to confront contemporary international complexity.

The term 'governance' refers originally to the decision-making processes in the administration of an organisation. This concept concerns both nation states and organisations. But governance has acquired a stronger political meaning since it has been connected to processes of democratisation from bottom up and to claims of validity coming from differentiated groups of civil society. Entities and stakeholders, who aim at a more direct participation in the governance of the public realm, underline the limits of the rights of citizenship because they refer only to citizens. Governance indicates thus a more articulated way of approaching decision making, taking into account a broader set of social actors and institutions. Governance should, therefore, reflect a higher grade of democratisation in the administration of a territory.

On the basis of this premise, the European Commission delivered a White Paper on European governance concerning "the way in which the Union uses the powers given by its citizens" (Commission of the European Communities, 2001, p 3). The aim of this document is to open up the policy-making process to get more people and organisations involved in shaping and delivering EU policy. It promotes "greater openness, accountability and responsibility for all those involved" and, therefore, the scope to "get more people and organisations involved in shaping and delivering EU policy". It states: "to improve the quality of its policies, the Union must first assess whether action is needed and, if so, whether it should be at Union level. Where Union action is required, it should consider the combination of different policy tools." But the principles of good governance (that is: openness, participation, accountability, effectiveness and coherence) in Europe also concern a more general meaning of global governance. In fact, "The Union should seek to apply the principles of good governance to its global responsibilities. It should aim to boost the effectiveness and enforcement powers of international institutions." To this end the Commission will: "Improve the dialogue with governmental and nongovernmental actors of third countries when developing policy proposals with an international dimension.

Propose a review of the Union's international representation in order to allow it to speak more often with a single voice" (Commission of the European Communities, 2001, p 5).

The international political constellation is composed not only of autonomous national states and supernational institutions but also of NGOs, cross-borders social actors and networks. Such bodies represent an overlapping global civil society and have become increasingly relevant in the present geopolitical context. The rising exchange of experiences through migration and networks (Calloni, 2002) indicate new forms of cosmopolitanism intended to counteract the presence of armed conflicts and aggressive forms of fundamentalism in the explosive mix of religion and politics.

The international order has changed: the 'empires' have been redefined and states try to reconstruct new geopolitical powers through new areas of influence (Hardt and Negri, 2000). In the case of international controversies, as the war in Iraq has shown, nation states are ambiguous about the will and the decisions taken by supernational institutions, such as the United Nations, and also about the opinions expressed by their own citizens. Nevertheless, the nationalist and statist approach is inadequate in proposing stable resolutions and strategies for solving international political conflicts and coping with problems (such as the environment, poverty, health and sustainable development), which are both worldwide and specific to each country. A global perspective (Kaldor, 2003) is thus needed in order to deal with marginalisation and the search for adequate and diversified social policies related to specificity of local needs in different regions.

Cosmopolitanism can become a political project if connected to forms of governance where social actors and stakeholders are actively involved in the decision making. A political cosmopolitanism should include:

> Multilayered governance and diffused authority. A network of democratic fora from the local to the global. Enhancing the transparency, accountability and effectiveness of leading functional NGOs; and building new bodies of this type where there is demonstrable need for greater public coordination and administrative capacity. Use of diverse forms of mechanisms to access public preferences, test their coherence and inform public will formation. Establishment of an effective, accountable, international police/military force for the last resort use of coercive power in defence of cosmopolitan law. (Held, 2004b)

Liberty can be reached only in the struggle against poverty, illiteracy, disease, scarcity of resources, oppression, violence, by empowering the agency of social actors and their capabilities. In this case, domestic political institutions should accomplish this process, reinforcing the power of supernational organisms and agreeing common strategies but at the same time respecting local diversities. However, the recent events in Israel indicate that nation states at both the domestic and international level relinquish power only with the greatest reluctance. But, even though it is necessary to be politically realistic and to keep in mind that in recent wars humanitarian rights and the Geneva conventions concerning crimes of war, genocides and torture against prisoners have been neglected (Robertson, 1999; Gutman and Rieff, 2002; Power, 2002), nevertheless the normative idea of social and humanitarian justice should illuminate the way to reach common policies and strategies against the humiliation, deprivation and violation of all human beings.

New forms of 'global/local' marginalisation cannot be approached by employing the traditional means of political citizenship. Political rights should be thus related to a broader notion of social and cosmopolitan citizenship. The boundaries of politics are limits which can be rethought and become a resource for a cosmopolitan democracy (Habermas, 2004), developing collective overlapping actions, able to give voice and to include at the centre of the public arena 'marginal' and neglected social actors. The stereotyped image of the 'others' could be thus challenged, including the 'strangers' in our own life horizon as a constitutive part of our personal and political identity.

References

Anderson, B. (1991) *Imagined communities. Reflections on the origins and spread of nationalism*, London and New York: Verso.

Anheier, H., Glasius, M. and Kaldor, M. (eds) (2003) *Global civil society*, Oxford: Oxford University Press.

Archibugi, D., Held, D. and Kohler, M. (eds) (1998) *Reimagining political community. Studies in cosmopolitan democracy*, Stanford CA: Stanford University Press.

Aristotle (1981) *The politics*, London: Penguin.

Aristotle (1998) *The Nichomachean ethics*, Oxford: Oxford University Press.

Barry, B. (2000) *Culture and equality: An equalitarian critique of multiculturalism*, Cambridge: Polity Press.

Benhabib, S. (ed) (1996) *Democracy and difference: Contesting the boundaries of the political*, Princeton, NJ: Princeton University Press.

Benhabib, S. (2002) *The claims of culture: Equality and diversity in the global era*, Princeton, NJ: Princeton University Press.

Berger, P. and Luckmann, T. (1967) *The social construction of reality. A treatise in the sociology of knowledge,* London: Penguin.

Berlin, I. (1969) *Four essays on liberty*, Oxford: Oxford University Press.

Bobbio, N. (1990) *L'età dei diritti*, Torino: Einaudi.

Bobbio, N. (1999) *Teoria generale della politica*, ed by Michelangelo Bovero, Torino: Einaudi.

Calloni, M. (ed) (1997) *The changing welfare state: Citizenship, gender, and the family. Experiences of northern and southern Europe*, Conference papers, London: London School of Economics, Gender Institute.

Calloni, M. (2001) 'Gender relations and daily life: Towards a cross-cultural approach', in W. Beck, L. van der Maesen, F. Thomése and A. Walker (eds) *Social quality: A vision for Europe*, Boston, MA: Kluwe Law International, pp 69-86.

Calloni, M. (2002) 'International women's networks, social justice and cross-borders democracy', in I. Lenz, H. Lutz, M. Morokvasic, C. Schöning-Kalender and H. Schwenken (eds) *Crossing borders and shitfting boundaries. Vol II: Gender, identities and networks*, Opladen: Leske and Budrich, pp 179-202.

Calloni, M. and Lutz, H. (2000) 'Migration and social inequalities: the dilemmas of European citizenship', in S. Duncan and B. Pfau-Effinger (eds) *Gender, economy and culture in the EU*, London: Routledge, pp 143-70.

Cohen, J., Nussbaum, M. and Howard, M. (eds) (1999) *Is multiculturalism bad for women?*, Princeton, NJ: Princeton University Press.

Commission of the European Communities (2001) *European governance: A White Paper*, Brussels, 25.7.2001, CM (2001) 428.

Eder, K. (1992) 'Il paradosso della cultura. Oltre una teoria della cultura come fattore consensuale', *Fenomenologia e Società*, vol 15, no 2, pp 17-39.

European Union (2004) 'Treaty establishing a Constitution for Europe', *Official Journal of the European Union*, vol 47, C 310, 16 December.

Fraser, N. and Honneth, A. (2003) *Redistribution or recognition? A political-philosophical exchange*, London: Verso.

Fukuda-Parr, S. (2003) *Reading in human development,* Oxford: Oxford University Press.

Geddes, M. (2000) 'Tackling social exclusion in the EU? The limits to the new orthodoxy of local partnership', *International journal of urban and regional research,* vol 24, no 4, pp 782-800.

Giddens, A. and Diamond, P. (eds) (2005) *The new egalitarianism*, Cambridge: Polity Press.

Gutman, R. and Rieff, D. (eds) (2002) *Crimes of war: What the public should know*, New York, NY: Norton & Company.

Habermas, J. (1992) *Faktizität und Geltung*, Frankfurt a.M.: Suhrkamp.

Habermas, J. (1996) *Die Einbeziehung des Anderen. Studien zur politischen Theorie*, Frankfurt a.M.: Suhrkamp.

Habermas, J. (2004) *Der gespaltene Westen*, Frankfurt a.M. : Suhrkamp.

Habermas, J. and Derrida, J. (2003) 'Nach dem Krieg: Die Wiedergeburt Europas', *Frankfurter Allgemeine Zeitung*, 31 May.

Hardt, M. and Negri, A. (2000) *Empire*, Cambridge, MA: Harvard University Press.

Held, D. (1996) *Democracy and the global order. From the modern state to cosmopolitan governance*, Stanford, CA: Stanford University Press.

Held, D. (2004a) *A globalizing world? Culture, economics, politics*, London: Routledge and the Open University.

Held, D. (2004b) 'Cosmopolitanism: globalization tamed', Unpubished manuscript.

Held, D. and McGrew, A. (2003) *Global transformations reader: An introduction to the globalization debate*, Cambridge: Polity Press.

Hobbes, T. (1982) *Leviathan*, London: Penguin.

Kaldor, M. (2003) *Global civil society: An answer to war*, Cambridge: Polity Press.

Kant, I. (1991) 'Perpetual peace', *Political writings*, Cambridge: Cambridge University Press.

Kymlicka, W. (ed) (1995) *The rights of minority cultures*, Oxford: Oxford University Press.

Kymlicka, W. (ed) (2000) *Citizenship in diverse societies*, Oxford: Oxford University Press.

Lemke, C. (2001) 'Social citizenship and institution building: EU-enlargement and the restructuring of welfare states in East Central Europe', Working paper, Hannover: University of Hannover.

Liebert, U. (2004) 'Europeanization and citizenship: mechanisms of exclusion and inclusion', Paper presented at the 14th Biennial Conference of Europeanists: 'Europe and the World: Integration, Interdependence, Exceptionalism?' Chicago, March 11-13.

Locke, J. (2003) *Two treatises of government and a letter concerning toleration*, New Haven, CT: Yale University Press.

Macintyre, A. (1988) *Whose justice? Which rationality?*, London: Duckworth.

Magnusson, L. and Strath, B. (2004) *A European social citizenship? Preconditions for futures policies from a historical perspective*, Brussels: PIE-Peter Lang.

Margalit, A. (1996) *The decent society*, Cambridge, MA: Harvard University Press.

Marshall, T.H. (1992) *Citizenship and social class*, London: Pluto.

Miller, D. and Walzer, M. (eds) (1995) *Pluralism, justice and equality*, New York, NY: Oxford University Press.

Moller Okin, S. (1998) 'Feminism and multiculturalism: some tensions', *Ethics*, vol 108, no 4, pp 661-84.

Nussbaum, M. (2003) *Women and human development: The capabilities approach*, Oxford and New York: Cambridge University Press.

Nussbaum, M. and Glover, J. (eds) (1995) *Women, culture, and development. A study of human capabilities*, Oxford: Clarendon Press.

Parekh, B. (2000) *Rethinking multiculturalism: Cultural diversity and political theory*, Basingstoke: Macmillan.

Pennacchi, L. (1997) *Lo Stato sociale del futuro: pensioni, equità, cittadinanza*, Roma: Donzelli.

Pogge, T. (ed) (2001) *Global justice*, Oxford: Blackwell.

Power, S. (2002) *A problem from hel: America and the age of genocide*, New York, NY: Basic Books.

Rawls, J. (1971) *A theory of justice,* Harvard, MA: Harvard University Press.

Robertson, G. (1999) *Crimes against humanity: The struggle for global justice,* London: Allen Lane.

Rousseau, J.-J. (1968) *The social contract*, London: Penguin.

Sandel, M.J. (1982) *Liberalism and the limits of justice,* Cambridge: Cambridge University Press.

Sen, A. (1992) *Inequality re-examined,* Oxford: Clarendon Press.

Sen, A. (1999) *Development as freedom,* New York, NY: Knopf.

Sen, A. (2000) *Social exclusion: Concept, application, and scrutiny*, Manila: Office of Environment and Social Development, Asian Development Bank.

Sophocles (2003) *Antigone*, Cambridge: Cambridge University Press.

Spinelli, A. (1988) *Battling for the Union: 1979-86*, Luxembourg: Office for Official Publications of the European Communities.

Spinelli, A. (1996) *La rivoluzione federalista: Scritti (1944-1947)*, Bologna: il Mulino.

Taylor, C. (ed) (1991) *Multiculturalism and the politics of recognition,* Princeton, NJ: Princeton University Press.

UNDP (United Nations Development Programme) (2000) *Human development report,* Oxford: Oxford University Press.

Walzer, M. (1985) *Sphere of justice: A defence of pluralism and equality*, Oxford: Blackwell.

Young, I. (1990) *Justice and politics of difference*, Princeton, NJ: Princeton University Press.

Young, I. (2000) *Inclusion and democracy*, New York, NY: Oxford University Press.

SEVEN

Citizenship and the activation of social protection: a comparative approach

Jean-Claude Barbier

The activation of social protection is one of the most important current transformations of social protection across Europe. However, there is disagreement about how it should be interpreted. The purpose of this chapter is to point out that:

- The concept of activation can be used in both a broad and narrow sense. In the broader sense, it reaches well beyond what is usually described as 'activation' (all sorts of welfare-to-work programmes and making work pay policies).
- There is no such thing as one universal activation rationale: instead, a diversity of solutions persists for activation in both the broad and narrow sense.
- The assessment of the meaning and impact of activation does not require knowledge about formal rules only, but also about the broader context as well as about the praxis of activation.
- Such an assessment can be made from mapping the consequences of activation on citizenship. For this purpose, we will need an analytical and robust notion of citizenship. On the basis of this, we shall bring some empirical evidence of actual transformations and reforms that have happened under the general banner of activation.

Activation of social protection: the broad sense

In the late 1990s, following the reforms in Denmark and the New Deal strategy in the UK, the activation slogan became fashionable internationally. For instance, the OECD was happy to popularise the Danish *aktivering*. However, little attention was given either to the diversity of historical and societal embeddedness of the reforms or to their special scope. Logically, the activation motto has consistently figured very high on the European employment strategy (EES) agenda.

As a scientific concept, activation can be constructed as describing a tendency observable in the transformation of all national systems. Activation is the introduction (or reinforcement) of an explicit linkage between, on the one hand, social protection and, on the other hand, labour-market participation. Redesigning these systems has led to enhancing the various social functions of paid work and labour-force participation, in increasingly compulsory forms in many national cases. The programmes potentially activated certainly go beyond traditional active labour-market policies (ALMP) or French-style *insertion* policies (Barbier and Théret, 2001). They also comprise benefit programmes (unemployment insurance and various assistance schemes for working age groups, including disability and some other family-related benefits); pension systems and most particularly, early retirement programmes and policies which aim at reforming the tax and benefits systems. Two types of programmes stand out, which, in political documents, are generally termed 'welfare-to-work' programmes and 'making work pay' policies. In this sense, an activation rationale has increasingly informed not only labour-market policies, but more broadly, the reforms of social protection (Barbier, 2002, 2004a, 2004b, 2004c).

From the individual's point of view, activation programmes are supposed to provide incentives or sanctions, but also, in some cases, a wide array of offers of services (for instance counselling, job searching and training, as well as wage subsidies). This is where activation and citizenship strongly meet. On the other hand, from a system perspective, social protection is activated in the sense that the delivery of services and benefits mainly targets working-age people in some sort of work activity. It is also activated in the sense that funding mechanisms and the allocation of resources are designed so as to foster increased job creation or, to put it differently, to be employment-friendly. This is certainly not alien to the quality of citizenship if we consider that equal access to jobs can be seen as one of its dimensions.

Finally, it should be noted that activation is not an entirely new phenomenon but must be analysed in the context of national histories. In the Scandinavian countries, as well as in Germany or Austria for instance, an important dimension of social policy has long been devoted to vocational training, an active policy tool par excellence (Barbier and Ludwig-Mayerhofer, 2004). Moreover, the policy goal of full employment was always historically deeply integrated into the social protection rationale in the Nordic countries (especially Sweden and

Norway), where it was also linked to a very strong commitment to work.

Absence of convergence: two ideal-types, a third yet to emerge

We have shown that activation strategies across Europe could be captured and stylised along two ideal-types: a liberal, and a universalistic. With some (often American) exceptions (Gilbert, 2002; Handler, 2003), most of the literature would agree that these types converge only in procedures but not in substance (Barbier and Gautié, 1998; Torfing, 1999; Morel, 2000; Wood, 2001; Goul Andersen et al, 2002; Jørgensen, 2002; Schmid and Gazier, 2002; van Berkel and Møller, 2002; Serrano Pascual, 2004; Barbier and Ludwig-Mayerhofer, 2004). Remarkably, both ideal-types are linked to Beveridgean systems: the universal, generous Scandinavian version and the liberal British version of a safety net for the poor, respectively. The liberal type chiefly stresses relationships with the labour market, which, when aggregated, are assumed to yield social equity and efficiency. ALMPs as well as social policies thus take on a limited role that is restricted to inciting individuals to seek work, providing quick information and matching services, as well as investing in short-term vocational training. Individuals are also the target of tax credits or in-work benefits in order to 'make work pay'. Activation includes measures inciting people to be as active as possible across their life-course, including pension reforms dispensing with any fixed age for retirement. Here, activation entails both recommodification and efforts to reduce social expenditure. This liberal type of activation is sometimes characterised as 'workfare': however, this is a misnomer, not only because workfare is embedded in a particular US tradition, but because the term applies to only a small area of social protection (assistance).

On the other hand, the universalistic type not only caters for the provision of complex and extended services to all citizens, but simultaneously guarantees relatively high standards of living for the assisted. Hence, the role of the market is not unilaterally prevalent. Activation is applied in a relatively egalitarian manner and the negotiating between the demands of individuals and society is balanced. A fully active society would then yield employment opportunities tailored to a variety of needs and skills in the context of relatively good-quality jobs. It also entails cost containment and reforms of income compensation, but the use of tax credits and subsidies plays a limited role, if any.

The relationship of activation to full employment constitutes an important difference between both ideal-types. Additionally, in the universalistic type, new forms of activation have seen the state assuming the role of an 'employer of last resort', when the market has failed to deliver jobs.

We have discussed the possibility of a third ideal-type of activation which would match the now traditional tripartition of welfare regimes. In fact, France has shown mixed elements from both types, a fact which stems from its hybrid legacy of Beveridgism and Bismarckism (Barbier and Théret, 2003, 2004). Italy, on the other hand, seems to oscillate between both types. Some of the measures proposed recently in Germany might seem to indicate a new 'state-market mix'. Yet, so far, no clear third ideal-type has emerged.

Assessing effects of the activation of social protection on citizenship

The assessment of the consequences of activation on individuals' social rights ought to reach beyond the domain of assistance and labour-market policies to include the impact of these reforms upon their access to quality jobs. Yet, so far, existing evaluation studies have concentrated on the former (such as micro-evaluations of participants in terms of their access to the labour market and econometric studies of these effects on their labour-market participation), and mainly on formal changes, but very seldom on actual ones. Hence it is important to complement this very narrow picture. At this point, Goul Andersen's suggestion of using the notion of citizenship as a "perspective and a benchmark" is welcome (see Chapter Five). Before turning to operationalising it in the area of activation, the role of 'social citizenship' in the French context ought to be mentioned briefly.

Social citizenship in the French discussion

Although it is extensively discussed by researchers familiar with Beveridgean welfare regimes and with social citizenship as a special aspect within a broader notion of citizenship, this concept is not common in the French literature. Although discussed in a small number of papers (Théret, 1992; Birnbaum, 1996; Hassenteufel, 1996), it has remained marginal in the French debate over social protection. Partly, the reluctance to adopt a French equivalent of social citizenship has to do with the normative tradition of the Republican approach to citizenship (Schnapper, 1994; Schnapper and Bachelier, 2000). But it also pertains to other theoretical approaches. Extending the framework of the French regulation school of economists, Théret (1992, 1998) has remarked that the "wage-labour nexus" is not only an economic, but also a political nexus that sets the private status of wage-earners as equal and free in general (1992, p 19). Hence, he is able to speak of a "wage-earner citizenship". We have used this approach empirically when analysing the French RMI (*revenu minimum d'insertion*) (Barbier and Théret, 2001). In this work we explained that, because of the particular historical legacy of the French system, the traditional Rousseauist perspective of citizenship tended to render impossible or, at least highly problematic, any implementation of welfare-to-work programmes along the British model.

Operationalising the concept of citizenship

If we set these particular theoretical caveats apart and follow Goul Andersen, we may focus on the first elements he suggests (rights and duties; social and economic conditions), nevertheless bearing in mind the two others (participation and identities). His analytical concept helps comparing transformations which have occurred across the European nations as consequences of the activation of social protection systems. True, the main aspect considered here pertains to social rights (benefits and services), but, their linkage to political and social participation cannot be ignored, as we will see.

Moreover, we argue here that the question of rights and obligations ought to be contextualised, in order to avoid a simple extension of what is empirically observable in the Anglo-Saxon world. In other words, while developments in various countries show that entitlements to social benefits and services have been redefined across the board, it is impossible to capture the meaning of this in terms of a universally downgraded social citizenship. Indeed, decontextualised concepts of rights as against obligations fail to help us grasp how the actual substance of social citizenship and, more broadly, citizenship in general, has been affected. This, we contend, is the reason why it is important to bring ample empirical material to the discussion.

It is obviously much easier to identify the procedural altering of rights and entitlements of persons eligible for welfare-to-work-type programmes than to take into account their actual implementation (Barbier and Ludwig-Mayerhofer, 2004). It is even more difficult to assess the far-reaching consequences of reforms in tax and benefit systems (including tax credits or the subsidising of labour costs). As a determining factor for citizenship, full employment certainly does not belong to all contexts. Yet, the impact of activation policies like the UK welfare to work, the Danish *aktivering* or the French *insertion* programmes on the rights is bound to be profoundly marked by the overall economic circumstances of the country where the policies are implemented. When 'quality jobs' are available and numerous on the market, the quality of citizenship cannot but be very differently affected by programmes which activate people, when compared to instances where the jobs are missing, or where only dead-end or precarious jobs are available. The substantive nature of the demand to take a job is different in both cases. This is why we add to Goul Andersen's types of actually implemented rights, access to quality jobs in a context of full employment (see Table 7.1).

To sum up, activation has been implemented in the context of hugely differing systems, some providing universal benefits and services of a high quality and generosity, some delivering only targeted, low, flat-rate benefits, others privileging citizens who are insured. If the technical parameters of benefits (duration, percentage of basic wages) have been changed almost everywhere, this process has not left European citizens in the same situation, either individually or collectively. These changes do not convey the same meaning in a context where activation is forced on individuals and in another where it is negotiated. Not only the implementation of sanctions, but the very notion of a sanction differs substantially. Additionally, citizens, parties and unions may be very differently involved in the devising, managing and legitimating processes of the reforms.

The norm of active participation in work is accepted in most countries, and the conditionality of benefits has generally been reinforced. Yet to interpret this general procedural change as testimony for a common substantive turn across Europe and the Anglo-Saxon world remains far-fetched. A key question resides in the identification of national 'normative frameworks' (Barbier, 2004d), which are particularly difficult to compare cross-nationally: acceptable in some national contexts, reforms introducing stricter demands can be seen as unacceptable in others. Some examples of these national-specific forms of acceptability in the recent years are described below.

While the UK has clearly seen increased demands from individuals in return for benefits and services of better quality – recently with the various New Deals – sanctions and compulsion remained privileged policy tools there, and these reforms were associated with a gradual extension of tax credits (Barbier and Ludwig-Mayerhofer, 2004). While reforms triggered only limited opposition in the country, important public movements and demonstrations often took place in the Latin countries when the unions' members disagreed with the reforms. In France in 1993, when the Balladur government tried to introduce a reduced minimum wage for the young, extensive demonstrations by the young forced the cancellation of the reform. In 2002, the Spanish unions and their members rejected tightened requirements for the acceptance of jobs in terms of transportation time. After large demonstrations the government withdrew the reform. Even within one particular country, intranational or regional patterns of implementation may prevent one single substantive pattern, as has been demonstrated both in France (Mahé, 2002) and in Denmark (Larsen et al, 2001). The role of street-level bureaucrats as well as other agents who participate in implementation of activation should also be carefully considered. Sometimes reforms may eventually not be implemented at all, as indicated by repeated failures to decrease the caseloads of recipients of disability benefits, both in Britain and the Netherlands. On the other hand, in France and in Italy (Barbier and Fargion, 2004), a common failure to provide citizens with universal benefits and services meant that there was little actual implementation of a political discourse which stressed obligations in the sense of punitive programmes.

France: activating the insured and 'assisted' unemployed

French activation reforms so far have borrowed either from the liberal or the universalistic ideal-types outlined above. Thus, a sector of well-established and mostly wage-based employment programmes certainly amounts to significant activation. Similarly, social services, family and housing benefits have so far been spared any systematic linkage to work incentives. Furthermore, while activation was introduced from the late 1970s, unemployment insurance and assistance have only recently been at the forefront of the public debate: reforms have tended to target remaining regulations leading to possible 'inactivity traps', especially for minimum income benefits' recipients. Finally, the gradual extension of reductions to social contributions has taken a leading role in the dynamics of activation. This was recently embedded into the working-time reduction process, along with marginal tax credits and crucially linked to the medium-term reform of social contributions in the areas of funding social protection as a whole (Barbier and Théret, 2004). These prominent features have been introduced and implemented in the context of an extremely low creation of jobs.

Hence the access to quality full employment has never featured among the universal rights of citizenship in France from the late 1970s.

We will now focus the empirical analysis on two key programmes: PARE (*Plan d'aide au retour à l'emploi* – the standard unemployment insurance individual plan) and the RMI (*revenu minimum d'insertion* – the standard assistance minimum income, which, since 1988, has also been associated with a personal plan – *contrat d'insertion*). Both apply to working-age beneficiaries and have been affected by the activation dynamics in the 1990s.

The criteria against which we assess a transformation of the dimensions of citizenship are presented in Table 7.1. Five dimensions are explored: individual freedom of choice and autonomy[1] (to what degree individual choices are taken into account by the administration); the availability of associated various quality services (counselling, support, social services, etc.); the generosity (and duration) of benefits; conditionality and sanctions for noncompliance; participation of the social partners and other actors in policy formulation and implementation. We will also see whether gender and age equality of opportunity actually exists (dimension 7). Final comments will recall the impact of full employment (dimension 6).

Table 7.1: Criteria for analysing the impact of reform upon citizenship

	Goul Andersen's definition	**Citizenship criteria used in the French case**
Rights (actually implemented)	(civil, political, social) for social rights: eligibility, level, adequacy, duration, conditionality, sanctions	1. Freedom of choice and autonomy 2. Quality services 3. Generosity and duration 4. Sanctions and conditionality
Participation	political and social participation	5. Participation in the formulation and the implementation of policies and programmes (role of actors, social partners, democratic debate, demonstrations)
		6. Access to quality full employment 7. Inequality across genders and ages; differences insured/assisted

Reform 1: PARE

From July 2001, PARE has been the standard provision for all the new unemployed who claim unemployment insurance. Along with access to the benefit, it comprises an individualised project (involving the negotiation of an action plan, PAP (*projet d'action personalisé*), which entails the offer of services (skill assessment, job search and counselling, vocational training courses and so on). The reform was kicked off by demands from MEDEF (Mouvement des Enterprises de France), the employers' association, arguing that the previous system was too passive. Despite its rather long period of implementation, only limited evaluation data are available today.

Freedom of choice and autonomy

The possibility of individual choice should be checked against obligations imposed upon the unemployed. One of the main justifications for the PARE reform was that it would lead to more adequate and effective choice. Basically, new entrants eligible to benefits discuss their plan with advisors from the administration, taking into consideration their skills and job experience, as well as the local or wider labour-market conditions. Although there seemed to be general acceptance of PARE, qualitative (and fragile) indications show that, due to their increased workload, PES employees use 'creaming' practices when the unemployed are considered to be able to look for themselves. Thus, the formal rights of the unemployed seem to be curtailed by the lack of resources. Yet, in the absence of empirical data, we are left with conjectures about the fact that this activation reform has tended at the same time to upgrade services (although not for all) and reduce the choice for training.

Offer of quality service

France's ranking among the European countries is intermediate, in terms of its employment expenditure. Whereas, in theory, programmes for the long-term unemployed have been designed as universal, the number of places has always been limited, leading to unequal access to programmes and the insufficient coverage of services. In the case of temporary employment in the public and non-profit sector, for instance, the ratio of offers to the number of potential participants has varied from less than 10% to 27% and has decreased in the 1990s (Simonin, 2002, p 2). This is one of the typical features of the hybrid French system, where programmes are defined on a universalistic basis but provision is de facto limited. This feature also explains that, in periods of low employment creation combined with the limited provision of places, the PES could not enforce strict rules for certain categories of the unemployed (Demazière, 1992). It has also been shown that, before the present reform, less than 20% of the insured had access to specific activation measures (Tuchszirer, 2002, p 4).

Whereas the PARE reform was presented as an opportunity to extend the unemployed's freedom of choice, this assumption cannot be vindicated so far for lack of representative evidence. The PAP mainly obliges the unemployed to have their skills assessed, to undertake training or to take an 'acceptable' job. Thus the employment agencies are committed to deliver a variety of active measures, including training and counselling. The implementation of individual projects should be assessed in-depth at least every six months and is supposed to lead to various levels of offers of services, according to the difficulties experienced by the beneficiary. One key element here lies again in the anticipation of a possible quantitative discrepancy between the formal offers and the actual potential beneficiaries, given the level of resources available. One of the main fears expressed by critics of the reform is the risk that it will increase the already existing dualism and inequality of services between the more employable and the 'hard-to-place' persons.

Generosity and duration of benefits

Because of the reform, benefit rates were increased and the previous rule according to which they were decreasing over time was abolished in 2001. Thus generosity was improved overall. Compared with the minimum wage (*salaire minimum interprofessionnel de croissance* [SMIC]),[2] benefits remain less generous[3] than in the Scandinavian countries, but are much more generous than in the UK. Moreover, the decision to lower the duration of benefit as from January 2004 was cancelled by the government after its defeat in the regional elections and after the courts ruled that the reform was unlawful. While the ratio of the unemployed eligible to insurance (versus assistance) decreased in the 1980s and 1990s (Daniel and Tuchszirer, 1999), this trend was reversed in the course of the PARE reform. Yet, mean figures conceal wide discrepancies between part-timers and full-timers. All in all, the duration of benefits remained practically unchanged, whereas the conditions for eligibility were eased for recipients with a limited job experience and benefits upgraded: in this respect, activation has been synonymous with enhancing social rights.

Sanctions and conditionality

Again, evaluation data is lacking as to the precise effects attributable to the enhanced activation dynamics. In France, there is no automatic link between being registered as unemployed and eligibility to benefits. Rates of leaving the PES register have remained rather constant for years. Motives for leaving the register have never been analysed comprehensively, and the sanction indicator reveals only part of the information. The 2001 reform has not altered formal provisions regarding sanctions, although, here again, we lack precise data about actual implementation. However, formal sanctions used to be marginal: the monthly mean number of sanctions in 1991 was about 4,000 (to compare with 130,000 leavers of the register for unknown reasons) and rose to more than 16,000 in 1993. Subsequently, it decreased again to a level of about 7,000, but at the beginning of 2001, the rate had risen again to about 16,000 and by 2004 to about 30-40,000. It is likely that much of this should be attributed to the PARE reform. If the proposed January 2004 reform had been implemented, activation would certainly have meant a further downgrading of rights.

Participation in policy formulation and implementation

PARE has been implemented by the unemployment funds which are jointly administered by social partners. Compared with previous reforms of the unemployment insurance that were passed by stealth, there was an intense debate about the reform. Political debates and trade unions' action eventually succeeded in containing potential orientations towards introducing stricter regulations for active job-seeking and new definitions of what a 'decent job'[4] was. The main dimensions debated were: what legitimate demands should be imposed on the insured? What actual quality of service provision was being offered, as opposed to rhetorical promises and formal rules? Would the new system decrease or reinforce the existing dualism of service provision to the insured unemployed and the assisted unemployed? What new balance was to be established between the role of the unemployment insurance system managed by the social partners on one hand, and, on the other hand, the role of the state, as the actor responsible for the employment service and for guaranteeing the principle of equal treatment? Here, one of the matters at stake was the potential increase in influence of the employers' organisations, but another was the division between trade unions, as two of the main French representative unions, CGT (Confédération Générale du Travail) and FO (Force Ouvrière), refused to sign the new unemployment insurance agreement. With hindsight, the reform process brought an increase of the participative dimension of citizenship.

Age and gender: equality of opportunity

In the past, the quality of offers of activation measures and the level of unemployment compensation have been highly unequal between men and women and for the young and older people. Preliminary analyses indicate that these inequalities have largely continued (Tuchszirer, 2002). Moreover, because of insufficient funding, the already existing dualism will be reinforced between those eligible to insurance and social assistance, and between the hard-to-place and the more employable. This inequality is a permanent feature of the French system, and one that is experienced – although with lower prevalence – even in universalistic systems such as Denmark (Bredgaard, 2001; Abrahamson, 2001). Recent surveys about the comparative access of women and men to employment programmes show that gender inequality still prevails: programmes closer to the mainstream labour market are gender-biased in favour of men, whereas the less effective vocational training programmes and *insertion* programmes are gender-biased the other way round. Again, it would seem that the implementation of this reform has not altered the bias against the young and women in France.

Reform 2: the RMI

The RMI vividly exemplifies the hybrid nature of the French regime, enhancing particular features related to its history. From its start (1988), it was designed as a universal benefit and as a right explicitly linked to citizen participation in the community: in this respect, the RMI belongs to a Republican universalistic model. At the same time, it was also designed as a safety-net benefit: in this respect, it belongs more to a liberal welfare model.

Freedom of choice and autonomy

A distinctive RMI feature has been – despite its 2004 reform – the absence of any work obligation[5]. Whereas local implementation obviously introduces different interpretations, a punitive orientation has never prevailed. The plans discussed with beneficiaries are on the basis of an individualised contract, where choices are taken into consideration. Yet, the degree to which they are effectively considered might vary according to the judgement of social workers and local labour-market conditions. It is assumed that all recipients should engage in a series of activities, which, in the medium term or long term, should result into integration in the labour market (*insertion professionnelle*). However, as is the case in the treatment of the long-term unemployed (Demazière, 1992) the imposition of a strict work obligation has always been relative: only about half the recipients are registered at the public employment service.

Up to 2004, and in a comparative perspective, the RMI's activation rationale was certainly neither punitive nor negatively affected by an explicit link with the beneficiaries' citizenship, despite the lack of resources and of employment opportunities on the market. Yet, in 2004, the government tried to introduce a new scheme for the RMI recipients who had been eligible for two years (estimated to be about 15% of one million) with downgraded contracts. Because of intense political controversy over a scheme that was intended to placate the more right-wing sections of the current political majority, it is not clear (at the moment of writing – 2005) whether and how the programme will eventually be implemented in the French *départements* (local authorities).

Offer of services

Because of the limited number of places available in employment programmes, the proportion of the RMI recipients effectively eligible has been lower than the proportion of the insured unemployed, although when labour-market conditions were favourable, this proportion grew. Clearly, they have had access to a narrower and a lower range of quality choices. However, many recipients have access to social services other than directly work-related activities (such as traditional social services, counselling and medical or housing support). Only a part[6] of *contrats d'insertion* have an *insertion économique* or *professionnelle* content (a work or training content). Moreover, according to their choice and strategies, the RMI recipients may be engaged in employment of some sort without having signed any *contrat d'insertion*. All in all, the situation displays a lower quality of services for the assisted persons than in the case of the insured together with a clear lack of universality.

Generosity and duration

The RMI rates for one person are fixed at half the minimum wage in order to ensure that job-taking always leads to increased income. New regulations have tended to reinforce these incentives. Certainly less generous than comparable benefits in the Scandinavian countries, rates compare more favourably with the UK ones. A high proportion of beneficiaries are long-term recipients. Recent statistics showed, for instance, that 9% had been eligible since the start of the programme in 1989[7]. Long-term RMI recipients and especially those living alone thus undoubtedly belong to the socially excluded in France, entitled to a low-value benefit and a lower quality of citizenship.

Sanctions and conditionality

On the other hand, conditionality is very limited, in contrast with the UK and probably even with the Danish situation. When the law was passed in 1988, a controversy arose about the compensation beneficiaries were supposed to give society in return for their benefit. Yet, the RMI was eventually introduced as an explicit entitlement, differential and non-conditional (Belorgey, 1996). Whereas some MPs opposed any linkage between the entitlement and the recipient's behaviour, this was not the case for the majority. The compromise resulted in what Belorgey has termed an 'ambiguous situation', where the benefit emerged somehow in between a totally non conditional benefit and a benefit conditioned by the compliance of beneficiaries with participation in the *insertion* actions they are presented with. However, only 5% to 6% of the claimants have been sanctioned for not complying.

One interesting study of two contrasted cases shows that at least two types of implementation may occur at local level, with significantly differing sanctions (Mahé, 2002). In a first type, little stigma is attached to the benefit, which is effectively implemented in a universal manner, with a rather strict sanction regime. A key factor here is that the local labour market yields interesting opportunities. Sanctions, in that case, are considered more legitimate. In a second local situation, the target population was globally less employable, while local labour-market opportunities were scarce. In this situation, only the more employable left the programme early, while social workers tended to classify the others as traditional targets for medium-term or long-term income support. In that case, sanctions were rarer and certainly were considered illegitimate both from the social workers' and from the beneficiaries' point of view.

Participation in policy formulation and implementation

Access to and exercise of political citizenship's rights figure explicitly among the legislation's objectives (article 1, 1988 RMI Act). Before the Raffarin conservative government in 2004, despite recurring controversy over its effectiveness in terms of actual integration in jobs (and allegations about insufficient incentives), no government had tried to reform the programme. Yet, even with this current punitive reform, the basic tenets of the programme should not been altered for the majority of recipients. Fears are, however, expressed among experts about the future impact of the complete decentralisation of the RMI. Local funding restrictions may well emerge as a real factor in jeopardising the citizenship of recipients in the future.

Age and gender: equality of opportunity

In terms of age groups, the RMI is a typically biased programme. Because it is a third tier of the unemployment compensation system, the profile of beneficiaries points to persistent inequalities on the labour market. This is especially true for long-term recipients, who are more likely to be in the age bracket 50-54. The gender bias in the programme is associated with other characteristics. For instance, female recipients are more prone to sign *insertion contracts*, but these predominantly contain orientations towards training courses and temporary employment in the non-profit and public sectors.

Incapacity to universalism and reluctance to take the punitive route

From analysing two emblematic activation reforms in France (and contrasting them with the British and Danish cases) four conclusions may be drawn.

First, France has remained firmly on an intermediary path between the generous Scandinavian system and the liberal UK approach. After the reforms, the common tendency to activate across the three countries leaves them in the same relative position against one another. However, once activated, the French system still remains hybrid: it clearly manifests its 'incapacity to universalism' in practice, although it sticks to it rhetorically. On the other hand, it is also unable (or unwilling) to take the UK route of strict punitive, self-help programmes.

Rights that are theoretically designed as universal are de facto targeted. This leads to polarisation, including the emergence of a working poor stratum in French society. Accordingly, the French state has achieved only a limited de facto function of the employer of last resort and employment services have certainly been of a lower quality than, for instance, in the Scandinavian countries. Moreover, the generosity of benefits is much lower than in these latter countries, when compared with minimum market wages.

In such circumstances, the limited enforcement of work obligations appears as logical. The (relatively) limited pressure is linked to both a de facto acknowledgement of scarce labour-market opportunities and the acceptance of a certain norm of freedom of choice and of a balance between legitimate individual needs and the legitimate demands of society. This activation pattern also appears to be consistent with a wider mix of policies, which, since the late 1980s, has aimed at a reduction of employers' social contributions. As a result, the French transformation displays at the same time elements of an upgraded social citizenship and opposite elements, depending on schemes, programmes, locations, modes of implementation, target populations and groups.

A second feature is gender bias. French policy makers have only recently begun to address seriously the gender question. This is linked to the gender division of labour, but also to the de-familialisation issue. Still, in this respect, France is different from other countries in the continental cluster, as the French social protection is much more de-familialised than that of Italy, Spain and Germany.

The third important characteristic is linked to the treatment of the young. The young have remained eligible to lower-quality social benefits and programmes provision overall. This is also linked to the French familialistic tradition: many rights, entitlements and benefits for the young still rely on the family policy system and are not individualised. Moreover, the young experience worse conditions than adults and older employees in terms of unemployment and the precariousness of their employment (Barbier, 2004d).

Finally, a fourth dimension concerns the particular form taken by political participation as part of the wider wage-earner citizenship (mostly in the sense of policy formulation and programme implementation). In their own specific way, both activation reforms studied above display a common element.

In the RMI programme, *insertion professionnelle* retains a positive function of political integration. It is explicitly marked by political citizenship as an objective higher than mere participation in the labour market; accordingly, participation in social or intermediate activities is also valued. Although it is more and more questioned, such participation has not disappeared as, for instance it largely has done in the UK. This in no way precludes the possibility that future activation reforms will not depart from this situation; however, innovations will have to account for their consistency with the legacy, and especially with the role of associations.

The PARE reform illustrates another aspect of the complex interaction of political and social rights. Compared to Scandinavia, collective participation is marked by the dominant role of government and a relatively subordinated role ascribed to social partners. Yet, contrary to British reforms, the French record has demonstrated that a significant margin is opened to dissent, negotiation and action from unions, union members and civil society. During the 1990s, four significant social movements took place. The first one (in the winter of 1995) was organised over pensions in the public sector and defeated the government; the second (in the winter of 1997-98) was organised by the unemployed's organisations. A third moment was the reform of the unemployment insurance in the early 2000s and a fourth accompanied the pensions' reform of 2002-03, when the government was successful.

All in all, it is very clear that an activation dynamics has been at work within the French system of social protection. However, the empirical evidence reviewed here militates against an analysis in terms of a generalised downgrading of social citizenship's rights, in the direction of an overwhelming liberal welfare system, dominated by labour-market requirements. Yet, for all their solidaristic promises, activation reforms of the 1980s and the 1990s have obviously not delivered their promise of integrating all in the labour market.

Conclusion

Very often, the literature draws a far too simple picture of the consequences of activation upon the rights of citizenship. This has often been done in the light of the so-called workfare programmes, which are only a small part of the whole process of activation. It has also been said, too often, that, overall, social rights are curtailed or even dispensed with along with the activation reforms.

Yet, collective action and negotiation have had an important impact on the outcomes of activation reforms. Some were rejected because, we contend, a specific national form of wage-earner citizenship was seen by collective actors as jeopardised. With the analysis of two typical French reforms – put into a comparative perspective with the Danish and British cases – we have also seen that a detailed analysis of the operational dimensions of citizenship can be fruitfully conducted, in order to capture the precise empirical impact of the activation reforms. Here, broad generalisations are of little help and complex developments appear, which stress international and intranational diversity, but also illustrate their consistency with the well-known path-dependent division of the worlds of welfare. Although social rights have been deeply transformed across Europe, the particular instances studied here indicate that no universal downgraded form of citizenship has emerged. All the same, extending the present conclusions in a representative manner entails the conduct of wide-ranging empirical research across many countries.

Notes

[1] Note here an echo to the transitional labour-market approach (Schmid, 2002, p 398).

[2] Hourly SMIC: 6.67€ (5.28€ after social contributions) (1 July 2002). Monthly rate (169 hours): 1127,23€ (829.77€ after social contributions). During the period of implementation of the new legal working time, slightly different rates applied in firms, depending on whether or not they had adopted the new legal working time (the transition period lasted until 2004).

[3] Statistics for 2000 (Pommier and Cohen-Solal, 2001) show that the mean monthly amount was 5,202 FF (793€) and that 75% of recipients eligible for the insurance benefit received between 2,000 FF (304€) and 6,000 FF (912€) monthly. The monthly benefit for the under 50s who had contributed more than four months amounted to 75% of the previous wage under 970€ (as of August 2002); between 970€ and 1,061€, the daily rate is 24€; from 1,061€ to 1,754€, the daily rate is 40.4% of the previous wage + 9.94€ per day; and from 1,754€ to 9,408€, 57.4% of the previous wage.

[4] At the time of going to press (July 2005) French law does not define what a decent job is: rather, reasons are defined in broad principles, which allow the unemployed to refuse a job (or training) offer.

[5] Unfortunately, as we have shown, Lødemel and Trickey (2000) have considered the RMI as workfare, along with programmes which displayed heterogeneous characteristics, like the German social assistance, the French *emplois-jeunes*. Indeed, they defined workfare in such minimalist terms ("programmes and schemes that require people to work in return for social assistance", p 6) that nothing specific existed to compare them with the original programmes in America.

[6] This part is not easily calculated, because of the limits of the monitoring system. Statistics showed that in 1993 two thirds of activities mention either job search or various forms of work. More recent data indicate that about 40% of recipients had signed only a *contrat d'insertion* (Blanpain, 2000).

[7] Because it is a universal benefit, the RMI caters for a very heterogeneous population. Although recent data are lacking as to a precise quantitative categorisation of recipients, a very common assessment among practitioners is that the RMI target group comprises one third of recipients that leave the programme rapidly (Afsa and Guillemot [1999] showed that one third left in less than six months). At the other end of the spectrum, one third experience important problems preventing them from a rapid return to the labour market. Recent national statistics estimate the proportion of recipients present in the programme for more than four years at around 25% (Blanpain, 2000).

References

Abrahamson, P. (2001) 'L'activation des politiques sociales scandinaves, le cas du Danemark', in C. Daniel and B. Palier, *La protection sociale en Europe, le temps des réformes,* Paris: DREES, Documentation française, pp 123-40.

Afsa, C. and Guillemot, D. (1999) 'Plus de la moitié des sorties du RMI se font grâce à l'emploi', *INSEE Première*, no 632, February.

Barbier, J.-C. (2002) 'Peut-on parler d' "activation" de la protection sociale en Europe?', *Revue française de sociologie*, vol 43, no 2, April-June, pp 307-32.

Barbier, J.-C. (2004a) 'Systems of social protection in Europe: two contrasted paths to activation and maybe a third', in J. Lind, H. Knudsen and H. Jørgensen (eds) *Labour and employment regulation in Europe*, Brussels: PIE-Peter Lang, pp 233-54.

Barbier, J.-C. (2004b) 'Activation policies: a comparative perspective', in A. Serrano Pascual (ed) *Are activation policies converging in Europe? The European employment strategy for young people*, Brussels: European Trade Union Institute, pp 47-84.

Barbier, J.-C. (2004c) 'A comparative analysis of "employment precariousness" in Europe', in M.T. Letablier (ed) 'Learning from employment and welfare policies in Europe', pp 7-18, available online at http://www.xnat.org.uk/.

Barbier, J.-C. (2005) 'The European employment strategy, a channel for activating social protection?' in J. Zeitlin, P. Pochet and L. Magnusson (eds) *The open method of coordination in action: The European employment and social inclusion strategies,* Brussels: PIE-Peter Lang, pp 417-66.

Barbier, J.-C. and Fargion, V. (2004) 'Continental inconsistencies on the path to activation: consequences for social citizenship in Italy and France', *European Societies,* vol 6, no 4, pp 437-60.

Barbier, J.-C. and Gautié, J. (1998) *Les politiques de l'emploi en Europe et aux Etats Unis,* Cahiers du CEE, Paris: PUF.

Barbier, J.-C. and Ludwig-Mayerhofer, W. (eds) (2004) 'The many worlds of activation', *European Societies,* Special issue on activation policies, vol 6, no 4, pp 423-36.

Barbier, J.-C. and Théret, B. (2001) 'Welfare to work or work to welfare, the French case', in N. Gilbert and R. Van Voorhis (eds) *Activating the unemployed: A comparative appraisal of work-oriented policies,* Rutgers, NJ: Transaction Publishers, pp 135-83.

Barbier, J.-C. and Théret, B. (2003) 'The French social protection system: path dependencies and societal coherence', in N. Gilbert and R. Van Voorhis (eds) *Changing patterns of social protection,* Rutgers, NJ: Transaction Publishers, pp 119-67.

Barbier, J.-C. and Théret, B. (2004) *Le nouveau système français de protection sociale,* Repères, Paris: La Découverte.

Belorgey, J.M. (1996) 'Pour renouer avec l'esprit initial du RMI', in 'Vers un revenu minimum inconditionnel', *Revue du MAUSS semestrielle,* no 7, premier semestre, Paris: La Découverte, pp 297-9.

Birnbaum, P. (1996) 'Sur la citoyenneté', *L'Année sociologique,* vol 46, no 1, pp 57-85.

Blanpain, N. (2000) 'Les allocataires du RMI inscrits durablement dans le dispositif', *Recherches et prévisions,* CNAF, no 61, September, pp 75-83.

Bredgaard, T. (2001) 'A Danish jobtraining miracle', in H. Jørgensen (preface) and J.C. Barbier (ed) *Working Papers,* Aalborg: CARMA.

Daniel, C. and Tuchszirer, C. (1999) *L'Etat face aux chômeurs,* Paris: Flammarion.

Demazière, D. (1992) *Le chômage en crise? La négociation des identités des chômeurs de longue durée,* Lille: Presses Universitaires de Lille.

Gilbert, N. (2002) *Transformation of the welfare state: The silent surrender of public responsibility*, Oxford: Oxford University Press.

Goul Andersen, J., Clasen, J., van Oorschot, W. and Halvorsen, K. (2002) *Europe's new state of welfare*, Bristol: The Policy Press.

Handler, J. (2003) 'Social citizenship and workfare in the US and western Europe: from status to contract', *Journal of European Social Policy*, vol 13, no 3, pp 229-43.

Hassenteufel, P. (1996) 'L'Etat providence et les métamorphoses de la citoyenneté', *L'Année sociologique,* vol 46, no 1, pp 127-49.

Jørgensen, H. (2002) *Consensus, cooperation and conflict: The policy making process in Denmark*, Cheltenham: Edward Elgar.

Larsen, F., Abildgaard, N., Bredgaard, T. and Dalsgaard, L. (2001) *Kommunal aktivering: Mellem disciplinering og integration*, Aalborg: Aalborg Universitetsforlag.

Lødemel, I. and Trickey, H. (2000) *An offer you can't refuse: Workfare in international perspective*, Bristol: The Policy Press.

Mahé, T. (2002) 'Le RMI à Rennes et à St Etienne: des dynamiques locales différentes', *Recherches et prévisions*, CNAF, no 67, Paris, pp 67-75.

Morel, S. (2000) *Les logiques de la réciprocité, les transformations de la relation d'assistance aux Etats Unis et en France*, Paris: PUF.

Pommier, P. and Cohen-Solal, M. (2001) 'L'indemnisation du chômage en 1999 et 2000', *Premières informations-Premières synthèses*, vol 46, no 1, November, DARES, ministère de l'emploi et de la solidarité.

Schmid, G. (2002) 'Towards a new employment compact', in G. Schmid and B. Gazier (eds) *The dynamics of full employment*, Cheltenham: Edward Elgar, pp 392-435.

Schmid, G. and Gazier, B. (ed) (2002) *The dynamics of full employment*, Cheltenham: Edward Elgar.

Schnapper, D. (1994) *La communauté des citoyens, sur l'idée moderne de nation*, Paris: Gallimard.

Schnapper, D. and Bachelier, C. (2000) *Qu'est-ce que la citoyenneté*, Folio actuel, Paris: Gallimard.

Serrano Pascual, A. (2004) 'Conclusion: towards convergence of European activation policies?', in A. Serrano Pascual (ed) *Are activation policies converging in Europe? The European employment strategy for young people*, Brussels: European Trade Union Institute, pp 497-518.

Simonin, B. (2002) 'Vers une unification des contrats emploi solidarité et des contrats emploi consolidés', *CEE 4 Pages*, no 51, mai, Noisy le Grand.

Théret, B. (1992) 'Esquisse d'une conception topologique et régulationniste de l'interdépendance entre le rapport salarial et l'Etat-providence', *Cahiers du GRETSE*, no 11, December.

Théret, B. (1998) 'La régulation politique, le point de vue d'un économiste', in J. Commaille and B. Jobert (eds) *Les métamorphoses de la régulation politique*, Paris: LGDJ, pp 83–118.

Torfing, J. (1999) 'Workfare with welfare: recent reforms of the Danish welfare state', *Journal of European Social Policy*, vol 9, no 1, pp 5–28.

Tuchszirer, C. (2002) *Réforme de l'assurance chômage, du PAP au PAP-ND, le programme d'action personnalisée pour un nouveau départ*, Document de travail, no 02.02, February, Noisy le Grand: IRES.

van Berkel, R. and Møller, I.H. (2002) *Active social policies in the EU: Inclusion through participation?*, Bristol: The Policy Press.

Wood, S. (2001) 'Labour market regimes under threat? Source of continuity in Germany, Britain and Sweden', in P. Pierson (ed) *The new politics of the welfare state*, Oxford: Oxford University Press, pp 368-409.

EIGHT

The active society and activation policy: ideologies, contexts and effects

Jørgen Elm Larsen

This chapter focuses on the role of activation policy in the active society and especially on the employment and social integration effects of the Danish active line in labour market and social policy. First, the concepts of the active society and activation are investigated. Second, it is shown how the idea of the active society and activation is put into practice in different ways depending on particular ideological and institutional settings. Third, a closer look is taken of the Danish active line which has been promoted as 'best practice' since in the 1990s by the OECD and EU Commission in the field of labour market and social policies. Fourth, the employment and social integration effects of the Danish active line are investigated. Finally, in conclusion some of the most important lessons from the Danish case are highlighted.

The active society and activation

The overall aim of the politics of the active society is to promote active and self-reliant citizens. There is a widespread consensus among the OECD and EU countries about the blessings of the active society. The active society is perceived as the best or only way of combating poverty and social exclusion (OECD, 1990). Influenced by recommendations from the OECD (1994) and the European Commission (1997) the call for a shift from passive income transfer payments to active employment measures within social protection systems has become more and more popular. However, it would be a mistake to argue that the active society has replaced the welfare society. It seems more reasonable to argue that there is a growing emphasis on governing society through activating the individual in numerous ways – preferably through labour-market participation, but also through voluntary social and community work.

The concept of an active society is, however, a very imprecise one, which embraces very different approaches of whom to make active and on what terms. Although the values and practices that national policies are based on vary greatly across national welfare states, one common and clear notion in the concept of the active society is self-reliance. Self-reliance is a dominating element in the reshaping of social policy (Halvorsen, 1998). To be self-reliant one normally has to work. Accordingly, one of the cornerstones of the active society is an activation policy. Active labour-market policies are no new phenomena, especially in the Nordic countries (Hvinden et al, 2001), but there is clearly a difference between the old active labour-market policy and the new activation policy.

The call for an active society and activation policy first and foremost implies a direct linkage between different kinds of social protection systems and labour-market participation. Accordingly, today there is no longer a clear distinction between labour-market policy and social policy, since the active society aims at making all citizens active regardless of what kind of income transfer payments they receive. In that sense social policy is much more labour-market orientated than before. However, under the banner of such policies there are major differences between countries in how they try to achieve the goals of the active society. Activation can perhaps best be perceived as a broad framework for reforming or restructuring welfare states that takes on different forms and involves different types of policies depending on the specific national setting.

Workfare: the American way

Workfare programmes in the US have aimed at "end welfare as we know it by work-for-your-welfare" (Walker, 1999, p 540). The Anglo-Saxon countries (Britain, Australia and New Zealand) adopted related policies. Workfare programmes like the American one may reduce welfare dependency but they do not not seem to be effective in reducing poverty. These kind of workfare programmes force welfare clients to work at the bottom of the labour market in low-paid jobs and with few possibilities of achieving new qualifications which could offer the possibility of mobility at the same time as such policies, especially in the cities, have left the hardest-to-employ behind (Peck, 2001).

Activation: the European way

During the past decade, most European welfare states have adapted some kind of activation policy in their overall unemployment policy. The new active line in labour market and social policy has been introduced under different names in the different European welfare states. These active measures have been of prime importance in reforming welfare systems and in stimulating or forcing labour-market participation of the unemployed and other social benefit claimants, but these different activation policies, however, do not follow a common track and they often do not lead in the same direction. Furthermore, activation policies and workfare policies are often conflated, but it is misleading to treat activation and workfare as one and the same thing, because workfare and activation in principle refer to rather different approaches and strategies. The reason why activation and workfare programmes are often mixed up is not least due to the broad implication of the term 'activation' in OECD and EU publications on the issue. However, several scholars have pointed out the importance of distinguishing between different types of workfare and activation policies. Some scholars make a welfare regime-like distinction between workfare and activation approaches (for example van Berkel and Møller, 2002), but most studies distinguish broadly between two types of approaches: for example 'work first' or 'social investment' (Barbier, 2001), 'sanctions' or 'incentives' (European Employment Observatory, 1997), 'tightening' or 'activation' (European Foundation, 1999) and 'curtailing existing rights' or 'expansion of opportunities' (Lødemel and Trickey, 2001).

In general, 'work first' approaches are connected to liberal welfare states and the 'social investment' approaches of the Scandinavian welfare states in particular. According to Barbier (2001) the two polar examples in Europe are the UK, representing the most pure form of workfare, and Denmark, representing the most pure form of activation social investment. The Danish activation approach aims at improving the employability of those who are out of work by offering opportunities such as training, better skills and work experience, while the workfare approach tends to restrict access to benefits, reduce levels of compensation and restrict the duration of payments, among other things (Drøpping et al, 1999; European Foundation, 1999; Barbier, 2001). In practice, however, the opportunity and the sanction approach are often combined using both the carrot and the stick in making unemployed people 'active'.

Different national and institutional contexts in the EU countries

There is no common definition of activation in EU countries: in some countries activation is focused on labour-market integration while in others activation covers a broader sense of integration policies (Hanesch and Balzter, 2001). Activation policies therefore cover a wide range of institutional realities shaped by national histories and institutions which have constructed different types of workfare and activation regimes (Peck, 2001; van Berkel and Møller, 2002). It has been shown that most European schemes departed from a pure workfare model in several ways. First, 'work-for-benefits' was only one of the alternatives that unemployed people were offered, since opportunities for employment in subsidised jobs with higher earnings than the benefits available, or with a normal wage, was also an option in most schemes. Second, in most cases the unemployed would not lose all of their welfare benefit for non-compliance (Gallie, 2000). However, there are major differences between the EU countries in regard to the comprehensiveness of the schemes. In the Netherlands the magnitude and diversity of measures are probably greater than in any other EU country. In Austria and in Germany, where activation traditionally has not played an important role in relation to social assistance claimants, activation policies have become much more important in the 1990s (Hanesch, 2001). In the southern European countries, activation policies are of recent date, modest in scope and display major regional differences (Gallie, 2000; Hanesch, 2001). In general, it has also been questioned whether EU countries actually have changed the balance between passive and active measures as recommended by OECD and the European Commission. When spending on passive measures has been reduced this rather seems to have been a result of tightening access to benefits rather than of improving performance in active measures (Hvinden et al, 2001). However, this tightening also implied an obligation to be more work orientated and especially for social assistance claimants (Lødemel and Trickey, 2001; Saraceno, 2002).

The Danish active line

During the 1990s a so-called 'job miracle' was created on the Danish labour market. Unemployment fell from 12% in 1993 to 5% in 2002 and overall employment rose from 2,531,000 in 1993 to 2,720,000 in 2001. One explanation for this job miracle was that the Danish model combines a high degree of flexibility with a generous and tight security net and an active labour-market policy (Madsen and Pedersen, 2003).

Since the introduction of the European employment strategy in 1998 there has been an intense focus on the Danish active labour-market policy. The Danish Active Labour Market Policy (ALMP) model belongs to a Scandinavian family that has a long tradition for performing ALMP. Due to the good performance of the Danish labour-market model in the 1990s the EU Commission used the Danish success story to promote the European employment strategy (Auer, 2002), calling the Danish model 'best practice' in the field of social and labour-market policy (Torfing, 2003).

The most important change in the Danish model in the 1990s was the introduction of the so-called 'active line' in the labour market and especially in social policy. The term 'activation' was officially introduced for the first time in Danish social policy in connection with the youth allowance scheme in 1990, but the turn from passive income support of the unemployed to active employment policies had been underway since the 1970s. The labour-market reform implemented in 1994, covering both the insured and the not-insured unemployed and the 'Law on Active Social Policy' implemented in 1998, extending activation to all unemployed social assistance claimants (almost) regardless of their personal and social problems, constituted the peaks of the new Danish active line.

The underlying principle behind this line, which was increasingly emphasised throughout the 1990s, was that unemployed people in receipt of public income transfers should be participating in activities which bring them closer to the labour market and which are beneficial to unemployed individuals and to society as a whole (Rosdahl and Weise, 2001). Increasingly, active measures have become both a right and an obligation for social assistance claimants, and non-compliance is sanctioned by partially withdrawing support. However, in a survey it was found that while the municipalities claim that in 2000 86% withdraw assistance in case of non-compliance, only 20% of those unemployed who refused to participate in activation measures experienced the withdrawl of assistance, and 10% experienced its reduction or were sanctioned in other ways (Harsløf, 2001).

The primary purpose of activation is to bring people back into employment by maintaining or developing their human capital. However, in the 'Law on Active Social Policy' it was stated that the activation of social assistance claimants with problems other than unemployment can also mean participation in social activation. This is because such measures are supposed to enhance their quality of life and prevent their social and personal problems from escalating.

The driving force and motives behind the active line relates to both the micro and macro level. There was a growing concern and consciousness about the negative social impact of unemployment on the individual as well as on society as a whole (Madsen and Petersen, 2003). But the main argument for activation among most political parties, trade unions and employer's organisations was that it is an important instrument for combating structural unemployment. Due to the falling unemployment at the beginning of the 1990s there was a fear of a lack of employees, and the activation policy was seen as a means to mobilise and qualify all available personnel. In general, activation was positively evaluated, although the exact meaning and content of the practice diverged from one camp to another. For some it was purely an active labour-market measure while for others it also implied a moral demand about 'something for something' (Torfing, 2003).

The Danish active line follows an international trend in the OECD and EU countries (Abrahamson and Oorschot, 2003), but there is no such thing as a universal or converging active line. There may be a converging political rhetoric about the active society and reforms introduced under the banner of activation, but the specific type of activation that is implemented is embedded in the nation's political, economic, cultural and institutional history (see Barbier, Chapter Seven).

Comparatively speaking, Denmark has been in the forefront in terms of the comprehensiveness of activation measures and Denmark has also restricted access to unemployment benefits. During the 1990s, Denmark moved from having the most easily accessible unemployment benefit system in Europe to making the same demands for eligibility as, for example the UK and Germany (Kvist, 2002). Among the Nordic countries Denmark has the tightest rules for eligiblity for unemployment benefits. At the same time, the obligations of the unemployed to work or participate in activation measures have changed from being the least restrictive to being among the most restrictive in Europe (Kvist, 2002). This development clearly emphasises that Danish activation policy contains disciplining elements. On the other hand, Denmark is often singled out for placing its main emphasis on improving the labour-market performance of the unemployed by developing their human capital rather than forcing the unemployed to work and disciplining and punishing them (Torfing, 1999).

Effects of the Danish activation policy

Since the Danish active line has been highlighted as 'best practice' by, among others, the European Commission it seems reasonable to ask: what are the positive effects of the Danish active line? This is, however, not an easy question to answer. The effects of activation policy are often difficult to estimate, and there are several effects to take into account if one intends to give a comprehensive picture of the many different effects of the activation policy.

In the following the most important results from studies of different types of effects of the activation policy are highlighted. Most studies of activation effects, however, cover only limited aspects of the many types of effects that can be related to activation policy (to be discussed later).

Since effects can be measured in different ways, a simple distinction is made between labour-market integration and the social integration effects of activation policy. Labour-market integration is normally measured by the employment effects of activation policy, while social integration is normally measured by the impact of an activation policy on the everyday life and well-being of unemployed individuals.

Labour-market integration effects

Generally, evaluations show that the labour-market integration effects are much higher for those who receive unemployment benefit than for those who receive social assistance. But it is difficult to conclude whether the activation measures in themselves have been successful. It is impossible to know what the conditions of the unemployed would have been if they had not received an activation offer – especially in a period with growing employment rates. Recent econometric analyses have tried to take this into account in studies of the probability of finding a job. Three types of effects have been studied: the motivation effect, where unemployed people find jobs or leave the labour force before the obligation to activation occurs; the 'lock-in effect' where unemployed people are less active in job seeking while participating in activation measures and the 'activation effect' where, due to their participation in activation, the unemployed get a job.

The motivation effect of activation is considerable, in that the probability of the unemployed finding a job increases greatly before the obligation to participate in activation occurs. However, to date this applies only to unemployed people with insurance. Unemployed social assistance claimants do not leave the social assistance system (Geerdsen and Graversen, 2002).

There seems to exist a considerable lock-in effect during activation periods (Rosholm, 1998; Bolvig et al, 2002). The lock-in effect seems to be especially extensive in relation to educational or training measures.

The employment effect of activation depends on the type of measure employed. Private job training, but also public job training has a small but positive effect (Rosholm, 1998). The activation effect of educational and training measures is negative, since they prolong the period of receiving social assistance (Bolvig et al, 2002). However, the long-term effects of education have not been researched.

Effects of activation policy on long-term unemployment

From 1995 to 1999 there was an increase of 25% in the number of unemployed people participating in activation measures and in the same period the number of unemployed dropped considerably (from 10.4% to 5.7%). However, the activation policy has in recent years shown little success in bringing the remaining long-term unemployed into the labour market. Many of those who had remained unemployed during the employment boom are characterised by having social problems in addition to being unemployed, especially those who are characterised by having long-term spells of social assistance payments. Most long-term social assistance claimants who left the system are not in employment, but are now on permanent public support, especially in receiving early pensions (Abrahamson and Oorschot, 2003).

It has been difficult for the social security offices (SSO) in municipalities and the public employment services (PES) to implement the objective of placing unemployed people with social and personal problems in activation measures, and especially in measures that produce the best effects in terms of labour-market integration. Today, municipalities put weight on the social integration of unemployed individuals, instead of their integration in the labour market. According to them, a significant part of the unemployed (on average 65%) are characterised by having social and personal problems (Larsen et al, 2001). Both caseworkers in the municipalities and the unemployed themselves are of the opinion that long-term unemployed individuals with severe social and personal problems cannot be integrated in the labour market via participation in activation measures. Between one third and two thirds of unemployed social assistance claimants are not participating at all in activation measures (Larsen et al, 2001). The municipalities claim that activation for certain groups is pointless because they are not affected even by economic incentives (Weise and Brogaard, 1997) or by threats of sanctions in general. They are perceived by the caseworkers as being outside the reach of the universe of help, pedagogy and discipline (Larsen, 2002). However, studies of social activation projects that were introduced under the 'Law on Active Social Policy' in 1998 have shown that social activation can create some kind of social integration and improve the everyday life of the most vulnerable part of the long-term unemployed (Jensen, 2002; Kristensen, 2003).

Action plans

In principle, the unemployed and the caseworker have to agree on an action plan which outlines what is to occur with regard to matters such as education and job training and when it should happen. The personal situation, needs and wishes of the unemployed have to be taken into consideration and negotiated. According to several studies (Brogaard and Weise, 1997; Langager, 1997; Weise and Brogaard, 1997), the majority of unemployed can – to a greater or lesser degree – influence the drawing-up of these action plans. However, a considerable number of long-term unemployed people receiving unemployment benefits say that they have little influence (25%), or no influence (9%) in the drawing-up of the action-plans (Eskelinen et al, 2002). Many experience poor contact with and insufficient advice from the caseworkers at the PES. For example, 62% of the long-term unemployed said that they had insufficient advice about job-seeking and employment possibilities and 37% wished that they had a more frequent contact with the PES (Eskelinen et al, 2002). Complaints about being sent out to activation measures with very short notice and without their consent are also common (Caswell et al, 2002; Eskelinen et al, 2002; Braun and Nielsen, 2002). This is even more pronounced among long-term unemployed social assistance claimants. Many do not even have, or are not informed about having, an action plan (Larsen, 2003) and more than 40% of all unemployed social assistance claimants who have an action plan do not experience it as being of any benefit to them or that it is beneficial to only a limited degree (Weise and Brogaard, 1997). Among the long-term unemployed receiving unemployment benefits as many as 73% find that the action plan was of no use to them and only 27% found that it had been a good tool for planning the future (Eskelinen et al, 2002).

In general, there seem to be diverging experiences and satisfaction with actions plans and the contact with the PES and SSO, depending on the length of the period of unemployment. Short-term unemployed individuals have a more positive judgement of action plans and of the contact with the PES and SSO than the long-term unemployed. However, this is hardly surprising, since positive experiences and satisfaction are often related to positive outcomes.

Classification of the unemployed at the SSO

At the SSO in the municipalities the most typical classification of the unemployed social assistance claimants is a polar distinction between those who are ready and prepared for the labour market and those who are not. However, there are often no clear criteria for each category and caseworkers often have different assessments of individual claimants. Accordingly, the unemployed often do not understand the criteria used in their own classification and if they try to change it their caseworkers often do not listen to them. Not surprisingly, many social assistance claimants experience being forced to participate in activation projects that they are not motivated for or do not find suitable for their own specific needs and wishes (Ebsen and Guldager, 2002; Larsen, 2003). Of all social assistance claimants who participated in local activation projects, 44% perceived no goal to their participation beyond the activation itself (Harsløf, 2001).

At the same time, the purpose of activation measures, the selection of different groups of unemployed for these measures and the methods employed on the activation projects often harmonise poorly (Mik-Meyer and Berg Sørensen, 2000; Braun and Nielsen, 2002; Larsen, 2003). Because those who are classified as not being prepared for the labour market belong to a large and very heterogeneous group, but are often placed on the same activation projects, there is a risk that neither resource-strong nor resource-weak individuals gain from participating in these projects. In these projects methods that on the one hand aim at personal development and on the other at labour-market integration are mixed up (Bach, 2002; Larsen, 2003). Because many of the participants' self-conception is not in agreement with the project managers' and instructors' conceptions of the unemployed, they often do not see any purpose in carrying out the programmed activities (Mik-Meyer and Berg Sørensen, 2000; Braun and Nielsen, 2002; Larsen, 2003).

Is activation a profitable business?

Several attempts have been made to estimate the economic impact of the Danish activation policy. Such estimations are normally based on a simple model where the costs of the activation policy are compared with the positive employment effects of activation and thus the reduced costs of income transfer payments to unemployed people. However, the indirect effects of activation policy are difficult to estimate, but they may not be less important. These are, for example, a better life quality for the unemployed participants, or welfare benefits for the society as a whole in form of, for example, services for pensioners and the renewal of local communities. On the other hand, it is also possible that unemployed people are activated in jobs that otherwise would have been ordinary jobs.

It has been estimated that the Danish activation policy costs about 20 billion DKK per year (Jensen et al, 2002). According to the Economic Council (Det Økonomiske Råd, 2002) the activation policy has a negative impact on the economy since the positive employment effects do not match the costs of the policy. The deficit is estimated to about 6 billion DKK per year. However, estimations made by the Danish National Institute of Social Research (for example, Bach, 2002) show a positive impact of the activation policy on the economy. But even in the most positive estimations, for example from the Ministry of Labour (Larsen, 2000) the employment effect of activation is quite limited.

Social integration effects

Pro and cons in relation to activation policy cannot only be measured by its economic impact on society. The social impact of activation is also important, for example, in the way the activation policy influences the living conditions and everyday life of unemployed people and social relations in society as a whole. Does the activation policy contribute to a more coherent and inclusive society by socially integrating unemployed people in meaningful activities that improve their well-being or their employability? In what follows we will take a look into some aspects of the socially integrative effects of the activation policy.

The great majority of those who participate in activation projects are generally satisfied with their work environment and working conditions (Hansen, 2001). However, quantitative as well as qualitative studies of activation show that the motives for unemployed individuals to participate in activation and their experience of activation are ambiguous. Only 5% say that they have refused to participate in activation measures, but 55% of those who do participate in activation measures say that they do so because of the risk of losing financial support. Even though very few are in practice sanctioned in this way the possibility of being sanctioned seems to motivate a majority of unemployed to participate in the activation measures. On the other hand, the possibility of being sanctioned is not the only motivation for participating in activation measures since about 30% of those who mention sanctions as a motivational factor also mention positive motives for participating (Harsløf, 2001). In other words, there are mixed motives for participating and many clients are ambivalent about their activation. However, the overall assessment of activation from most of those in activation projects is that their well-being improved during the period in which they have been activated (Hansen, 2001; Bach, 2002; Larsen, 2003). In one survey (Hansen, 2001), more than half of those who had participated in an activation measure answered that to a high degree or to some degree, they had a more exciting life, a brighter outlook on the future, had gained more self-respect, felt themselves to be more responsible and more integrated in society. Therefore, even the most critical studies of activation find it hard to conclude that the consequences for those activated are all but negative. It seems that what is important for most unemployed individuals is that work on the projects is meaningful, that activation establishes time and space regularities in their everyday life, and that they experience social contact and communion with other people during the day. Attempts to reduce or eliminate forced aspects of activation programmes and to create trust and respect between the unemployed and the employees on the projects are of prime importance.

Conclusion

Although activation is used as a framework in reforming social and labour-market policies in EU countries, the specific type of activation policy that is implemented is embedded in the nation's political, economic, cultural and institutional history. In the promotion of the European employment strategy the EU Commission used the Danish success story and the Danish model was highlighted as 'best practice' in the field of social and labour-market policy. It is obvious that some lessons can be learnt from the Danish case, but it is less clear how and if these lessons are of any use in other labour-market and social-policy settings.

First of all, it seems fair to say that the evidence on the effects of Danish activation policy are far from conclusive. There are big gaps in our knowledge, especially about the more indirect effects of activation, for example, in terms of how and if the activation of unemployed people creates a more inclusive and coherent society and how it might affect citizenship rights. However, the evidence put forward so far by the different studies referred to in this chapter suggests that the direct employment effect of activation in the best-case scenario is limited. On the other hand, the socially integrative effect of integration seems to be comprehensive for most unemployed individuals. Among other things, the majority of unemployed people feel that, due to their participation in activation measures, they feel themselves to be more socially integrated into the society.

However, their experiences also show that when activation takes place in a closed universe where both caseworkers, job supervisors, project managers and instructors consider activation as a end in itself, then activation does not contribute towards reducing the negative consequences of being on public support, but rather strengthens the clientalisation of the unemployed and their future in repeated activation programmes. In particular, the repeated participation of older people in activation measures over a period of many years seems to be counterproductive by creating frustration and anger among the unemployed.

References

Abrahamson, P. and Oorschot, W. v. (2003) 'The Dutch and Danish miracles revisited: a critical discussion of activation policies in two small welfare states', *Social Policy and Administration*, vol 37, no 3, pp 288-304.

Auer, P. (2002) 'Flexibility and security: labour-market policy in Austria, Denmark, Ireland and the Netherlands', in G. Schmid and B. Gazier (eds) *The dynamics of full employment*, Cheltenham: Edward Elgar Publishing, pp 81-105.

Bach, H.B. (2002) *Kontanthjælpsmodtagere: Aktivering og arbejdsudbud*, København: Socialforskningsinstituttet.

Barbier, J-C. (2001) *Welfare to work policies in Europe: The current challenges of activation policies*, Working paper no 11, November, Centre d' études de l'emploi.

Bolvig, I., Jensen, P. and Rosholm, M. (2002) *The employment effects of active social policy in Denmark*, Working paper, Afdeling for Nationaløkonomi. Aarhus: Aarhus Universitet.

Braun, T. and Nielsen, A. (2002) *Metoder i aktivering af 'svagt stillede dagpengemodtagere': Spørgeskema og interviewundersøgelse*, Copenhagen: Arbejdsmarkedsstyrelsen.

Brogaard, S. and Weise, H. (1997) *Evaluering af Lov om kommunal aktivering: Kommuneundersøgelsen*, Copenhagen: Socialforskningsinstituttet.

Caswell, D., Eskelinen, L. and Hansen, S.L. (2002) *Langtidslediges erfaringer med Arbejdsformidlingen og aktivering*, Copenhagen: AKF Forlaget.

Det Økonomiske Råd (2002) *Dansk Økonomi. Efterår 2002*, Copenhagen: Det Økonomiske Råds sekretariat.

Drøpping, J.A., Hvinden, B. and Vik, K. (1999) 'Activation policies in the Nordic countries', in M. Kautto, M. Heikkilä, B. Hvinden, S. Marklund and N. Ploug (eds) *Nordic social policy: Changing welfare states*, London: Routledge, pp 133-58.

Ebsen, F. and Guldager, J. (2002) 'Kommunal klassificering af langtidsledige', in M. Järvinen, J.E. Larsen and N. Mortensen (ed) *Det magtfulde møde mellem system og klient*, Aarhus: Aarhus Universitetsforlag, pp 61-80.

Eskelinen, L., Hansen, S.L. and Caswell, D. (2002) *Langtidsledige, aktivering og arbejde*, Copenhagen: AKF Forlaget.

European Commission (1997) *Modernising and improving social protection in the European Union*, Brussels: European Commission.

European Employment Observatory (1997) *Activation of labour-market policy in Europe. Trend 28*, Brussels: European Commission.

European Foundation for the Improvement of Living and Working Conditions (1999) *Linking welfare and work*, Dublin: European Foundation.

Gallie, D. (2000) *Unemployment, Work and Welfare*, Paper presented to the seminar 'Towards a learning society: innovation and competence building with social cohesion for Europe', Quinta da Marinha, Guincho, Lisbon, 28-30 May 2000.

Geerdsen, L.P. and Graversen, B. (2002) 'Øger udsigten til aktivering de lediges jobsøgning?', *Samfundsøkonomen*, no 7, pp 12-19.

Halvorsen, K. (1998) 'Symbolic purposes and factual consequences of the concepts "self-reliance" and "dependency" in contemporary discourses on welfare', *Scandinavian Journal of Social Welfare*, vol 7, no 1, pp 56-64.

Hanesch, W. (2001) 'Activation: narratives and realities. a seven countries comparison', Paper presented at the 5th Conference of the European Sociological Association 'Visions and Divisions', in Helsinki, 30 August-1 September.

Hanesch, W. and Balzter, N. (2001) *Activation policies in the context of social assistance*, Report 4. Helsinki: National Research and Development Centre for Welfare and Health.

Hansen, H. (2001) *Arbejde, aktivering og arbejdsløshed: integration i det hele liv*, Copenhagen: Samfundslitteratur.

Harsløf, I. (2001) *The integrative dimension of activation. results from a survey among social benefit claimants*, Working Paper 12, Copenhagen: Socialforskningsinstituttet.

Hvinden, B., Heikkilä, M. and Kankare, I. (2001) 'Towards activation? The changing relationship between social protection and employment in western Europe', in M. Kautto, J. Fritzell, B. Hvinden, J. Kvist and H. Uusitalo (eds) *Nordic welfare states in the European context*, London: Routledge, pp 168-97.

Jensen, P., Larsen, J.E. and Rosholm, M. (2002) 'Aktivering: mål eller middel?', *Samfundsøkonomen*, no 7, pp 4-11.

Jensen, S.M. (2002) *Nye veje i den by- og boligsociale indsats. Anden delrapport fra evalueringen af seks projekter*, Copenhagen: Center For Forskning I Socialt Arbejde.

Kristensen, C.J. (2003) 'Myndiggørelse gennem legitim perifer deltagelse: et teoretisk bud på et mål for aktiveringsindsatsen', in J. Andersen, A.M. Beck Tyroll, C.J. Kristensen and J.E. Larsen (eds) *Empowerment i storbyens rum: et socialvidenskabeligt perspektiv*, Copenhagen: Hans Reitzels Forlag, pp 162-84.

Kvist, J. (2002) 'Changing rights and obligations in unemployment insurance', in R. Sigg and C. Behrendt (eds) *Social security in the global village*, Brunswick: Transaction Publishers, pp 227-45.

Langager, K. (1997) *Indsatsen overfor de forsikrede ledige*, Copenhagen: Socialforskningsinstituttet.

Larsen, C.A. (2000) *Employment miracles and active labour-market policy: a critical review of the Danish evaluations*, Aalborg University, Department of Economics, Politics and Administration, Centre for Comparative Welfare State Studies.

Larsen, J.E. (2002) 'Marginale mennesker i marginale rum', in M. Järvinen, J.E. Larsen and N. Mortensen (eds) *Det magtfulde møde mellem system og klient*, Aarhus: Aarhus Universitetsforlag, pp 148-84.

Larsen, J.E. (2003) 'Aktiveringspolitikkens mange ansigter', in J. Andersen, A.M. Beck Tyroll, C.J. Kristensen and J.E. Larsen (eds) *Empowerment i storbyens rum: et socialvidenskabeligt perspektiv*, Copenhagen: Hans Reitzels Forlag, pp 114-61.

Larsen, F., Abildgaard, N., Bredgaard, T. and Dalsgaard, L. (2001) *Kommunal aktivering: Mellem disciplinering og integration*, Aalborg: Aalborg Universitetsforlag.

Lødemel, I. and Trickey, H. (2001) *An offer you can't refuse: Workfare in international perspective*, Bristol: The Policy Press.

Madsen, P.K. and Pedersen, L. (2003) 'Miraklernes værksted', in P.K. Madsen and L. Pedersen (eds) *Drivkræfter bag arbejdsmarkedspolitikken*, Copenhagen: Socialforskningsinstituttet, pp 12-25.

Mik-Meyer, N. and Berg Sørensen, T. (2000) *Metoder i aktivering og forrevalidering: Observation og interview*, Århus: Forlaget Gestus.

OECD (1990) *Employment outlook 1990*, Paris: OECD.

OECD (1994) *New orientations for social policy*, Paris: OECD.

Peck, J. (2001) *Workfare states*, New York, NY: Guilford Press.

Rosdahl, A. and Weise, H. (2001) 'When all must be active: workfare in Denmark', in I. Lødemel and H. Trickey (eds) *An offer you can't refuse: Workfare in international perspective*, Bristol: The Policy Press, pp 159-80.

Rosholm, M. (1998) 'Evaluating subsidized employment programmes in the private and public sector', in M. Rosholm (ed) *Modelling transitions in the labour market*, Ph.D. Series 98-03, Afdeling for Nationaløkonomi, Aarhus: Aarhus Universitet.

Saraceno, C. (ed) (2002) *Social assistance dynamics in Europe: National and local poverty regimes*, Bristol: The Policy Press.

Torfing, J. (1999) 'Workfare with welfare: recent reforms of the Danish welfare state', *Journal of European Social Policy*, vol 9, no 1, pp 5-28.

Torfing, J. (2003) 'Den stille revolution i velfærdsstaten', in P.K. Madsen and L. Pedersen (eds) *Drivkræfter bag arbejdsmarkedspolitikken*, Copenhagen: Socialforskningsinstituttet, pp 12-25.

Van Berkel, R. and Møller, I.H. (2002) 'The concept of activation', in R. van Berkel and I.H. Møller (eds) *Active social policies in the EU: Inclusion through participation?*, Bristol: The Policy Press, pp 45-71.

Walker, R. (1999) '"Welfare to work" versus poverty and family change: policy lessons from the USA', *Work, Employment and Society*, vol 13, no 3, pp 539-53.

Weise, H. and Brogaard, H. (1997) *Aktivering af kontanthjælpsmodtagere: En evaluering af Lov om kommunal aktivering*, Copenhagen: Socialforskningsinstituttet.

NINE

Individualising citizenship

Asmund W. Born and Per H. Jensen

Activation policies are at the core of the changing face of welfare. Previous analyses of the activation phenomenon have focused on whether activation policies fit into or cause changes in different welfare regimes (Torfing, 1999; Barbier, 2004; Barbier and Ludwig-Mayerhofer, 2004). Similarly, a significant number of studies have demonstrated that activation policies rebalance the relationship between rights and obligations (Kildal, 2001; Kvist, 2002; Gilbert, 2002; van Oorschot and Abrahamson, 2003). Conversely, the number of studies examining the field-level administration of activation programmes is limited (Handler, 2003; Olesen, 2003). In other words, our knowledge concerning the implementation of activation policies is relatively rudimentary.

This chapter is aimed at contributing to filling this gap in our understanding of the implementation of activation policies. More specifically, the article will present reflections concerning the so-called 'individual action plan' (IAP) that serves as an instrument in the activation efforts in countries such as Denmark. Activation in Denmark is not allowed to proceed in an abstract, unstructured manner. Prior to being activated, an IAP has to be drawn up. It explicitly has to account for the content and purpose of the activation (OECD, 1995), that is, the means of activation that are employed (such as education or job-training), have to be tailored to fit a well-defined ultimate objective. The client has to engage in dialogue with a social worker to negotiate the IAP. This dialogue must be built on the basic understanding that the unemployed person is genuinely interested in becoming integrated in the labour market. Subsequently, another basic premise for this dialogue is that the IAP embodies an attempt at balancing the wishes of the individual with the needs of the labour market (as failure to grant consideration to the needs of the labour market will render integration in the ordinary labour market impossible). Mutual rights and obligations must be specified in the negotiations and, by signing an IAP, unemployed individuals are obliged to act in the manner agreed upon. Conversely, the administration is obliged to make the resources available that render it possible for the unemployed persons to fulfil the IAP objectives. Thus, an IAP assumes the form of a mutual contract between the agency and the client.

The unique aspect of an IAP is that its creation depends upon the active and committed participation of the unemployed person. In this respect, an IAP represents an attempt at remedying the 'passivisation' of the unemployed person that was typical in the past, that is, reducing the unemployed person to a client. An IAP makes it possible for the unemployed person to function as a responsible and reflexive citizen, as it activates unemployed individuals in the solution of their own employment problem. Thus, the citizen becomes as self-regulated and reflexive decision maker by being granted membership and/or ownership of the public administration (Andersen, 2004). The claim can thus be made that an IAP represents the emergence of self-government or the formation of an administrative citizenship (Jensen, 1997). An administrative citizenship refers to the right and obligation of an individual to participate in the processing of all aspects of their own case.

Clear parallels can be drawn between the IAP and the citizenship concept (expounded in Chapter One in this volume). First, on the discursive level, the IAP represents a 'discursification' of new forms of 'civicness'. The IAP institutionalises new expectations of citizens, namely, that they are reflexive, responsible and capable individuals. Second, the citizen has both a right and obligation to have an IAP drawn up. Conversely, this right and obligation serves to oblige the welfare state to procure resources that are tailored to the individual. Thus, the unemployed person has a legal right to be activated in a goal-oriented manner on the basis of an IAP. Third, the citizen participates in a self-administration process, which makes it possible to customise and adjust the measures aimed at an individual. Lastly, the actual drawing-up of the IAP can have considerable significance for the unemployed person's own role perception. The notion of one's 'own role perception' raises the issue of whether the system treats the unemployed with consideration and respect, that is, whether the citizen is subject to a humiliating or dignified treatment, and whether the activation creates opportunities for the unemployed people to make progress with their lives.

Several first-order analyses of the IAP have been marked by scepticism and criticism (Larsen et al, 2002; Handler, 2003; Jørgensen, 2004). In keeping with Lipsky's (1980) classic analyses, it has been argued that the relationship between the social worker and the client is fundamentally asymmetrical; that the financial resources are permanently insufficient; that rules and circulars are not respected; that 'creaming' takes place and the clients are manipulated. Consequently, citizens pursuing a vision of a good life therefore will be disappointed. However, this type of observation sets the scene most of all for a technical criticism of the system. The ensuing demand is that new resources must be added and that social workers must modify their social work practice so that they are better prepared to negotiate with their clients regarding how the policy is to be tailored in relation to the individual.

On this first-order level, the following section will present a sketch of how the IAP functions in Denmark. The purpose is not to determine whether to apply an optimistic or pessimistic view on administrative citizenship. Such a judgement is not possible, as controversies will always exist as to how institutionalised practices should be described and understood. Rather, the overall aim of this chapter is to account for the extremely important role played by the IAP in Denmark as it conditions the formation of the self, regardless of whether the IAP itself is ambiguous and woven in layers of ambiguities.

The specific goal of this chapter, however, is to present reflections concerning the IAP in a citizenship perspective on an empirical, or second-order level. The argument is that the IAP negotiations institutionalise particular expectations in terms of the way the individuals should be and act, as well as representing a new type of identity production in the form of a contract (the way one is a person). On this basis, the claim is that IAP as a form of administrative citizenship in the late modern ad hoc society is rendered a necessary condition for the realisation of other forms of citizenship, namely, economic, social and political citizenship.

The Danish experience with the IAP

In Denmark, the client relationship has been 'contractualised' in relation to many areas of social policy. The IAP has thus become a commonly utilised instrument in social work (Andersen, 2003). In relation to unemployed persons in particular, the IAP was introduced to beneficiaries of unemployment benefits in 1994 and to beneficiaries of welfare benefits in 1998. The general purpose of the IAP in relation to unemployed people is to bring about integration into the labour market. Employment, however, is not a realistic goal for all beneficiaries of welfare benefits. In those instances where it is not a realistic goal, the aim of the IAP is to stabilise and improve the general life situation of the individual, and to prevent the development of further social problems and social exclusion. In particular circumstances, an IAP can thus be intended to support integration into local communities. Thus, according to the Ministry of Social Affairs, participation in local communities is considered to be "a goal in itself, as it is regarded as being good for the individual – even if it fails to lead to self-maintenance" (Socialministeriet, 2000).

Analyses of IAP dialogues that are based on qualitative methods and approaches provide contrasting results and point in opposing directions. Carstens (1998, 2002), who has observed ten IAP dialogues in which social welfare recipients were involved, claims that the caseworker fundamentally defines the content of the IAP, thereby dictating a specific course of action to the client. According to Carstens, IAP dialogues are therefore nothing more than a farce. They are inscrutable to clients and merely serve to contribute further to their sense of dependency and impotence. On the other hand, Olesen, who has employed so-called "initiative-response analyses" in observing 32 dialogues where unemployment benefit recipients were involved, claims that IAPs can actually function as "continous dialogues" with "a certain equality between the dialogue partners" (Olesen, 1996, p 4), as many of the unemployed individuals manage to "use the IAP dialogue and the activation efforts very constructively" (Olesen, 1999, p 63). Olesen distinguishes between 'satisfactory' and 'unsatisfactory' conversations (in the data material in question, he deems 17 to be satisfactory and 15 to be unsatisfactory). Satisfactory dialogues are conversations that actually function as a planning instrument that make it possible for clients to get on with their lives, while unsatisfactory conversations result in stop-gap solutions or opportunities that the unemployed person has no faith in. Olesen further concludes that, more than anything else, unsatisfactory dialogues bear the character of traditional casework approaches rather than assuming the form of actual dialogue or negotiations (Olesen, 2001, p 16).

One can also pin down the dialogical character of the IAP by asking those activated whether they themselves feel that they have had any influence on their own IAP. A number of survey-based studies from 1997 indicate that the unemployed persons who were questioned experienced their IAPs very differently (Brogaard and Weise, 1997; Langager, 1997; Weise and Brogaard, 1997). Some were positive and felt that they had subject status, while others were critical, and felt that they had object status. Thus, findings indicate that two thirds of the unemployment benefit recipients who were activated during the first two years of unemployment reported that they had had a decisive influence on their activation, compared to 56% of those who were activated after two years of unemployment. A total of 85% of all recipients of unemployment benefits were satisfied with their IAP. Among the activated recipients of welfare benefits, only 16% felt that the social worker or other municipal officials had determined the content of their IAP. More recent data, however, points towards slightly different tendencies. Clement (2004) thus concludes that 44% of the beneficiaries of welfare benefits and 23% of the beneficiaries of unemployment benefits felt that their IAP was forced upon them. The long-term unemployed, in particular, did not feel that they have been involved in the process aimed at facilitating their return to ordinary work (Caswell et al, 2002).

Unemployed persons can feel obliged to enter into an IAP, otherwise they risk losing their benefits. Benefits can be discontinued on two grounds: firstly, beneficiaries may forfeit their unemployment benefits because the benefit period terminates after four years of unemployment. Secondly, if the unemployed person refuses to engage in an IAP dialogue or refuses to comply with the content of an IAP, they risk losing their entitlement to welfare and unemployment benefits. All in all, however, relatively few persons lose their entitlement to unemployment and/or welfare benefits.

In 1999, for example, about 388,000 persons entitled to unemployment benefits were unemployed for shorter or longer periods (Danmarks Statistik, 2000, p 149). It is estimated that the total number of persons forfeiting their rights to unemployment benefits in 1999 was between 600 and 1,500 (Arbejdsløshedskassernes Samvirke, 2002). That is, a total of about 0.25% of the recipients of unemployment benefits forfeited their rights to these benefits in 1999. Those forfeiting their rights to unemployment benefits are entitled to welfare benefits.

If social welfare clients refuse to comply with the IAP, they risk losing their welfare benefits entirely, or are exposed to the withholding of up to 20% of their welfare benefits. While the level of absenteeism and truancy in the activation schemes is remarkably high (Sørensen, 2000, p 17), it is rare that clients are deprived of their welfare benefits, as this can have detrimental social and psychological effects that would merely serve to exacerbate the individual's situation (Ebsen et al, 1999; Sørensen, 2000; Boll and Christensen, 2002). This lack of sanctions leads one to believe that social workers prefer to demonstrate loyalty towards their professional ethic rather than towards any given legislation. Moreover, if integration is to succeed, social workers also depend on the acceptance and confidence of their clients, as well as their active participation. The social worker will therefore occasionally turn a blind eye to breached agreements or act as the client's advocate in relation to the authorities (Henriksen and Prieur, 2004).

That is not to say, however, that it is possible to draw simple and unambiguous conclusions on the functioning and appropriateness of IAPs. There are numerous ambiguities inherent in these plans and they are scarcely reduced by the fact that there are no objective, scientific standards and criteria for assessing the appropriateness of IAPs on the first-order level. This sets the stage for the recognition that the assessment of IAPs in general depends on the individual researcher's understandings and intentions, just as vague and relative criteria for assessment secure a foothold in the debate. This problem is as great as the discussion as to whether the IAP is good for an individual and whether pastoral care is exercised or not: it is not possible to gain an understanding of the IAP as a symptom of new tendencies affecting the development of society.

Activation plans and contract

The remainder of this chapter will be devoted to a discussion of the IAP as a system of regulation. Thus, instead of focusing on the learning-to-labour perspective, the IAP may be regarded as a technology that meets the late modern demands on the self as decision maker. Furthermore, the IAP may be construed to be a symptom of more general phenomena in society. There is little doubt that the individual subject is emphasised on the discursive level in all sections of society. The subject–IAP combination is found in schools, where children are to plan their own learning processes; in hospitals, where the patients are expected to be responsible for their own personal health; and in working life, where the employee is encouraged to assume responsibility. In effect, there is no longer a common point of reference. Communal notions of a good life, communal notions of rights and obligations and communal notions regarding society's developmental goals no longer serve as a given institutional element framing encounters among people. On the contrary, everything that is construed as held in common and shared is constituted in the planning and contractual encounter.

This development has had profound effects on the constitution of the individual. The subject is no longer conceived as a stable unit in a system of social coordinates; instead, it has become an ongoing process of self-constitution: at one moment 'a minister of health', at the next responsible for the workplace. In this process of self-construction, the individual encounters new technologies. These new technologies affect internal processes of subjectification, typically installing modalities by which the individual may observe herself as an object to be modelled. This overall societal development (the discourse on the self) combined with the development of new self-technologies (contractual self-observation) constitute the field of IAP.

The human resource management society and a new 'self-technology'

The tendency towards dialogues concerning individual planning and developmental goals have impacted the sphere of the working life far beyond social affairs – and labour-market departments. Human resource management (HRM) has become a widespread management philosophy focusing on the development of co-workers, strategies for the individual, career planning, competence assessments and the relevant tools for the development of the self (Spencer and Spencer, 1991; Beardwell and Holden, 1997). HRM has also found its way into many universities (to use an example close to home), where various staff groups (including scientific staff) engage in annual dialogues with the management. During such performance reviews, the strong and weak sides of individuals are addressed in order to compel employees to reflect upon themselves and their own position in the social realm, and, of course, to elucidate the relevant competencies and ambitions.

At such performance reviews, the language created by industrialisation and collectivisation ('we want', 'we demand', etc) is not applicable. Instead, a new idiom – the language of self-strategising – is employed. Using this idiom, the individual employees articulate that they as individuals have defined the goal of getting from point A to point B in X number of days[1].

When disregarding the close linkage between benefits and dialogue, which provides the client with tactical possibilities that are different from those available to the employee in the ordinary labour market, the activation dialogue and plan appear to be identical to the HRM-based review. There is no significant difference between IAP dialogues and performance reviews in the ordinary labour market. They are future-oriented dialogues in which dialogical power is constituted in a schematised form. The employer/social worker position is typically constituted as the position from which one is in control over the economy, whereas employees and clients have been granted expert power: they possess expertise in their own images of the future, which the employer/social worker depends on if there is to be any dialogue at all. Regarded in terms of a dialogue, the interaction is marked by a profound asymmetry, as one part is performing as a role-in-action (a manager) and the other is the present topic of conversation (the one who must be activated). On one side, there is an administrator of a system, on the other, the administrator of oneself as a subject.

That which emerges on the horizon is a homology between the ordinary labour market and the 'activation market'. Both performance reviews and IAPs provoke self-reflection. The two arenas draw on the same language and similar means of negotiating solutions. Both arenas expect conscious and reflexive participation in the social realm and reflection is, in both arenas, the self-staging method. Individualisation is the machine and dialogue, planning and contract represent the technologies. Lurking in the background are voluntaristic ideals and risk-running as a life form (Giddens, 1991; Sennett, 1998; Beck, 2000; Baumann, 2001, 2003).

This staging has effects on the relationship between action, language and experience. First of all, the relationship between classificatory concepts and their social references changes. They become flexible and loosely coupled elements varying with their context and strategic usefulness. Universal categories (such as 'work') are dissolved and reappear with new and varying significance through negotiations. The meaning of words and concepts is established and transformed during these very negotiation processes. Instead of being institutionally based and taken for granted, the semantics and concepts become the result of the negotiations and are therefore renegotiable in the next and subsequent dialogues.

Second, there is also a change in the way people's position in the labour market is perceived as a cause–effect relationship on a linear time axis, where the terms of the future are conditioned by the actions of the past. In a planning dialogue, where the subject is under construction, the relationship between future and past is transformed into a variable, and the imagined future defines the relevant past. However, during the negotiation process, individuals being activated are never aware whether it is their ability as negotiating subjects or their actual plans that are at stake. The horizon of time is future-oriented as long as the administrator believes in the negotiating capacity of the other. When in doubt, the past takes over and the administrator questions the very qualities of the subject, such as by saying that you cannot become activated as this or that, because your past shows this or that. Any past–future relationship can be redefined in every dialogue and at every level[2].

The fact that it is possible to link together situationally charged concepts with situationally created pasts and futures links together the decision-making process and the conception of the self in a mutual constitution, wherein even the evaluation of successes or failures is a joint one ("My social worker and I negotiated the wrong choice of instrument when we planned my future"). Such planning mistakes can always be dealt with, of course. One can always reconsider one's life and devise a new plan, which is exactly what Giddens is aiming at with the "politics of second chances" (Giddens, 1991, p 185).

This type of loop forces individual rationality away from the classic rationality of decision making towards what Luhmann refers to as the new rationality: future-oriented risk assessment. Consequently, a self-generating stress factor enters dialogues and decisions, whether one is inside or outside the labour market, in the form of coerced reflection and the risks associated with making decisions (Luhmann, 1991).

Thus, activation and IAP schemes are not exclusively about inducing new ethics among unemployed and marginalised persons. Instead, they indicate a general shift towards individualisation and system-induced reflexivity. By focusing on dialogue as an occasion to create an identity and images of work and life as a basis for action, the operation is projected as a positively loaded opportunity for self-reflection. On the level of self-technology, this type of regulation is indicative of a shift in technology. The basic concept is not 'beware of thyself'; rather, in the vocabulary of Foucault, it becomes 'care of thyself' (Townley, 1995).

In the self-technology of 'beware of yourself', the individual is conceptualised as a stable unit and dialogues regarding the self focus on stability and the deviation from stability; the method being the clinical and control-oriented intervention of the pastor, the therapist or the social worker. The technology of 'care of thyself' is built around another concept of self. In this instance, the self is a movement, an ongoing handling of the relationship between the past and future of the individual within individuals themselves. In the fashion of the late stoics, the point here is to beware of what you want to do, to register what you actually did and then ponder the reasons and implications for so doing. Within this very operation, the self emerges as a mobile output of or input to the ongoing process of emerging (Foucault, 1986, 1988; Townley, 1995, 1998). In the activation plan perspective, the alleged shift has two implications: it links activation planning to overall societal change (a new dispositif), and it points towards the internal division of the individual into an observer and an actor, which has consequences for the IAP.

In terms of activation and IAPs, this means that the individual is accorded autonomy and opportunities for self-regulation in the fight against unemployment. It is therefore emphasised that the politics of second chances is an integrated element in life–political arrangements (Giddens, 1991). In our perspective, however, these second chances are not about allowing individuals to try over and over again until they succeed. The politics of second chances means that one is constantly offered a new chance to (re–)narrate oneself in a new manner in the social realm. In terms of activation, a second chance does not entail being told that in six months you will be assigned a workfare job if you fail to adopt the proper moral character. On the contrary, it means that in six months you will get the chance to narrate yourself in relation to the social realm, that is, you are given a new opportunity to do what we all do: to create and sustain your identity through the reproduction and renewal of your self-narration, which is a figure of reflection penetrating many, if not all, areas of society.

HRM society and a new dispositif

Organising the relationship between man and work/life as a self-created and partially planned relationship moves the well-known mechanisms of discipline and socialisation into the micro space of interaction and the body. Instead of the disciplinary mechanisms inherent to industrial society, forming a disciplinary dispositif that runs along the distinction normal/abnormal[3], one may postulate that a new dispositif is at work: because the very disciplining has been internalised within the individual as a means of being-in-the-World, and because the form of operation has shifted. Instead of disciplining with reference to an absolute, God or reason, there is an ongoing subjectification, in the sense that the individual is duplicated into an observing self who employs planning technologies when observing herself. Instead of the panopticon of the prison based on the economy of surveillance, we live in an economy of synopticon, wherein the very surveillance itself is privatised, leaving the second-order activity of support to public policy (Giddens, 1991; Deleuze, 1992).

From a sociological point of view, a negative consequence of this development of sociality is the dismantling of the collective realm, which has rendered the new labour market and social policy both possible and necessary. The growing tendency to individualise through reflexive self-staging processes that are subsequently shaped into micro spaces of negotiation, makes it increasingly difficult to collectivise language and meaning, as statements become polysemic in the sense that their semantic possibilities are not fixed through a general institutionalisation; instead they are fixated in the very process of contract making, step by step.

A shift is taking place in inclusion and exclusion itself, as exclusion and marginalisation no longer adhere by necessity to well-known systemic lines (such as one's position in the educational system, profession, job duration, age or gender). Inclusion and exclusion are instead linked to isolated interactions and actions and to visions of the future and willingness to accept risk (how one chooses to make use of the educational system). Consequently, exclusion and marginalisation become invisible, along with integration and social diversity. This is a characteristic feature of the changing sociality that increases society's capacity to absorb exclusion while maintaining the form of integration itself (Luhmann, 1997; Born and Jensen, 2002). Furthermore, this is exactly the core of the new dispositif. It operates exclusively on the level of operations, where it functions along the difference between risk and possibilities, hiding exclusion in the in-betweens of operations.

HRM society and contractual subjectivity

Only through, and not prior to, dialogue, reflection and choices does one become a subject and an individual, that is, an individual who is always open to redefinition. In fact, it is even becoming institutionalised as the way to approach life. Schoolchildren in the third grade in Denmark must practise self-strategising coached by their teacher resulting in contracts for the next semester, and every second television programme, labelled reality-TV, revolves around emerging subjectivity and negotiation.

When regarding the contract as a formal contract between the individual and the system represented by the teacher, the employer or the social worker, the entire point is lost. Returning to the 'care of the self' technology, the basic property was the doubling of the self. Without a stable unity of self, the self emerges in the ongoing observation of self, and the contract is a method by which self-observation is actualised under rather ambiguous conditions. On one side, it presupposes that the contract partner is an instrumentally rational individual who will play the game and feel obliged by the contractual conditions. These conditions on the other side are themselves produced and reproduced in the very contractual situation as a part of the operation.

Administrative citizenship

Observing the IAP on the level of operation makes several layers of insights relevant. First, the activation and planning dialogues are important events, so to speak, 'fatal moments' (Giddens, 1991), or moments ripe with possibilities and risk: moments where the subject might face transformation of the self and the relevant context. Second, the dialogue has assumed the form of the contract, which implies that there are two parts that are actually able to commit themselves to a contract. However, the object becomes quite opaque, as the contract is about the contractual ability (subjectification) of the one part. During the negotiations, the one to be activated never knows what is being discussed – my expertise in my own life or my future. Third, the line of argument was that this contractual subjectification has penetrated society and become a new dispositif in which the subject is an ongoing emergence from event to event: this is characteristic of the new citizenship.

In effect, citizenship is no longer a spatial organiser. It has turned temporal. The issue is not about time becoming the topic of citizenship, but about temporality as a generative principle penetrating the operations of citizenship; its logics of practice, so to speak (Bourdieu, 1992). Whenever citizenship is active, it functions along the logics of temporality, not spatiality. Citizenship is no longer a geographic concept delimiting a borderline within which exists an all-encompassing citizenship granting subjectivity in general. Instead, it has become an event or operation characterised by the actualisation of the distinction between competent or incompetent participant/subject. Consequently, citizenship is preconditioned by the capacity and willingness to negotiate.

In relation to social citizenship, the result is that the access to resources is no longer guaranteed from the outside: rather, it depends on a double capacity connected to the event of dialogue. First and foremost, the applicants are able to construct themselves as a future potentiality, and secondly, they have the dialogical capacity and risk willingness to do so in the situation, never knowing whether the dialogue is about the future or present ability.

In relation to economic citizenship, the point is that the market and exchange value of individuals are not predetermined entities. By contrast, the market and market value is established in the moment of negotiations, that is, upon receiving acceptance as a negotiating partner. Economic citizenship does not lie along the division between labourer and employer; instead, it is along the distinction between the entrepreneur and the irrelevant.

Finally, this temporality has profound effects on the political citizenship. If political citizenship is perceived as the access to decision making concerning the distribution of societal resources, this must logically presuppose an overarching shared political community and that no longer exists. On a less abstract level, this means that streams of relevant societies varying with the topic and strategy at hand have been substituted for the unity of society as a frame of reference. Considered in the perspective of society as a lasting structure, the result is the disappearance of society itself. Seen from the level of ongoing interaction, this is not the effect. This is owing to the very nature of the contract. In a society where the frame of reference is constituted in the contract, the very choice of topic and strategy has become generically political and under the condition of temporality, the contract must be sensitive to the present context, as well as to imagined future ones.

Conclusion: IAPs and administrative citizenship

As IAPs are oriented towards the creation of the individual subject, the scope of the labour-market policy has shifted. Instead of being orientated towards the behavioural aspects of labour market and society, the IAPs focus on the basic cognitive prerequisites associated with this subjectivity. Participation and citizenship is no longer to be taken for granted as a question of legitimate actions or participation within the frame of a shared society. Instead, it has become a question of perceiving oneself and society through specific lenses. It has become an administrative citizenship, wherein inclusion or exclusion is a private affair that remains hidden on the societal level. Self-government has become a societal practice and the IAP a technology for subjective learning and relearning.

In this light, the IAP contract is not between individual and system or between individuals; rather, it is a productive machine providing an arena for learning and practising social sensitivity. Through the practical combination of subjectification, choice of topic and the evaluation of effects and strategies, the IAP serves as the grounds for that which has been termed learning through peripheral legitimate participation, that is, the participation through which one enters a community of practice, the late modern ad hoc society (Lave and Wenger, 1991).

In the late modern ad hoc society, administrative citizenship has for all intents and purposes become the proverbial ticket for admission to the economic, social and political citizenship or a ticket of admission to the various arenas in society, as it is one's negotiations and self-presentation that determines access to participation. Participation itself, however, will always remain fragmented. Via the contract, one negotiates clearly defined and delimited forms of participation and this participation will always be temporary. Participation is always up for debate, negotiation and reformulation.

Notes

[1] Employee development reviews (appraisals) have been introduced in all large companies and almost all larger public institutions in Denmark. See Holt Larsen et al (1989) for a description of the language and purpose of the appraisals. For a Foucauldian critique, see Townley (1999).

[2] Richard Sennett discusses this point empirically (1998, Chapter 3).

[3] By 'dispositif', we refer to the Foucauldian understanding of a discursive and praxis regime, namely, the rules and regulations for transporting forms of communication and interaction (and control) from one situation to another (Foucault, 1975).

References

Andersen, N.Å. (2003) *Borgerens kontraktliggørelse*, Copenhagen: Hans Reitzels Forlag.

Andersen, N.Å. (2004) 'Kontraktliggørelse af borgeren - om indskiftning af pligt til frihed', *Nordiske Organisasjonsstudier*, vol 6, no 1, pp 4-26.

Arbejdsløshedskassernes Samvirke (2002) *Rapport om udfaldstruede og marginaliserede medlemmer*, Copenhagen.

Barbier, J.-C. (2004) 'Systems of social protection in Europe: two contrasted paths to activation, and maybe a third', in J. Lind, H. Knudsen and H. Jørgensen (eds) *Labour and employment regulation in Europe*, Brussels: P.I.E.-Peter Lang, pp 233-53.

Barbier, J.-C. and Ludwig-Mayerhofer, W. (2004) 'The many worlds of activation', *European Societies*, vol 6, no 4, pp 423-37.

Bauman, Z. (2001) *Community: Seeking safety in an insecure world*, Cambridge: Polity Press.

Bauman, Z. (2003) *Liquid love*, Cambridge: Polity Press.

Beardwell, I. and Holden, L. (1997) *Human resource management: A contemporary perspective* (2nd edn), London: Pitman Publishing.

Beck, U. (2000) *The brave new world of work*, Cambridge: Polity Press.

Boll, J. and Christensen, T.Q. (2002) *Kontanthjælpsmodtagere og arbejdsmarkedet*, Copenhagen: Socialforskningsinstituttet.

Born, A.W. and Jensen, P.H. (2002) 'Second order reflections on the concepts of inclusion and exclusion', in J.G. Andersen and P.H. Jensen (eds) *Changing labour markets: Welfare policies and citizenship*, Bristol: The Policy Press, pp 257-79.

Bourdieu, P. (1992) *The logic of practice*, Cambridge: Polity Press.

Brogaard, S. and Weise, H. (1997) *Evaluering af Lov om kommunal evaluering*, Copenhagen: Socialforskningsinstituttet.

Carstens, A. (1998) *Aktivering: Klientsamtaler og socialpolitik*, Copenhagen: Hans Reitzels Forlag.

Carstens, A. (2002) '"Motivation" i visitationssamtaler på aktiveringsområdet', in M. Järvinen, J. E. Larsen and N. Mortensen (eds) *Det magtfulde møde mellem system og klient*, Aarhus: Aarhus Universitetsforlag, pp 28-60.

Caswell, D., Eskelinen, L. and Hansen, S.L. (2002) *Langtidslediges erfaringer med Arbejdsformidlingen og aktivering*, Copenhagen: AKF Forlaget.

Clement, S.L. (2004) *Betinget velfærd*, Aalborg: Aalborg Universitet.

Danmarks Statistik (2000) *Statistisk Årbog 2000*, Copenhagen.

Deleuze, G. (1990) 'Pourparlers – postscript to the societies of control', *L'Autre*, no 59, pp 3-7, October.

Ebsen, F., Guldager, J. and Hagen, U. (1999) *Arbejdsløse og aktivering*, Copenhagen: Samfundslitteratur.

Foucault, M. (1975) *Surveiller et punir*, Paris: Editions Gallimard.

Foucault, M. (1986) *The care of the self: The history of sexuality vol 3*, London: Penguin Books.

Foucault, M. (1988) 'Technologies of the self', in L.H. Martin, H. Gutman and P.H. Hutton (eds) *Technologies of the self: A seminar with Michel Foucault*, Amherst, MA: University of Massachusetts Press.

Giddens, A. (1991) *Modernity and self-identity. Self and society in the late modern age*, Cambridge: Polity Press.

Gilbert, N. (2002) *Transformation of the welfare state, the surrender of public responsibility*, Oxford: Oxford University Press.

Handler, J.F. (2003) 'Social citizenship and workfare in the US and western Europe: from status to contract', *Journal of European Social Policy*, vol 13, no 3, pp 229-43.

Henriksen, L.S. and Prieur, A. (2004) 'Et nyt perspektiv på magt i det sociale arbejde', *Dansk Sociologi*, vol 15, no 3, pp 101-12.

Holt Larsen, H., Relster, E. and Nielsen, J. (1989) *Medarbejdersamtaler: Nøglen til personaleudvikling*, Copenhagen: Teknisk forlag.

Jensen, P.H. (1997) 'Decentraliseringens moralske og forvaltningsmæssige udfordringer belyst ved den ny arbejdsmarkedsreform', in P. Gundelach, H. Jørgensen and K.K. Klausen (eds) Det lokale: Decentral politik og forvaltning, Aalborg: Aalborg Universitetsforlag, pp 315-41.

Jørgensen, H. (2004) 'Labour market and employment policies activated?', in J. Lind, H. Knudsen and H. Jørgensen (eds) Labour and employment regulation in Europe, Brussels: P.I.E.-Peter Lang, pp 199-209.

Kildal, N. (2001) 'Workfare tendencies in Scandinavian welfare politics', SES papers no 5, Geneva: International Labour Office.

Kvist, J. (2002) 'Changing rights and obligations in unemployment insurance', in R. Sigg and C. Behrendt (eds) Social security in the global village, International Social Security Series no 8, New Brunswick: Transaction Publishers, pp 227-45.

Langager, K. (1997) Indsatsen over for de forsikrede ledige, Copenhagen: Socialforskningsinstituttet.

Larsen, J.E., Mortensen, N. and Thomsen, J.P.F. (2002) 'Magtens mange facetter i mødet mellem system og klient', in M. Järvinen, J. E. Larsen and N. Mortensen (eds) Det magtfulde møde mellem system og klient, Aarhus: Aarhus Universitetsforlag, pp 185-97.

Lave, J. and Wenger, E. (1991) Situated learning, legitimate peripheral participation, New York, NY: Cambridge University Press.

Lipsky, M. (1980) Street-level bureaucracy, New York, NY: Sage Publications.

Luhmann, N. (1991) Risiko und Gefahr, in Soziologische Aufklärung 5: Konstruktivistische Perspektiven, Opladen: Westdeutscher Verlag.

Luhmann, N. (1997) Die Gesellschaft der Gesellschaft, Frankfurt a. M.: Suhrkamp.

OECD (1995) Employment outlook, Paris: OECD.

Olesen, S.P. (1996) Mødet mellem velfærdsstaten og den arbejdsløse/ den arbejdsmarkedspolitiske samtale: Et eksempel på forskning I socialt arbejde, Aarhus: Den Sociale Højskole i Aarhus.

Olesen, S.P. (1999) Handleplanssamtaler, Intentioner og aktører, Aalborg: Aalborg Universitet Carma, Arbejdstekst nr. 1.

Olesen, S.P. (2001) 'Handlingsplansamtaler. En hån mod de arbejdsløse eller konstruktivt samspil med systemet', Tidsskrift for Arbejdsliv, vol 3, no 3, pp 7-28.

Olesen, S.P. (2003) 'Client, user, member as constructed in institutional interaction', in C. Hall, K. Juhila, N. Parton and T. Pösö (eds) Constructing clienthood in social work and human services. Interaction, identities and practices, London: Jessica Kingsley Publishers, ch 13.

Sennett, R. (1998) *The corrosion of character: The transformation of work in modern capitalism*, New York, NY: Norton and Company.

Socialministeriet (2000) *Socialpolitik som investering, Socialpolitisk Redegørelse 2000*: Sammenfatning, Copenhagen.

Sørensen, T. (2000) *Metoder i aktivering og forrevalidering*, Aarhus: Forlaget Gestus.

Spencer, L.M. and Spencer, S.M. (1991) *Competence at work: Models for superior performance*, London: John Wiley & Sons.

Torfing, J. (1999) 'Workfare with welfare: recent reforms of the Danish welfare state', *Journal of European Social Policy*, vol 9, no 1, pp 5-28.

Townley, B. (1995) '"Know thyself": self-awareness, self-formation and managing', *Organization*, vol 2, no 2, pp 271-89.

Townley, B. (1998) 'Beyond good and evil: depth and division in the management of human resources', in M. Foucault, *Management and organization theory*, London: Sage Publications, pp 191-210.

Townley, B. (1999) 'Nietzsche, competencies and Übermensch: reflections on human and inhuman resource management', *Organization*, vol 6, no 2, pp 285-305.

van Oorschot, W. and Abrahamson, P. (2003) 'The Dutch and Danish miracles revisited: a critical discussion of activation policies in two small welfare states', *Social Policy & Administration*, vol 37, no 3, pp 288-304.

Weise, H. and Brogaard, S. (1997) *Aktivering af kontanthjælpsmodtagere*, Copenhagen: Socialforskningsinstituttet.

TEN

Gender equality, citizenship and welfare state restructuring

Birte Siim

One of the crucial themes that has emerged as a background and premise for feminist scholarship and debates is the gendering of inequality during the past 30 years inspired by feminist politics. Gender equality has become part of the political agenda in western democracies and social movements have taken up the struggle for women's equal rights all over the world. Feminist scholars have studied the gendered links between the family, the state and the market and have re-conceptualised the division between public and private, between paid and unpaid work and care and between equality and difference (Hobson et al, 2002). Equality is contested as a concept and as a cultural norm and there is a debate about the meaning of gender equality and the means to achieve it. Gender equality is about recognising the equal moral worth of women and men. It has been defined by the European Commission as "a situation where all individuals can develop their capacities and can make choices without being constrained by gender stereotypes or restrictive roles; and where different behaviors, goals and needs of women and men are equally recognised, valued and promoted" (cited in Liebert, 2003, p 12). From this perspective an equality policy is a set of public policies that seeks to promote gender equality as a societal value and norm by adopting equitable programmes and measures. Arguably, gender equality is an important normative ideal, although equality is no longer high on the political agenda (Phillips, 1999).

Today the European welfare states are at a crossroad and new forms of inequality have become visible. One of the challenges is to analyse the interconnection between gender equality and other kinds of inequalities in relation to race, ethnicity and class. Citizenship has become a key concept in social and political theory embedded in debates about equal rights and resources to overcome inequality. Since the 1990s it has been employed as both a normative and analytical framework to analyse the inclusion and exclusion of women and marginalised social groups (Lister, 1997). The notion of citizenship refers both to rights, belonging and participation (Bellamy et al, 2004). It has been connected with the nation state, and the double process of globalisation and immigration represent new challenges to link the framework of citizenship with transnational governance (Hobson and Lister, 2002, Bellamy et al, 2004).

In this chapter I use the framework of citizenship[1] to study the barriers and potentials for gender equality in the era of globalisation and welfare state restructuring. In this frame, citizenship has two dimensions: a welfare state dimension designating social policies, as well as a democratic dimension designating the participation and identities of citizens (Siim, 2000). The focus is on the interplay between political, social and civil rights, as well as the interconnection between rights, participation and power. The framework is based on the belief that politics matters and the notion of agency provides a link between demands for equal civil, political and social rights. Agency refers both to individual actors and to the capabilities of collective agency to influence politics and policies on all levels of decision making. The focus on agency makes it possible to address their gendered roles and activities as parents, workers and citizens and the interconnection of the different arenas of state, market and civil society (Siim, 2000).

There is no universal story of citizenship and recent research indicates that although there are certain characteristic features of modern citizenship, it has evolved in very different ways in different European countries (Bellamy et al, 2004). Gender relations and welfare systems are also dynamic concepts embedded in national histories, institutions and cultures (Siim, 2000; Hobson et al, 2002). The European welfare regimes represent different vocabularies and dynamics of citizenship and gender that can illuminate the complex processes of exclusion and inclusion of women and men as workers, parents and citizens (Bussemaker and Voet, 1998). The various gender regimes[2] have a different a logic based on rules and norms about gender relations that influence the construction of policies and have implications for gender equality.

The analysis of gendered inequalities can be divided in different dimensions; for example civil, social and political rights (Siim, 2000) in relation to different arenas, for example democratic politics, the labour market and the family and in differentiations among women. The relative autonomy of politics and welfare state institutions can be seen as mediating variables between labour-market dynamics and policy outcomes (Korpi, 2000).

This chapter first gives an overview of the dynamic of welfare state restructuring in the era of globalisation and discusses the implication of these shifts in policy logic from a male breadwinner model to a dual breadwinner or an adult worker model[3] for gender equality and inequality. Feminist scholarship has stressed that the implementation of the new adult worker model depends upon the national policy contexts that create different opportunity structures for social actors to influence social policies (Hobson et al, 2002; Sainsbury, 1999).

Second, it looks at the trend towards individualisation and changes in the organisation of care work in post-industrial societies, discussing the potential for gender equality on the basis of the Nordic example, often seen as an inspiration for gender equality. Here gender equality has been high on the political agenda, although gender equality policies have not reduced the gender-segregated labour market. An expansion of childcare services and an extension of the daddy quota have accompanied women's increased labour-market participation (Borchorst, 2002) and there has also been a substantial increase in women's political representation (see Bergqvist et al, 1999).

The last section addresses the role of European integration in relation to gender equality and social policies and the tendency towards convergence and divergence in the European welfare state. One of the central objectives presented at the Lisbon Summit was to increase the number of women in the labour force as well as to expand childcare provision (Lisbon European Council, 2000). What are the implications of this for European social policies and what is the normative gender equality model behind EU social policies (Mahon, 2002)?

Gender equality in the era of welfare state restructuring and globalisation

Globalisation has become a new buzzword and there are many competing interpretations of what it means, but academic debate has placed little attention on the gendered script of globalisation. Feminist scholars have only recently started to address the gendered dimensions in the context of global economic, political and cultural processes (Hobson et al, 2002). Policy making within national contexts appears more and more bound to international policy arenas and discursive landscapes. This can be seen at both the discursive and the policy levels. New actors and new forms of claims are emerging in supranational forums and the EU has become a key actor influencing gender equality on the labour market (Liebert, 2003).

Comparative research has indicated that welfare states respond differently to the forces of globalisation and up till now there have been relatively strong 'path dependencies' in the way welfare regimes respond to perceived threats of globalisation, influenced by their national histories, political institutions and ideologies (Esping-Andersen, 1999). The different welfare regimes express a different policy logic that may have different implications for gender, class and ethnicity (Acker, 2000; Korpi, 2000). Comparative feminist research has identified different breadwinner-models, namely, variations in the work–family relation that express different dynamics between the state, the market and civil society (Lewis and Ostner, 1994). It follows that key concepts in social policy are gendered and often have different meanings for women and men, because they have different positions in the labour market and in the family (Hobson et al, 2002).

One example of this is the gendered link between commodification and decommodification. According to Esping-Andersen (1999) and the power resource school, decommodification is a key concept in comparative welfare research that explains variations in welfare state regimes. Wage labourers have traditionally fought for decommodification: a concept that refers to their right not to be obliged to sell their labour power in cases of average workers' risks, like old age, disability, sickness and unemployment. Feminist scholars have criticised this approach because it focuses on state–market relation and leaves out the state–family relation. Furthermore, it does not include social services or the gendered distribution between paid and unpaid work (Sainsbury, 1999; Borchorst, 2002). The implication is that decommodification does not apply to women unless welfare states have first helped them to become commodified through wage work. The argument is that in social policy commodification and decommodification is inseparable (Knijn and Ostner, 2002, pp 146-7).

The twin processes of globalisation and modernisation represent new challenges to European welfare regimes that have created barriers to gender equality as well as some potential for it. There are both new problems for women connected with the flexibilisation of the labour market (Lewis, 2001) as well as new openings connected with individualisation and with de-traditionalisation of family structures (Beck et al, 1994).

Feminist scholarship concerned with theorising social politics have identified key dilemmas and policy debates connected with the split between the public and the private sphere, paid and unpaid work and with commodification and decommodification (Hobson et al, 2002). The inclusion of working mothers on the labour market thus represents a shift in policy logic with large implications for the politics and economics of care (Boye and Leira, 2000). The tendency towards a shift from a male breadwinner to a dual-earner family has politicised the work/care nexus, and it has put childcare at the centre of the redesign of the contemporary welfare state (Mahon, 2002).

The policy logic of the modern welfare state was constructed around the work–welfare relationship based upon normative assumptions of women's care work and men's wage work. This involved a labour-capital settlement as well as a gender settlement conceptualised as the male breadwinner model. Feminist scholarship has shown how the male breadwinner model in different ways in different countries became a normative basis for social policy after the World War II (Lewis and Ostner, 1994). The model was a prescription that underpinned social policy as well as family law. The post-war gender settlement assumed full employment of a regular kind for men together with stable families, and social policy followed by routing benefits to the male head of households.

In European welfare states there has during the last 30 years been a gradual change in the assumptions of policy makers as well as in the identities and practice of women concerning women's wage work. There is an increasing political emphasis on the responsibilities of adults to engage in paid work, identified as the shift towards the dual-earner family. The male breadwinner model has been substantially eroded in two respects: by an increase in the labour-market participation of women and a decrease in that of men, and by the change in family structures towards increasing individualisation.

In terms of labour-market changes, feminist scholars have identified three clusters:

- What Jane Lewis has called the strong male breadwinner models: the UK, the Netherlands and Germany (Lewis, 1992).
- Continental countries such as France and Belgium that have a tradition of women working full time[4] (Daune-Richard, 2000).
- The Nordic countries that have been closest to a dual breadwinner or dual earner model, although there are important variations in the gender political models in the five Nordic countries (see Bergqvist et al, 1999; Korpi, 2000).

The second shift is in the mixed economy of care. Again feminist scholars have identified different patterns. In France and Belgium a general family support has given all children over the age of three a place in a publicly funded childcare centre. In the UK there is a market-oriented gender model, which means that provision is likely to be a mixture of kin, market provision, public provision and voluntary provision. As mentioned earlier, it is only in the Nordic countries where there has been a tradition for publicly funded childcare centres for the under three year olds (Leira and Saraceno, 2002).

The changes in respect to the labour–capital settlement have been widely attributed to globalisation, although there are different interpretations of the meaning and implications of these changes. Some find that internal factors, such as demographic change, are more important than external factors associated with the concept of globalisation in explaining the need for welfare state restructuring (Esping-Andersen, 1999). It has been noted that the two are not necessarily competing explanations. Rather, increasing individualisation with respect to family change and labour-market behaviour may go hand in hand, and are reinforced by the changing nature of the assumptions made by policy makers who are influenced by globalisation talk (Hobson et al, 2002).

Scholars also have different interpretations of the dangers of the globalisation discourse for women. As Jane Lewis (2001) has noticed, a major problem is that the change in the prescription for an adult worker model is not necessarily followed by a change in behaviour or in practical policy. This raises new questions. In terms of social policy, the question is to what extent welfare states redesign social policies to support working mothers, including a public infrastructure in terms of good quality and affordable childcare facilities to enable them to become full-time workers? In terms of identity, the question is whether all women, including single parents, who were earlier supported by the state, can be expected to behave as full-time workers. The dual-earner family means that families can no longer provide full-time care and this has created a caring deficit in western welfare states, that is, a gap between the need for care and the supply available (Leira and Saraceno, 2002). European welfare states have responded differently to the growing shortage of caring resources and their different childcare policies have implications for gender equality (Mahon, 2002).

From a gender perspective one key question is how the state responds to the challenge to take on new care responsibilities. Jane Lewis concludes, on the basis of the British case, that unless something is done on the care side of the equation work/care, there is a real danger of overestimating women's economic independence and capacity for self-provision, for example in relation to pensions (Lewis, 2001). There are different models for childcare, but in terms of gender equality, a more equal sharing of care work between women and men is seen as crucial (Mahon, 2002).

In continental Europe 'labour-market insertion' has been viewed as a means to combat social exclusion. The idea of active citizenship has been grounded in the responsibility to work. The new European welfare contract is moving from social contributions to individually defined contributions, premised on the ideal that all adults are in the workforce. Lewis, among others, has pointed out that this is an unreal assumption for many women, given the unequal gendered division of unpaid care work and the fact that a disproportionate number of women are employed in low-paid, part-time, often care-related jobs. This is especially true in Britain, where in addition the means-tested nature of the whole social security system tends to oppose individualisation (Lewis, 2001).

To sum up the dynamic of welfare state restructuring: the increased individualisation on the work and family front has different implications for gender and citizenship.[5] Feminist researchers generally agree that the trend towards individualisation and what has been called defamilisation, or the de-gendering of care, tends to increase gender equality because it decreases the reliance of individual women on the family and increases their economic independence (Saraceno, 1999; Liebert, 2003). More recently leading sociologists like Gøsta Esping-Andersen (1999) and Walther Korpi (2000) have supported the argument about the potentials for defamilisation to increase gender equality and justice. They tend, however, to overlook the fact that the dual earner model based upon individual benefits and increased contractualisation may lead to a care deficit (Leira and Saraceno, 2002). Jane Lewis and others have stressed that in the strong male breadwinner models, especially Britain, the Netherlands and Germany, the trend toward individualisation may at the same time increase class inequalities among women workers (Gerhard et al, 2002).

Towards a new gender model in the European welfare states?

Feminist scholars have argued that the family, its behaviour and its framing is, and will increasingly be found, at the core of social policy thinking and making (Leira and Saraceno, 2002; Mahon, 2002). There is, furthermore, a growing recognition in comparative welfare research of the key role of households in the post-industrial economy and of the importance of different European family policy models (Esping-Andersen, 1999; Korpi, 2000).

The family and care work is today central to welfare state redesign and European welfare states have developed social and family policies, including a mix of childcare arrangements to respond to the new social and economic demands. Feminist scholars have discussed these care-related policy reforms, strategies and models (Leira and Saraceno, 2002; Knijn and Ostner, 2002; Gerhart et al, 2002). Defamilisation indicates the extent to which economic and social rights are granted to individuals of all ages and family conditions – or are vice-versa contingent on family circumstances (Saraceno, 1999). Re-familisation shifts responsibility from the public to private families, for example, in the case of payments for care. Finally there is also a trend towards an increased marketisation of social services from the public sector to the market (Knijn and Ostner, 2002). The differentiation in the social policies above overlap with Rianne Mahon's (2002) identification of three dominant childcare models in Europe in the 1990s: a) the egalitarian Swedish-Danish, b) the neo-familial Finnish and French and c) the third way British and Dutch model that is different from the dominant neoliberal US model.

The recent political developments have sparked a new theoretical interest in gender, the family and care work in comparative social research (Korpi, 2000). Gøsta Esping-Andersen has argued that the household economy is the alpha and omega of any resolution of the main post-industrial dilemmas around equality and justice/solidarity (Esping-Andersen, 1999). He adds defamilisation to decommodification as key concepts in the welfare regime framework in order to analyse variations in welfare state regimes in relation to class and gender. This work has been criticised because it does not address the way social policy affects the gendered division of care in the family, especially men's role as fathers (Knijn and Kremer, 1997).

Knijn and Kremer (1997) have analysed how the right to give and receive care has created different caring regimes with different assumptions about gender relations and implications for gender equality. This caring approach cuts across the three welfare regimes, the liberal, conservative and social democratic and goes beyond the male breadwinner regime approach (Leira and Saracena, 2002, Mahon, 2002). Welfare states have during the 1990s developed different strategies towards the caring deficit and it has been noticed that care chains are becoming increasingly global, because it is more and more common for children and frail older people in the rich North to be taken care of by women from the poor South, who in turn pay women in their own country to take care of their own children or parents (Leira and Saracena, 2002; Knijn and Ostner, 2002). This development tends to increase class and ethnic differentiation among women.

Feminist research has discussed different normative gender models

(Fraser, 1997). An increase in women's economic independence and a decrease in family dependencies is, however, often seen as a key to gender equality that requires a radical recast of welfare responsibilities[6] (Leira and Saraceno, 2002; Mahon, 2002). Female independence requires a certain degree of individualisation of welfare obligations and the adoption of social policies committed to lessening the caring burden of the family. Defamilisation policies through the welfare state have until recently only been a political strategy in the Nordic countries, whereas the Conservative/familist and liberal welfare regimes have historically assigned a maximum of welfare obligations to either families or markets. It has been noted that familialistic policy appears counterproductive to family formation, and that female employment is positively related to fertility (Esping-Andersen, 1999). European integration has raised a debate about whether there is indeed a move towards a convergence in terms of European social and family policy towards more public support for working mothers and families, or whether they are moving along different paths of adjustment (Liebert, 2003).

During the 1990s both family and care work have come high on the political agenda in many western European welfare states, and the restructuring of care takes forms that can both challenge, cement or increase gender inequality (Mahon, 2002). Scandinavia, especially Denmark and Sweden, are today the only countries in which publicly funded services are generously provided for children under three years old as well as for older people (Leira and Saraceno, 2002). Strategies for restructuring of work and care may be determined by economic concerns as well as by the political pressure from the participation of ordinary citizens (Siim, 2000; Liebert, 2003).

Gender equality in democratic politics

Globalisation and European integration has diminished the power of the nation state, and political scientists have identified a democratic deficit in modern democracies. The evolution of women's democratic citizenship, defined as equal political participation and representation is contradictory (Marques-Pereira and Siim, 2002). On the one hand, there is a tendency in modern democracies towards a more equal or balanced representation between women and men – to include women directly in national political institutions through parity or quota systems. On the other hand, women tend to be absent from transnational governance on the European level, even though women's networks and organisations have increasingly used EU equality laws to push for equality reforms in the different European countries (Liebert, 2003).

In the Nordic[7] countries women have gradually been included in politics during the last 30 years, and here women make up about 40% of the representatives in political assembles. This trend can also be identified in other countries like Britain and Germany, where women today constitute one third of the representatives. The shift has been more sudden and dramatic in France, where women's demand for parity has resulted in a revision of the French Constitution (in 1999) and new legislation (in 2000) to include the principle of parity in local and national elections. As a result women's representation increased dramatically at the local level from 25 to 47.5%, and today women make up one third of the national assembly (Marques-Pereira and Siim, 2002; Reuter and Mazur, 2003).

This trend towards what is called a feminisation of the political elite is important, because it may open new spaces for women citizens to influence social politics. Surveys show that there is a gender gap in political attitudes in the sense that women are more positive towards public expenses than men are, but it is an empirical question what kind of care policies women support. Arguably women politicians have contributed to put care policies on the political agenda in the Nordic countries, but it is an open question whether women's representation can help to solve the growing shortage of caring resources. Redistribution policies divide women politicians who belong to different political parties that compete over scarce resources. In social politics, it is contested whether children, older people or the sick and handicapped, citizens or immigrants are the most deserving social groups. Women politicians also have different gender political projects and identities, and Nordic investigations indicate that they form alliances as well as compete over different childcare policies and models (Bergqvist et al, 1999).

Gender equality has only recently appeared on the political agenda in Europe triggered partly by demographic developments, and social politics has been ambivalent towards gender equality. It is therefore an important conclusion in a recent expert report to the EC that: "a comprehensive women-friendly policy of affordable day care and flexible leave arrangements is the sine qua non in the pursuit of multiple goals: more gender equality, raising female employment to offset smaller active populations and, as an added bonus, a broadening of the tax base" (Esping-Andersen et al, 2000, pp 4-5). The report is clearly inspired by lessons from Scandinavia, and it indicates that a women-friendly policy is a necessary but not sufficient policy, because it does not address the gender segregated labour market. The report therefore recommends that the women-friendly policy packet must be complemented with 'parent-friendly' employment policy that will change men's working time and career preferences.

This is an indication of a new emphasis on the family, care work and gender equality from European social scientists and policy makers that is the basis for a debate about childcare models in Europe. It raises both analytical and normative questions about the potential of the Nordic gender political model (Borchorst and Siim, 2002; Mahon, 2002). One problem concerns the labour-market dynamics towards globalisation and flexibilisation. Do European welfare states in times of welfare state restructuring and the decline of social democracy have the political will to adopt the Nordic welfare model based upon a large public sector? Another is linked to the silence in the report about the new challenges from immigration. It is a major political challenge to connect strategies towards gender equality with public policies to decrease other kinds of inequalities with regard to ethnicity and class. The third problem concerns the normative vision of 'the Nordic model' (see Borchorst and Siim, 2002). There are important variations in the Nordic gender models and differences in what counts as 'women-friendly' policies. On an analytical level it is useful to differentiate between 'women-friendly' policies and policies that promote gender equality. It is a further problem to assume that there will only be one norm for gender equality in Europe.

Gender equality and social care as European issues?

Today there are new problems of citizenship associated with globalisation, immigration and Europeanisation. Transnational governance has changed the role of the nation states, and comparative welfare research has noticed that European integration has been ambiguous in terms of individual, social and political rights (Bellamy et al, 2004; Liebert, 2003). The Maastricht and Amsterdam Treaties have given European citizens individual rights and obligations, for example the local right to vote and be elected, but European citizenship appears to be a "top-down" project that does concern ordinary citizens (Gerhart, 2004, p 109). The social dimension has strengthened the rights of workers, but at the same time the demands of the single market/currency has contributed to cutting public spending and increasing unemployment and part-time work. In terms of democratic governance the development has also been contradictory. The democratic influence of the European Parliament has been strengthened and the number of women has increased, but at the same time the centralisation of EU governance has weakened the influence of (women) citizens and the national democratic processes.

From a gender equality perspective, the consequences of European political and economic integration has also been ambiguous (Hobson and Lister, 2002): Equality policies have increased gender equality in the labour market, but the application of social rights is limited to paid work. The potential of EU law to influence gender politics and increase gender equality is contested. One position has highlighted the weaknesses of the EU law in relation to areas outside the labour market, for example the organisation of unpaid work and care of children, older people and disabled people. Another position has a more optimistic vision about the role of the EU in developing policies to address the social dimension (Liebert, 2003; Gerhard, 2004).

In the following I look briefly at the contradictory trend towards a social Europe on the basis of case studies of gender equality policies and childcare in Britain, France and Scandinavia. One example is Ulrike Liebert's recent overview of Europeanisation[8] and gender equality focusing on the advancement of gender equality rights over the past three decades on the basis of a comparative study in six member states (Liebert, 2003). She notes that European integration research has focused upon processes of homogenisation and convergence, whereas gender research has emphasised the varieties of Europeanisation between national diversity and common frames. The case studies confirm the general conclusions from comparative feminist research. The different gender regimes have influenced the implementation of the EC gender equality norms, although there is no straightforward link between domestic gender regimes and member state performance in implementing EC gender equality (Liebert, 2003).

Another example is Rianne Mahon's (2002) overview of contemporary European childcare models that illustrate both shifts and 'path dependencies' in political assumptions about gender relations and trends in social policies. She has identified the three dominant childcare models in France, Britain and Scandinavia and discusses the implications for gender equality.

The British gender regime has been characterised as a 'strong male-breadwinner model' with an emphasis on the private organisation of care work (Lewis and Ostner, 1994). In terms of gender equality in social rights Britain has historically been the laggard (Siim, 2000). Britain has been an extreme case of stubbornness towards EC gender equality norms, and the Conservative government refused to sign the Protocol attached to the Maastricht Treaty (Liebert, 2003). After the election of 1997 the Labour government chose to comply with EC social policy, but issues of parental leave and pregnant workers' rights were highly controversial. Liebert concludes that there has been a domestic gender policy shift in dealing with Europeanisation and that an old liberal frame has given way to a more positive New Labour frame for interpreting gender equality issues (Liebert, 2003).

Arguably the tendency of the New Labour government since 1997 towards a more active social state does represent a policy shift (Lister, 1998). The political ambition to support married women's employment, increase public childcare centres, as well as include women in politics, express a conscious break with the old masculine ethos of the labour movement. The social liberal discourse and institutions are changing with New Labour, and the feminist demand to include care work in the framework of citizenship has been put on the political agenda. Ruth Lister and others have noted that New Labour's social programme towards working mothers is ambiguous, because there is not enough public investment in childcare. Thus the active line in social policy that treats all women as workers has created special problems for lone mothers. It is a problem that New Labour has generally given priority to civil and political rights over social rights (Lister, 1998).

Rianne Mahon has also identified shifts in the Dutch and the British cases presented as a third way view on childcare that institutionalises one and a half worker model with women doing part-time work and parents paying a substantial part of the costs for childcare (Mahon, 2002). This illustrates the emphasis in the British political culture on the private obligations of parents, and especially the obligations of women to care for dependants (Siim, 2000).

The French gender regime has traditionally been positive towards women's wage work and is based upon a generous state support of families, including public day care services for older children (Lewis and Ostner, 1994; Korpi, 2000). France has historically been the laggard in terms of gender equality in political citizenship (Siim, 2000). Jospin's Socialist-led government in power in France since 1997 indicates a shift in the political programmes and politics bringing it closer to an individual model of social politics in the Nordic countries. Key aspects of the Republican French discourse and institutions changed with the Green–Red coalition government from 1997-2001. One example of this shift in the political discourse is the adoption of the feminist principle of parity – an equal balance between women and men in political institutions. Parity was first included through a constitutional change and later adopted in legislation (Marques-Pereira and Siim, 2002). Arguably this represents a shift that challenges the perception of Republican universalism embedded in political institutions and discourses. It can be interpreted as a step towards an acceptance of the ethos of democratic pluralism of political representation, although politics in France remains connected to 'elite politics' rather than 'everyday life politics' (Siim, 2000). The principle of parity applies only to politics, and it is an open question whether it will have any implications for family politics and for gender equality?

Rianne Mahon has identified a new familialism in France and Finland based upon subsidies for non-parental care in the home that breaks with earlier egalitarian ideals. This has resulted in a substantial growth in women's part-time employment (Mahon, 2002). One key problem is that citizenship is based upon a public/private split and the political culture is split between individualism and familialism (Siim, 2000). One indication for this is that care for the under three-year-olds is still primarily the responsibility of the family, while care for over three-year-olds is the responsibility of the state (Daune-Richard, 2000).

The Scandinavian citizenship model, based on universal social rights and a high degree of individualisation in social policies, has been interpreted as a potential for gender equality (Siim and Skjeie, 2004). The Scandinavian, and especially the Danish and Swedish, gender regimes have developed a dual earner model with public day care services for the under two-year-olds. Mahon argues that the Danish and Swedish model has during the 1990s managed to keep gender equality as a central principle of welfare state design (Mahon, 2002). Arguably the gradual inclusion of women citizens in the political elite has contributed to put care work and gender equality high on the political agenda. Scandinavian scholars have emphasised that the childcare model has not solved the problems with the gendered division of work and care[9] (Borchorst and Siim, 2002).

The Scandinavian welfare states have been based upon 'politics of redistribution' (Fraser, 1997) and till recently they have scored high on equality and gender equality. The homogeneity of the egalitarian discourse, institutions and policies is presently being challenged by immigration that has put demands for 'politics of recognition' that respect diversity and difference based on ethnicity on the political agenda. Immigrants must comply with the dual-breadwinner model and the dominant gender equality model, and there are new social differentiations based on ethnicity and a new marginalisation of immigrants in relation to politics. This challenges the citizenship model (Siim, 2004) and raises new questions about the interrelation between gender equality/inequality and other kinds of inequality (Pringle, 2003).

To conclude, the new conditions for equality/inequality connected with globalisation, European integration and welfare state restructuring makes it important to discuss the meaning of gender equality from cross-national contexts. Identifying the different gender regimes is one key to understanding the implications of globalisation and European integration for gender equality. Gender interacts with other kinds of diversity and differentiation, and it is an analytical challenge to understand the dynamic between gender equality/inequality and inequalities according to class and ethnicity. I suggest that globalisation increases the need for a post-national framework of citizenship based upon a new vision of equality and diversity able to include women and marginalised social groups in the democratic deliberation of the public good, not only in relation to local and national politics, but also in relation to European and transnational politics. From this perspective it is a major challenge for social, political and feminist theory to develop new forms of solidarity that are able to integrate recognition of differences in the language of citizenship – a reflective solidarity that expresses "support for the others in their difference" (Dean, 1996).

Notes

[1] The theoretical frame is presented in *Gender and citizenship: Politics and agency in France, Britain and Denmark* (Siim, 2000). The reflections in this chapter are also inspired by the dialogue between participants in the EC-project 'Gender and Citizenship Inclusion and Exclusion in European Welfare States' reflected in the the various articles as well as in the introduction to *Contested concepts in gender and social politics* (Hobson et al, 2002).

[2] Feminist scholars have been inspired by the welfare state regime studies of Gøsta Esping-Andersen and the power resource school to analyse variations and patterns in gender relations. Gender regime is explored by Diane Sainsbury in the book *Gender and welfare state regimes*. Here regime is defined as: "a complex of rules and norms that create established expectation, and a gender regime consists of rules and norms about gender relations, allocating tasks and rights to the two sexes" (Sainsbury, 1999, p 5). It thus refers to the "norms, principles, and policies informing the allocation of tasks, rights and life-chances" (Liebert, 2003, p 11). See also Rianne Mahon's article in *Social Politics*, vol 18, no 1, Spring 2001.

[3] The term the 'adult worker' or 'one and a half worker' model was coined by Jane Lewis to replace 'the male breadwinner model' as a normative ideal (2001). From the Nordic context the notion of a 'dual-breadwinner' or

'dual-earner' model has been used to capture both a practice and a norm (Siim, 2000; Borchorst, 2002; Korpi, 2000).

[4] Daune-Richard has noted that during the 1990s there was an increase of women's part-time work in France (Daune-Richard, 2000).

[5] There are also different theoretical interpretations of individualisation. The sociological theories of modernity presented by Ulrich Beck and Anthony Giddens interpret individualisation as a tendency toward de-traditionalisation and democractication of personal life (Beck et al, 1994), while communitarians like Etzioni tend to interpret the changing family structures negatively as a trend towards selfish individualism and a 'parenting deficit'.

[6] This is a normative position. Nancy Fraser has developed three normative gender models:
- a universal breadwinner model with wage work as the norm for both men and women;
- a care-giver-parity model based upon a family wage with women as caregiver and men as breadwinners and
- a universal caregiver model where care work is the norm and men are induced to become more like most women are now (Fraser, 1997, p 60)

[7] There are also important differences in the mobilisation models in the five Nordic countries, for example in the use of voluntary quotas in political parties to include women in politics. Denmark is different from Norway and Sweden because there is no gender quota in politics (see Bergqvist et al, 1999; Borchorst and Siim, 2002).

[8] Europeanisation is an interdisciplinary term that has become a key concept in political science. Ulrike Liebert defines Europeanisation as transnational processes that strengthens a European dimension as a feature that frames politics and policy within European states. This definition combines a social constructivist with an institutional perspective (Liebert, 2003, pp 14-15).

[9] The gendered division of care has even been exacerbated by the social policies of the new Conservative liberal government in power in Denmark since November, 2001 that has prolonged the maternity/paternity leave for all parents but at the same time has abandoned 14 days of the leave period reserved exclusively for fathers (see Borchorst and Siim, 2002).

References

Acker, J. (2000) 'Revisiting class: thinking from gender, race and organizations,' *Social Politics. International Studies of Gender, State and Society,* vol 7, no 2, pp 192-214.

Beck, U., Giddens, A. and Lasch, S. (1994) *Reflexive modernization. Politics, tradition and aesthetics in the modern social order,* Cambridge: Polity Press.

Bellamy, R., Castiglione, D. and Santoro, E. (eds) (2004) *Lineages of citizenship: Rights, belonging and participation in eleven nation-states,* Basingstoke: Palgrave.

Bergqvist, C., Borchorst, A., Christensen, A.-D., Ramstedt-Silen, V., Raaum, N. and Styrkarsdottir, A. (eds) (1999) *Equal democracies: Gender and politics in the Nordic countries,* Oslo: Oslo University Press.

Bergqvist, C., Kuusipalo, J. and Styrkasdottir, A. (1999) 'The debate about childcare policies', in C. Bergqvist, A. Borchorst, A.-D. Christensen, V. Ramstedt-Silen, N. Raaum and A. Styrkarsdottir (eds) *Equal democracies: Gender and politics in the Nordic countries,* Oslo: Oslo University Press, pp 137-57.

Borchorst, A. (2002). 'Danish childcare policy. Continuity rather than radical change', in S. Michels and R. Mahon (eds) *Childcare policy at a cross-road,* New York, NY: Routledge, pp 267-85.

Borchorst, A. and Siim, B. (2002) 'The women-friendly welfare state re-visited', *NORA, Nordic Journal for Women's Studies,* vol 2, no 10, pp 90-8.

Boye, T. and Leira, A. (eds) (2000) *Gender, welfare state and the market,* London and New York: Routledge.

Bussemaker, J. and Voet, R. (eds) (1998) 'Introduction', *Critical Social Policy,* vol 18, no 3, pp 375-96.

Daune-Richard, A.-M. (2000) 'Women's work between family and welfare state: part-time work and childcare in France and Sweden'. Paper given to the COST A13, working group, 'Gender issues', *Workshop on labour marginalisation/exclusion and caring,* Berlin, Wissenschaftsforum, 24-25 November.

Dean, J. (1996) *Solidarity of strangers. Feminism after identity politics,* Berkeley, CA: University of California Press.

Esping-Andersen, G. (1999) 'Social foundations of post-industrial economies', in G. Esping-Andersen (ed) with D. Gallie, D. Hemerich and J. Myles (2002) *Why we need a welfare state,* Oxford: Oxford University Press.

Fraser, N. (1997) *Justice interruptions. Critical reflections on the 'postsocialist' condition,* New York, NY and London: Routledge.

Gerhart, U. (2004) 'Gendered citizenship: a model for European citizenship? Considerations against a German background', in J. Andersen and B. Siim (eds) *The politics of inclusion and empowerment: Gender, class and citizenship,* Basingstoke: Palgrave, pp 100-15.

Gerhart, U., Knujn, T. and Lewis, J. (2002) 'Contractualisation', in B. Hobson, J. Lewis and B. Siim (eds) *Contested concepts in gender and social politics,* Aldershot: Edward Elgar pp 105-40.

Hobson, B., Lewis, J. and Siim, B. (eds) (2002) 'Introduction: contested concepts in gender and social politics', in B. Hobson, J. Lewis and B. Siim (eds) *Contested concepts in gender and social politics,* Aldershot: Edward Elgar, pp 1-20.

Hobson, B. and Lister, R. (2002) 'Citizenship', in B. Hobson, J. Lewis and B. Siim (eds) *Contested concepts in gender and social politics,* Aldershot: Edward Elgar, pp 23-53.

Knijn, T. and Kremer, M. (1997) 'Gender and the caring dimension of welfare states: towards inclusive citizenship', *Social Politics,* vol 4, no 3, pp 328-61.

Knijn, T. and Ostner, I. (2002) 'Commodification and decommodification', in B. Hobson, J. Lewis and B. Siim (eds) *Contested concepts in gender and social politics,* Aldershot: Edward Elgar, pp 141-69.

Korpi, W. (2000) 'Faces of inequality: gender and class and patterns of inequality in different types of welfare states', *Social Politics,* vol 7, no 2, pp 127-91.

Leira, A. and Saraceno, C. (2002) 'Care: actors, relationships and contexts', in B. Hobson, J. Lewis and B. Siim (eds) *Contested concepts in gender and social politics,* Aldershot: Edward Elgar, pp 65-83.

Lewis, J. (1992) 'Gender and the development of welfare regimes', *Journal of European Social Policy,* vol 2, no 3, pp 159-73.

Lewis, J. (2001) 'The decline of the male-breadwinner model: implications for work and care', *Social Politics,* vol 8, no 2, pp 152-70.

Lewis, J. and Ostner, I. (1994) *Gender and the evolution of European social policies,* Zentrum für Sozialpolitik, Bremen Universität (Centre for Social Policy Research), Arbeitspapier, no 4.

Liebert, U. (2003) 'Gendering Europeanisation: patterns and dynamics' in U. Liebert (ed) (2003) *Gendering Europeanisation,* Brussels: Peter Lang, pp 255-84.

Lisbon European Council (2000) Presidency conclusions, 23-24 March.

Lister, R. (1997) *Citizenship: Feminist perspectives,* Hong Kong: Macmillan (2nd edn 2003).

Lister, R. (1998) 'To Rio via the third way: the equality and "welfare" reform agenda in Blair and Brown's Britain', Paper given at the conference, 'Equality and the Democratic State Conference', Vancouver, November.

Mahon, R. (2001) 'Theorising welfare regimes: towards a dialogue', *Social Politics. International Studies in Gender, State, and Society,* vol 8, no pp 24-35.

Mahon, R. (2002) 'Child care: toward what kind of "social Europe"?', *Social Politics. International Studies in Gender, State, and Society,* vol 9, no 3, pp 343-79.

Marques-Pereira, B. and Siim, B. (2002) 'Representation, agency and empowerment', in B. Hobson, J. Lewis and B. Siim (eds) *Contested concepts in gender and social politics,* Aldershot: Edward Elgar, pp 170-94.

Phillips, A. (1999) *Which equalities?,* London: Polity Press.

Pringle, K. (2003) 'Paradise never attained rather than paradise lost?: some Nordic welfare systems in comparative perspective', Paper presented at Aalborg University, November.

Reuter, S. and Mazur, A. (2003) 'Paradoxes of gender-biased Universalism: the dynamics of French equality discourse', in U. Liebert (ed) *Gendering Europeanisation,* Brussels: Peter Lang, pp 47-83.

Sainsbury, D. (ed) (1999) *Gender and welfare state regimes,* Oxford: Oxford University Press.

Saraceno, C. (1999) 'Gendered politics: family obligations and social policies in Europe', Paper given to the European Sociological Association, Amsterdam.

Siim, B. (2000) *Gender and citizenship: Politics and agency in France, Britain and Denmark,* Singapore: Cambridge University Press.

Siim, B. (2004) 'Globalisation, democracy and participation: the dilemmas of the Danish citizenship model', in J. Andersen and B. Siim (eds) *The politics of inclusion and empowerment: Gender, class and citizenship,* Basingstoke: Palgrave, pp 64-83.

Siim, B. and Skjeie, H. (2004) 'The Scandinavian model of citizenship and feminist debates', in R. Bellamy, D. Castiglione and E. Santoro (eds) *Lineages of citizenship: Rights, belonging and participation in eleven nation-states,* Basingstoke: Palgrave, pp 148-66.

ELEVEN

New forms of citizenship and social integration in European societies

Birgit Pfau-Effinger

Introduction

In fordist industrial society, the term 'citizen' was constructed as employed citizens who, by virtue of their relatively strongly standardised employment biographies on the basis of full-time employment, received social rights that were connected to the cultural concept of 'decommodification', that is, rights to maintain a reasonable standard of living during periods beyond employment, including unemployment, retirement and illness (Esping-Andersen, 1990, 1999). The 'worker citizen' was, in many societies, also defined as the male breadwinner who, through his employment income and social security claims, was able to support a financially dependent wife and children. Housewives were seen as 'non-working' and therefore did not have their own social rights. Their citizenship status was indirect, meaning that it was derived from the employment position and citizenship of the male breadwinner (Lewis, 1992).

During the transition to a post-fordist service society, this basic cultural construction of citizenship has changed. The development can be characterised as a shift from a notion of citizenship as passive towards a model of active citizenship (Pfau-Effinger, 2003; Jensen and Pfau-Effinger, Chapter One). The main features of 'active citizenship' include autonomy, self-responsibility, flexibility, geographical mobility, a professional education and the ability to engage in civil society to fulfil one's own interests. In this context, claiming responsibility for one's own life and well-being is not seen as merely an option; to a increasing degree it also represents an obligation. At the same time, the active citizen is also the '*Sozialcharakter*' (societal character), who is expected to be particularly able to deal with the demands of a globalised and highly competitive European knowledge society.

The traditional model of the housewife family, where care was allocated to the group of housewives who stayed outside the employment system and provided hidden and unpaid care in the family has fundamentally eroded. By integrating themselves to an increasing extent into waged work, women have individualised themselves and have come to behave as active citizens whose main social integration is via the labour market. In this context, their social rights as family members have been increasingly individualised, whereas their derived social rights – for instance on the basis of survivor pensions – are losing importance (Lewis, 2002).

However, the question that needs to be answered is who, according to the new images of citizenship, is responsible for providing childcare? What is the place of care in this new concept of citizenship? How is the relationship of labour-market participation and childcare of the active citizen constructed?[1]

The model of the citizen worker and the state as carer

The shift towards active citizenship has been accompanied – often with a substantial time delay – by processes of formalising care and extending public care services. Care has become visible and paid (Anttonen and Sipilä, 2005). From the debate and analyses of comparative welfare-state research in the last few decades, it is evident that the formalisation of care work is mainly the result of changes in welfare state policies. In many European countries in recent decades, the state provision of social care services has been extended, in part even despite retrenchments in other welfare state activities (Pfau-Effinger and Geissler, 2002).

As Knijn and Kremer (1997) have pointed out, new social rights have also been introduced that have supported this development: the right of individuals to receive care if this is required. Accordingly, in several (western) European welfare states, an individual right for children to childcare has been established, as is the case in Germany and most of the Nordic countries. This type of right constitutes an important approach to 'freeing' women from the dependence that is connected with informal care in the family and promoting the inclusion of a higher proportion of women into the labour market (Lewis, 2002). This kind of policy has contributed to a strengthening of the role of women as autonomous, active citizens. The formalisation of care has contributed also to the creation of new jobs for women in formal employment, and in its role in the employment sector, the social service sector has supported the increase of jobs for women in many European countries (OECD, 2000). Particularly in the Scandinavian countries, in this process a higher degree of professionalisation, partly on the basis of academic qualifications, was also achieved and, as a consequence, jobs for women at a relatively high level were also created (Theobald, 2005).

In addition, in part there are also state forms of support, in which the needs for flexible childcare outside 'normal' working hours are covered. For example, for this purpose, in Finland there are free-of-charge offers from the community as well as organisations in the non-profit sector like the 'Mannerheim league for child welfare', which lend out qualified and regulated personnel on a short-term basis to households, for instance, for babysitting services (Tommiska, 2005).

To a certain degree, these developments have also been contradictory. In several European countries precarious types of employment in the social service sector are prominent. Also, in several countries the amount of public childcare is still rather unsatisfactory, which causes substantial problems in the everyday lives of women carers. Because of their responsibility for the tasks of family care, women are still partly marginalised in labour markets. During the transformations in some central and eastern European countries, such problems have increasingly emerged, as Sadar (2005), for example, shows for the case of Slovenia. The cash-for-care schemes, which were introduced in addition to or in place of public childcare, are also not without problem. Under such programmes, parents are provided with money with which they can buy childcare services. However, this carries the risk that qualitatively inferior offers will be chosen and that precarious forms of employment or undeclared work will be fostered (Daly and Lewis, 1998).

The model of the 'worker and carer' citizen

Parallel to the concept of autonomous citizenship with state childcare, in a number of welfare states there is a further concept of a link between citizenship and care that can be described as a worker and carer citizen model. It is based on an extended cultural construction of active citizenship that includes, besides formal employment, temporary phases of informal family care on a full-time or part-time basis. It takes into account the fact that a substantial proportion of childcare is still provided within the family and that family care − in so far as it is combined with other forms of care − is still seen as an element of a 'good childhood' in many countries. Accordingly, a new type of social right has been established, as Knijn and Kremer (1997) have pointed out: the right to give care, meaning the social right of parents, relatives or friends during temporary life phases to provide care for their children, frail elderly relatives or friends in their households.

Such social rights include forms of payment and independent social security for those who care, often as well as schemes of leave within the existing work contract, which in some cases allow caregivers to retain their work contract during periods of leave, thus guaranteeing their right to labour market integration after such leave has been taken (Daly and Lewis, 1998; Geissler and Pfau-Effinger, 2005; Ungerson, 2005). The focus of social rights is no longer limited to waged work. Instead, care work within the family or social networks has also, to an increasing extent, become the basis of active citizenship.

The introduction of the social right to give care is in principle based on a recognition by the welfare state of care as a form of work. Unlike other activities outside formal employment, it is therefore treated as an activity that is a basis for claims to financial support and inclusion in the social security system. However, the precise way in which it is defined as work is often unclear and contradictory, and it also differs between countries and schemes. As a consequence of the introduction of such new social rights, in this context new forms of family care, which I call 'semi-formal forms' of family childcare (Pfau-Effinger 2004a), have substantially gained in importance. One characteristic of these is that they are more or less included in social security systems and in part and to some degree, are paid.

In this respect, the societal concept of informal family work has changed considerably. The current discussion in comparative social policy research does not as yet take this sufficiently into account. The labour-force participation rates of women and the public provision of care in the formal sector are currently often also used as central indicators of the strength of a welfare state and its 'woman-friendliness' (Siim, 2000). Informal and formal care work in this context are often conceptualised as opposites, such that formal care employment is seen as modern and woman-friendly, for it relieves women from care work at home, while informal care work, by contrast, is often associated with the social exclusion of the caregivers (see also Cousins, 1998). According to this argument, informal care is linked to the traditional family model of the housewife marriage. Its main characteristics are that it is unpaid work, hidden from view in the family household, performed by women and, as it is excluded from the category of formal employment, it is unable to act as the main provider of income, prestige and social security, and is lacking in recognition. It is also argued that because of their responsibility for informal care work, women are also at risk of social marginalisation when they enter the labour market. Informal care is thus associated with the 'backwardness' of tradition, a residual element from the times of the housewife marriage that confined women to the household.

However, the concept of two opposites of formal and informal care is too crude and does not leave any room to examine the more recent development of informal work itself. Indeed, informal care work has been modernised in specific ways by the new type of welfare state policies that have established new social rights in relation to care work, and the boundaries of formalised, paid care work and informal care work have in part eroded (Geissler and Pfau-Effinger, 2005).

In addition, new forms of social inclusion based on care work have developed. The close link of informal family childcare with the housewife role has been dissolved. Instead, a new type of home-caring parent or more generally, home-caring relative has emerged, who treats home care as a transitional stage of the life course, receives financial transfers from the welfare state and is protected by social security systems. These new forms often represent temporary phases of leave in personal biographies otherwise centred around the formal employment system. As a consequence, informal care has lost a substantial part of its character as hidden and unpaid and its strong connection with the housewife marriage. This development often still goes unnoticed in the debate on the development of welfare states and work in societies.

The recognition of semi-formal childcare as work is also expressed in the fact that the parents who are given employment leave for informal family care are often recorded in the employment statistics as employed persons. However, this is treated in a far from uniform manner in different countries. The comparative analysis of care-work patterns therefore suffers from methodological and statistical problems. Haataja (2005) has shown that statistics on labour-market exclusion/integration of caring mothers are in part misleading, and that adequate methods for distinguishing between informal or semi-formal, family-based forms of care work and formal employment are broadly lacking.

Welfare regimes and the two concepts of citizenship and care

In this section I analyse how the different welfare states deal with this issue. I refer to the 'welfare regime' approach by Esping-Andersen

(1990, 1999). According to his argument, in the liberal welfare regime where the market is seen as mainly responsible for providing care outside the family, social rights are based on individuals and of a low quality. In the conservative welfare regime, in contrast, non-profit organisations are given a relatively strong role in the provision of childcare, social rights are in part family-based and the provision and the quality of social rights by the state is at a medium level. The role that is given to the state is strongest in the welfare values underlying social democratic welfare regimes, where the state is the main institution responsible for the organisation and provision of childcare and social rights are both individual and of a high quality.

According to this typology, one would expect that the model of the citizen worker with the state as carer is dominant in social democratic welfare states and the concept of the 'worker and carer' citizen to be established mainly in conservative welfare states. However, neither of the two concepts is limited to one specific welfare regime. Instead, both models of citizenship and care have been established in conservative as well as in social democratic welfare states, where they often coexist within the same welfare state and provide alternative options for parents to chose between public childcare and temporary phases of parental childcare at home.

Welfare regimes and the citizen worker with the state as carer model

In conservative welfare states like Austria and Germany, public childcare provision has been substantially extended in the last decade, and individual rights of children to be cared for have been developed, even though the provision of childcare, particularly for very young children and after school, does not yet match the demand of parents (Esch and Stöber-Blossey, 2002; Kreimer and Schiffbänker, 2005). France, another conservative welfare state, has a tradition of extensive state childcare, which has been expanding since the 1970s (Martin et al, 1998). With regard to social democratic welfare regimes, it is well known from comparative social policy analyses that these countries have established relatively generous systems of public childcare provision and individual rights of children to be cared for (Siim, 2000; Lewis, 2003).

Welfare regimes and the carer and worker citizen model

The concept of the active citizen as worker and carer has been established in conservative welfare states. This is true of conservative welfare states like France, Germany and Austria. In France, family policy has provided parents with generous, universal childcare payments that are not means-tested, and thus it exhibits social-democratic features. The payments, paid at the birth of a second and every following child, make it possible for parents to stay at home or work part-time until a child reaches the age of three, as a basic income is assured. In Germany, a relatively extensive parental leave system was established as early as the 1980s and since then has been modified several times. It is based on the continuity of the work contract of the carer in employment. During this leave, which can be taken until the child is three years old, the carer is integrated into the pension insurance and health insurance systems. Moreover, the person is entitled to childcare allowances of 300€ per month for two years or 600€ per month for one year. Several of the Federal States in Germany pay an additional childcare allowance (*Landeserziehungsgeld*). The take-up rate among German mothers is 95% (DIW 2002), whereas only a small number of men choose parental leave. In Austria, a similar programme of parental leave and childcare allowances for children up to the age of three years was established in 2002 (Kreimer and Schiffbänker, 2005).

In most countries the introduction of the social right to care was linked to an extension of the public childcare. In this respect, it contributed to guaranteeing freedom of choice in terms of how to organise care work, such as in Austria (Kreimer and Schiffbänker, 2005). Of additional significance is that it also alleviated the dependency of the provider of family care, which is most often the woman who is dependent on the male breadwinner. However, these childcare allowances are mostly not high enough to enable the financial independence of the care providers in the family. Instead, to a considerable degree they are still additionally dependent on financial support by the male breadwinner, or, if they are single parents, on welfare benefits. The new policy towards care has therefore not sufficiently contributed to dissolving the traditional male-breadwinner family model or to promoting gender equality in Austria and Germany (Geissler, 2002; Kreimer and Schiffbänker, 2005).

However, the concept of the active citizen as worker and carer is not limited to conservative welfare states, as one might have expected on the basis of the welfare regime approach. Even more generous schemes have been established in social democratic welfare states. In general, also with respect to the degree to which this model is supported, there is some convergence between the two types of welfare regime.

In Sweden, for example, an exemplary parental-leave scheme model had already been introduced by the 1970s, offering parents generous and flexible leave options and a replacement income for the greater part of their leave period (Daune-Richard and Mahon, 1998; Koistinen, 1999). The measures taken by the Norwegian welfare state to this end were also far-reaching: the most important instruments being the promotion of flexible periods for parenting and the introduction of a parental leave scheme in which a nearly full replacement income was paid. This leave can also be combined with part-time work. On the whole, it can be established that in the Scandinavian welfare states, programmes that allow the parents financial autonomy as caregivers are predominant.

More recently, some Nordic welfare states have also started to empower fathers of young children in their role as caregivers. In her analysis of policies on parental leave in the Nordic welfare states, Eydal (2005) shows how a new welfare state framework for new forms of social integration for fathers has been established in the last decade. The take-up rates are increasing, but are still lower than those for women, and family care by fathers is still limited to a shorter period compared with women. However, this is a considerable step towards a non-gendered worker and carer citizen model.

From a comparative perspective, it is clear that the development of welfare state policies in this respect differs in some areas but also shows some features of convergence, as such schemes on the basis of social rights to give care have been established in many (western) European countries, and recently even in the liberal welfare regime of Great Britain (Meyer, 2005).

It could be argued that this development of welfare state policies is based on a new, more comprehensive understanding of citizenship; one that is no longer limited to recognising only formal employment, but also takes into account the fact that external formal employment and other types of work exist and need to be supported and protected (Knijn and Kremer, 1997). Since these changes have often been highly controversial among the leading political actors, the transformation was, however, not linear but often contradictory, accompanied by time lags and on occasion even by reversals. In addition, the duration of parental leave, if it is paid, and the length of time during which it is paid, as well as the amount of money paid, differ substantially between European welfare states.

Welfare state policies and social practices of care work

In principle, both concepts of the relationship of citizenship and care – the autonomous worker citizen model with the state as provider of childcare, and the worker and carer citizen model – have been further developed in (western) European welfare states. On the one hand, the expenditure on social programmes may have been cut, but on the other, precisely in the area of family policy, an expansion of social security and services is a quite recognisable change in state systems. In many welfare states, during the course of the 1980s and 1990s, the public infrastructure for care of children and older people was expanded and many countries have introduced forms of payment when these tasks are taken over by the family, as well as elements of an independent social security for those who carry them out (Daly and Lewis, 1998). The extension of public childcare provision and the introduction of new social rights in relation to care aimed to promote the employment of mothers and to improve the conditions of informal care within families in many welfare states. In part, such policies, as Shirley Dex (2003) has shown, have also aimed to address general challenges like falling fertility rates, child poverty and children's educational achievement.

Mainly also in the context of social democratic welfare states, but also in part in conservative welfare states, the two models of citizenship and care coexist and constitute the framework of options for parental choice. However, the concrete social practices in the population vary. In countries like France, Finland and Sweden, the autonomous worker citizen model with the state as provider of childcare is dominant. Even if relatively generous policy programmes also exist that support a worker and carer option, most parents in these countries decide in favour of the autonomous citizen and state care option. The case of France has already been mentioned. However, in actual fact, few women, even those who have two children, and almost no men, take advantage of the opportunity to stay at home on the basis of the childcare allowances, although only about one half of children under three are in public childcare.

Finland, which has a relatively generous parental leave scheme, is another good example: after 11 months of fully paid maternity leave, parents can stay at home in the framework of a parental leave scheme until their child is three. During this time, a relatively generous childcare allowance is paid. However, the take-up rate of parental leave among mothers is far from comprehensive and most mothers who take up parental leave restrict this period to a couple of months (*Statistics Finland,* 2002).

In some other countries, parents are more oriented to choose the worker and carer option. These countries include Germany and Austria, and also Norway. In Germany for example, there is a similar parental leave scheme to that in Finland. Pay is less generous and limited to a part of the whole period although the take-up rate of parental leave by women is high. The situation is similar in Austria, where women chose the option of parental leave even if there is also public provision of childcare (Kremer and Schiffbänker, 2005). In Norway, on the other hand, where public provision of childcare is also relatively comprehensive, the possibility of part-time leave with nearly full financial compensation on the basis of the former full-time income is used extensively.

How can such differences in the social practices of parenthood be explained? In part, the ways in which the concrete policies are shaped and the degree of attractiveness of the two options may differ. However, this explanation is not sufficient. I argue that international differences with respect to family values can also substantially contribute to the explanation of such differences.

"Culture" is defined here as the "system of collective constructions of meaning by which human beings define reality" (Neidhard et al, 1986, p 11). It includes stocks of knowledge, values and ideals – in sum: ideas. Cultural values can be seen as switches on the pathways along which interests influence actions to be taken. Family values include cultural values and notions regarding the structure of the family and the gender division of labour. Cultural values in relation to differing dimensions of the family together form family models (Pfau-Effinger 1998; 1999; 2004a). Within such family models, values about what is a good or adequate childhood are combined with values relating to the adequate division of labour within the family and between the family and the employment system. They therefore imply suppositions about how, with its caring tasks, the family should function together with other societal institutions. The models can be characterised in terms of their central cultural ideas about the role of the family versus other societal institutions for the provision of care. To what degree is the family seen as mainly responsible for providing care, and which members of the family carry this responsibility? Moreover, how does this relate to values concerning the gender division of labour and gender hierarchy or gender equality?[2] It is possible that one specific family model is dominant in a society, or that different family models coexist or compete.

It is my argument that the differing ways in which the social practices of the women and the family are shaped in the framework of the institutional options and restrictions of the welfare state can, to a substantial degree, be explained on the basis of the given cultural values in relation to the family and care upon which they rest.[3]

Accordingly, the model of the autonomous citizen is most common in social practice where the dominant cultural model of the family is based on a dual breadwinner/external care model. The model posits that, as a principle, all women as well as men can be employed full time, and that childcare is essentially the responsibility of institutions outside of the family. In this model the state is seen as primarily responsible for organising access to care. This model is dominant in France, where full-time employment and the continuation of employment has become a clearly evident cultural pattern, even after the birth of a second child and beyond (Maruani, 2000; Daune-Richard, 2005). This is also the case in Finland (Pfau-Effinger, 2004a, 2004b). Today, this model is the framework for the social practice of women and men and the structure of the gender division of labour in these countries. These countries traditionally already had above-average full-time employment levels for women (OECD, 2000), and the number of women who work only part-time for family reasons is generally low (in France, 7%; [European Commission, 1998, p 12]). Although the number of part-time working mothers in Sweden is clearly greater, these part-time jobs entail a high number of hours at work and tend to resemble full-time positions with somewhat fewer hours than normal (Daune-Richard, 2005).

The worker and carer citizenship construction, on the other hand, is more prevalent in social practices in Norway, Germany and Austria. In these countries, informal and semi-formal family care plays a substantially more important role compared with the countries of the first group, indicated by relatively high rates of women in parental leave or relatively high rates of women in part-time work and part-time leave (for Norway, see Leira [2002] and Ellingsaeter [1999]; for Austria, see Kremer and Schiffbänker [2005]; for Germany, see Geissler and Pfau-Effinger [2002], and Pfau-Effinger [2004a]).

The dominant family model in these countries can be identified as a male breadwinner–female part-time carer model, as in West Germany and Austria. This is based on a vision of the full integration of women and men into paid economic activity. In this, however, it is expected that women, as mothers, may interrupt their gainful activity for a few years, after which they combine employment and responsibility for childcare through part-time work, until their children are no longer considered to require special care. As in Norway, the dominant family model is a more egalitarian model of a dual breadwinner–dual carer. In this model it is considered desirable that both parents are employed part-time and share the childcare between themselves, while entrusting the other part of the work to an outside institution (Waerness, 1998; Ellingsaeter, 1999; Leira, 2002).

Conclusions

The cultural construct of the citizen of European welfare states has shifted towards the model of the active citizen in different policy fields. In the field of policies towards family and care, two different approaches to active citizenship are relevant. In the first approach, the main focus is on the integration of a higher proportion of women into waged work. The second approach is based on the promotion of informal care in the framework of the family and the introduction of a new social right to care. Both approaches have been further developed in different welfare regimes and in part coexist within the same welfare state. The options from which women and parents are able to choose have therefore been substantially extended. In this respect, a certain rapprochement of the conservative welfare state towards social democratic welfare states is apparent. At the same time, the public provision of childcare and social rights in relation to care tend to be more generous in social democratic welfare states than in conservative welfare states. However, the ways in which these options are used in the social practices of the family differ in an international comparison. Differences in relation to the central family values in the different welfare states contribute to explaining this.

Notes

[1] The concept of 'social rights' comes from Marshall's (1950) theory of the historical development of citizenship. In this, the history of modern societies is seen as a process, in the course of which people have been able to extend their basic rights. Feminist researchers have used Marshall's theory to articulate injustices and inequalities in the rights of women and men which result from the special situation of women in many countries, which is that they are mainly responsible for caring tasks (see also Siim, 2000; Lister, 2003).

[2] In previous publications I have developed a classification of different cultural models of the family and the way in which it is related to gender and care (Pfau-Effinger, 1998, 2004a).

[3] For a socio-historical explanatory model by the author, see Pfau-Effinger, 2004b.

References

Anttonen, A. and Sipilä, J. (2005) 'European social care services: is it possible to identify models?', *Journal of European Social Policy*, vol 6, no 2, pp 87-100.

Cousins, C. (1998) 'Social exclusion in Europe: paradigms of social disadvantage in Germany, Spain, Sweden and the United Kingdom', in *Policy & Politics*, vol 26, no 2, pp 127-46.

Daly, M. and Lewis, J. (1998) 'Introduction: conceptualising social care in the context of welfare state restructuring', in J. Lewis (ed) *Gender, social care and welfare state restructuring in Europe*, Aldershot: Ashgate, pp 86-103.

Daune-Richard, A.M. (2005) 'Women's work between family and welfare state: part-time work and childcare in France and Sweden', in B. Pfau-Effinger and B. Geissler (eds) *Care and social integration in Europe*, Bristol: The Policy Press.

Daune-Richard, A.M. and Mahon, R. (1998) 'Suède: le modèle egalitaire en danger', in J. Jenson and M. Sineau (eds) *Qui doit garder le jeune enfant?* Paris: L.G.D.J.

Dex, S. (2003) *Families and work in the twenty-first century*, York/Bristol: The Policy Press/Joseph Rowntree Foundation.

DIW (Deutsches Institut für Wirtschaftsforschung) (2003) *Erwerbsverhalten von Frauen: Tvotz Annäherung immer noch deutliche Unterscheide Zwischen Ost und West*, Berlin: DIW.

Ellingsaeter, A. (1999) 'Dual breadwinners between state and market', in R. Crompton (ed) *Restructuring gender relations and employment. The decline of the male breadwinner*, Oxford: Oxford University Press.

Esch, K. and Stöber-Blossey, S. (2002) *Kinderbetreuung: Ganztags für alle?: Differenzierte Arbeitszeiten erfordern flexible Angebote*, IAT-Report 2002, Gelsenkirchen: Institut für Arbeit und Technik.

Esping-Andersen, G. (1990) *The three worlds of welfare capitalism*, Cambridge: Polity Press.

Esping-Andersen, G. (1999) *Social foundations of postindustrial economies*, Oxford: Oxford University Press.

European Commission (1998) *Care in Europe. Joint report of the 'gender and employment' and the 'gender and law' groups of experts,* Brussels: European Commission.

Eydal, G.B. (2005) 'Childcare policies of the Nordic welfare states: equal rights of mothers and fathers to parental leave in Iceland', in B. Pfau-Effinger and B. Geissler (eds) *Care and social integration in Europe,* Bristol: The Policy Press.

Geissler, B. (2002) 'Die (Un-)Abhängigkeit in der Ehe und das Bürgerrecht auf Care. Überlegungen zur Gendergerechtigkeit im Wohlfahrtsstaat', in K. Gottschall, and B. Pfau-Effinger (eds) *Zukunft der Arbeit und Geschlecht,* Opladen: Leske, pp 183-206.

Geissler, B. and Pfau-Effinger, B. (2002) 'Cultural change and family policies in East and West Germany', in A. Carling, S.S. Duncan and R. Edwards (eds) *Analysing families: Morality and rationality in policy and practice,* London and New York: Routledge, pp 77-83.

Geissler, B. and Pfau-Effinger, B. (2005) 'Change in European care arrangements', in B. Pfau-Effinger and B. Geissler (eds) *Care and social integration in Europe,* Bristol: The Policy Press.

Haataja, A. (2005) 'Family leave and employment in the EU: transition of working mothers in and out of employment', in B. Pfau-Effinger and B. Geissler (eds) *Care and social integration in Europe,* Bristol: The Policy Press.

Knijn, T. and Kremer, M. (1997) 'Gender and the caring dimension of welfare states: toward inclusive citizenship', *Social Politics,* vol 5, no 3, pp 328-61.

Koistinen, P. (1999) 'The lessons from the labour-market policies of Finland and Sweden', in J. Christiansen, A. Kovalainen and P. Koistinen (eds) *Working Europe: Reshaping European employment systems,* Aldershot: Ashgate.

Kreimer, M. and Schiffbänker, H. (2005) 'Informal family-based care work in the Austrian care arrangement', in B. Pfau-Effinger and B. Geissler (eds) *Care and social integration in Europe,* Bristol: The Policy Press.

Leira, A. (2002) *Working parents and the welfare state: Family change and policy reform in Scandinavia,* Cambridge: Cambridge University Press.

Lewis, J. (1992) 'Gender and the development of welfare regimes', *Journal of European Social Policy,* vol 2, no 3, pp 159-73.

Lewis, J. (2002) 'Gender and welfare state change', *European Societies,* vol 4, no 4, pp 331-58.

Lewis, J. (2003) 'Erwerbstätigkeit versus Betreuungsarbeit', in U. Gerhard, T. Knijn and A. Weckwert (eds) *Erwerbstätige Mütter. Ein europäischer Vergleich,* Munich: C.H. Beck, pp 29-52.

Lister, R. (2003) *Citizenship: Feminist perspectives* (2nd edn) Basingstoke: Palgrave.

Marshall, T.H. (1950) 'Citizenship and social class', reprinted in T.H. Marshall and T. Bottomore (eds) (1992) *Citizenship and social class*, London: Pluto Press.

Martin, C., Math, A. and Renaudat, E. (1998) 'Caring for very young children and dependent elderly people in France: towards a commodification of social care?', in J. Lewis (ed) *Gender, social care and welfare state restructuring in Europe*, Aldershot: Ashgate.

Maruani, M. (2000) *Travail et emploi des femmes*, Paris: La Decouverte.

Meyer, T. (2005) 'Political actors and the modernisation of care policies in Britain and Germany', in B. Pfau-Effinger and B. Geissler (eds) *Care and social integration in Europe*, Bristol: The Policy Press.

Neidhard, F., Lepsius, R.M. and Weiss, J. (eds) (1986) *Kultur und Gesellschaft. Sonderheft 27 der Kölner Zeitschrift für Soziologie und Sozialpsychologie*, Opladen: Westdeutscher Verlag.

OECD (2000) *Employment outlook*, Paris: OECD.

Pfau-Effinger, B. (1998) 'Gender cultures and the gender arrangement: a theoretical framework for cross-national comparisons on gender', in 'The spatiality of gender', Special issue of *Innovation: the European Journal of Social Science Research*, vol 11, no 2, pp 147-66.

Pfau-Effinger, B. (1999) 'Change of family policies in the socio-cultural context of European Societies', *Comparative Social Research*, vol 18, pp 135-69.

Pfau-Effinger, B. (2003) 'Aktivierte citizens', Arbeitsgesellschaft und globalisierung, Working Paper, Institut für Soziologie, Hamburg: University of Hamburg.

Pfau-Effinger, B. (2004a) *Development of culture, welfare states and women's employment in Europe*, Aldershot: Ashgate.

Pfau-Effinger, B. (2004b) 'Historical paths of the male breadwinner family model: explanation for cross-national differences', *British Journal of Sociology*, vol 55, no 3, pp 177-99.

Pfau-Effinger, B. and Geissler, B. (2002) 'Cultural change and family policies in East and West Germany', in A. Carling, S. Duncan and R. Edwards (eds) *Analysing families: Morality and rationality in policy and practice*, London/New York, NY: Routledge, pp 77-83.

Sadar, N. (2005) 'Labour market integration of women and childcare in Slovenia', in B. Pfau-Effinger and B. Geissler (eds) *Care and social integration in Europe*, Bristol: The Policy Press.

Siim, B. (2000) *Gender and citizenship: Politics and agency in France, Britain and Denmark*, Cambridge: Cambridge University Press.

Statistics Finland (2002) *Gender statistics*, available online at www.stat/fi/tk/he/tasaarvo_tulot_en.html.

Theobald, H. (2005) 'Labour market participation of women and social exclusion: contradictory processes of care employment in Sweden and Germany', in B. Pfau-Effinger and B. Geissler (eds) *Care and social integration in Europe*, Bristol: The Policy Press.

Tommiska, K. (2005) *Users and providers of informal work. A qualitative perspective,* Fiwe-project, WP4 National report, Finland, Tampere: University of Tampere.

Ungerson, C. (2005) 'Gender, labour markets and care work in five European funding regimes', in B. Pfau-Effinger and B. Geissler (eds) *Care and social integration in Europe*, Bristol: The Policy Press.

Waerness, K. (1998) 'The changing "welfare mix" in childcare and care for the frail elderly in Norway', in J. Lewis (ed) *Gender, social care and welfare state restructuring in Europe*, Aldershot: Ashgate, pp 207-28.

TWELVE

The outcomes of early retirement in Nordic countries

Laura Saurama

In western industrialised countries labour markets have traditionally been the arena of life through which individuals are integrated into the society. The labour markets do not provide only economic security for individuals, but also provide social contact. Fundamental changes in the labour market, globalisation and the development of the information society have lead to an increasing exclusion of individuals from the labour market. Unemployment and early retirement have become more common than ever in developed societies. This has affected also the life course of ageing people (Guillemard and Van Gunsteren, 1991). Nowadays individuals rarely leave the labour force at the official retirement age to take up their old age pension; rather it is more common that individuals exit the labour force due ill health or for other reasons many years before the official retirement age.

The aim of the welfare state is to guarantee its citizens a livelihood against unemployment, disability, old age and other risks which may reduce their full membership of the society. Full membership in a society is an often-used concept that refers to social, political and economic integration into the society. This view derives from T. H. Marshall's idea of the development of citizenship rights. Marshall (1950) identified civil, social and political rights as the key determinants of a civil society and citizenship for securing the well-being of citizens.

When labour markets fail to employ all willing and capable individuals it becomes the responsibility of the society to contribute to their economic security. The problem is that welfare states can contribute to individuals' economic security but they are much less able to compensate for the loss of social integration (Pixley, 1993). The idea that exclusion from the labour market, in the form of unemployment, is connected to exclusion from other arenas of life in the social, political and economic arena has been relatively widely studied. These studies have shown that the negative effects of labour-market marginalisation among the unemployed are significant (Burchell, 1994; Gallie et al, 1994; Åberg and Nordenmark, 2000).

Unemployment is usually the only definition of the labour-market marginalisation used in such studies. This is interesting, because many previous studies have pointed out that early retirement is, at least partly, a form of labour-market marginalisation. These studies regard early retirement as labour-market expulsion or as hidden unemployment (Walker, 1985; Casey and Laczko, 1989; Kolberg and Hagen, 1992; Hytti, 1998).

In this chapter early retirement and well-being are discussed further. The aim of this chapter is to evaluate what affect the early withdrawal of wage-earners from the labour market under early exit arrangements has on the three dimensions – social, political and economic – of well-being in the Nordic countries: Norway, Finland and Denmark. After this, labour-force participation in the Nordic countries is discussed together with the connection between early retirement and well-being. After presenting the data the results showing the well-being of the early retirees are introduced and discussed.

Early retirement in the Nordic countries

Traditionally labour-force participation rates have been high in the Nordic countries and the commitment to full employment has been regarded as high. This implies that early withdrawal from the labour force should be low in these countries. However, Finland has diverged from the Nordic pattern: unemployment increased during the recession in the early1990s and has since then remained at a relatively high level. Furthermore, early withdrawal from the labour force has increased, so that the pattern of early exit is closer to continental European countries than Nordic ones. In Denmark, too, the early exit is relatively common, although it is moderate, compared with Finland. In Norway and Sweden labour-force participation has remained at a high level.

In Finland and Denmark early retirement schemes offering a variety of pathways for exit[1] flourished until the mid-1990s These exit possibilities were not only utilised but even regarded as rights. However, in both these welfare states the early retirement policy changed significantly towards the end of the 1990s by restricting early exit and promoting rehabilitation (Gould and Saurama, 2004; Jensen, 2004). In Norway the pathways out of the labour force have been less numerous and also are taken up less. Here the policy emphasis, especially the disability pension policy, has been for a long time to promote employment and regain workability. At the same time the emphasis

Figure 12.1: Labour-force participation and unemployment among 55- to 64-year-olds (2001)

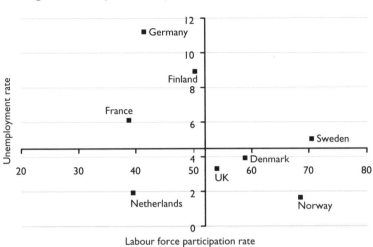

Source: OECD (2002)

has been on a right to work, rather than on a right to retire (Gould and Solem, 2000; Solem and Øverbye, 2004).

A comparison of the three Nordic countries is especially interesting when the meaning of the early retirement is considered and the different age cultures are regarded. What are the outcomes of early exit in these countries in terms of well-being? It can be assumed that in Finland and Denmark, where the early exit is more common and the rhetoric of early retirement stresses a right to retire more, the welfare outcomes could be less significant. However, in Norway, where the ethos of work and the right to employment is stressed, the welfare outcomes of early retirement may be more significant. Institutional factors, the pathways out of the labour market and entitlement criteria related to them, determine the level of well-being among the early retirees.

Labour-market marginalisation and well-being

The view that early retirees are to some degree excluded from the labour force is common among European researchers (Walker, 1985; Casey and Laczko, 1989; Hytti, 1998). Disability pensioners, who constitute the majority of the early retirees, lack employment opportunities due to their ill health or disability. In the case of a severe disability it is not a case of labour-market marginalisation; rather it is a question of the fulfilment of their social rights, namely, decommodification. But in case of less severe disability, retirement may be a result of weakened employment opportunities due to ill health.

The other types of early retirement, apart from disability-based early retirement, vary more in the reasons for early retirement. Firstly, there are so-called voluntary early retirement schemes and part-time pensions, which basically constitute a voluntary exit pathway. Even in an early retirement scheme that is based on a so-called voluntary decision to retire early an individual may feel that the decision to retire was not a voluntary choice. This makes it relevant to discuss early exit as labour-market marginalisation as involuntary early retirement constitutes labour-market marginalisation. Needless to say, in cases where the preretirement is a totally voluntary choice, the concept of labour-market marginalisation is not useful. Early retirement schemes, at least in Finland and Denmark, include also unemployment-based early retirement schemes. These schemes are clearly based on labour-market marginalisation or even hidden unemployment (for further discussion on retirement decisions, see Saurama, 2002, 2004).

Taking into account the fact that early retirement has been regarded as labour-market expulsion, it is interesting that the welfare outcomes of early retirement are less studied and even do not exist in the comparative research, while the effects of unemployment have been the subject of many studies. Studies concerning well-being have stressed the centrality of economic resources (Ritakallio, 1991; Halleröd and Heikkilä, 1999). However, labour-market marginalisation has been seen to be connected to social and political marginalisation (Pixley, 1993; Møller, 1995) and it has been shown that ill health often reduces social contacts and may lead to social marginalisation (Mutran and Reizes, 1981; Blekesaune and Øverbye, 2001).

As stated above, there is evidence that labour-market marginalisation, in the form of unemployment, is related to increased welfare problems. Increased welfare problems refer to social, political and economic problems or lack of social, political and economic resources, which are here termed 'diswelfare'. And, as such studies are lacking, it is interesting to examine whether early retirement is related to diswelfare. This chapter tries to fill the gap in our knowledge about well-being of early retirees. By comparing older people who are employed with early retirees and disability pensioners the chapter aims to discuss whether the labour market plays a major role in their well-being. If this is the case, the level of well-being should be found to be higher among older people who are employed. However, early exit per se is not necessarily connected with the level of well-being, as a lower level of well-being may be related to a lower socioeconomic status rather than to being in or out of the labour force. These are the questions that this chapter aims to investigate and discuss.

The research questions and the data

The welfare outcomes of early retirement are considered by comparing early retirees and disability pensioners with older people who are employed in three Nordic countries, Denmark, Finland and Norway, with the view to discovering whether early retirees and disability pensioners have more welfare problems than older people who are employed. If this proves to be the case, the early exit per se can be regarded as causally connected with diswelfare.

The data used in this chapter were collected during the research project, 'Unemployment, early retirement and citizenship: marginalisation and integration in the Nordic countries' (see Goul Andersen et al, 1998). Data include Finland, Denmark and Norway. From each country there is a sample of population and a sample of early retirees[2]. This allows comparing the social, political and economic resources as well as the health of older people who are employed, early retirees and disability pensioners.

The Danish data set was collected partly as a postal survey and partly by telephone interviews. In Finland and Norway all the data were collected by postal questionnaires. In the Danish data (18-67 years old) the response rate was 57% ($n=4,232$). In Finland the response rate of the population sample (aged 18-74) was 62.8% ($n=1,895$) and the response rate of the early retirees' sample was 51.3% ($n=1,532$). In Norway three data sets were collected, a sample of the population aged 20-67 (response rate 50%, $n=846$), a sample of disability pensioners (response rate 40%, $n=1,131$) and a sample of preretirees (response rate 63%, $n=426$).

In this chapter analysis is restricted to 55- to 64-year-olds and to individuals who have had an occupation (Table 12.1). This condition reduced the number of disability pensioners, especially in Norway, because the data also include disability pensioners who had not had a connection with the labour market before taking up their disability pension. The condition of prior occupation makes the comparison between countries more coherent.

In Finland and Denmark the early retirees include so-called voluntary early retirees, part-time pensioners and those with an unemployment pension. In Norway the early retirees constituted only those on voluntary early retirement schemes. The disability pensioners' category includes, in Finland and Denmark, both the relaxed disability

Table 12.1: Construction of the data (*n*)

55-64 years old	Denmark	Finland	Norway
Early retirees	865	486	150
Disability pensioners	237	510	427
Employed	270	134	143
Total	1,372	1,130	720

pensioners, for whom the pension is awarded on less strict medical criteria, as well as the ordinary disability pensioners.

The data are cross-sectional survey data collected during 1999-2000. Cross-sectional data are not the best kind of data to evaluate the effects of being out of the labour market, compared to those who are integrated into the labour market. This is because it does not allow the researcher to control whether the situation actually was the same before the early exit occurred. However, we must live with this deficiency, as these data are at the moment the most comprehensive data on early retirees in Nordic countries.

Results

Well-being among early retirees and older people who are employed

Well-being and the accumulation of welfare problems were investigated via four important resources: social, political and economic resources and health. These four dimensions of welfare resources are commonly used in the Scandinavian research tradition. The possession of these resources will be examined and after that, their cumulative consequences will be described and investigated.

As one might assume, self-rated health is poorest among disability pensioners (Table 12.2). The health status of these disability pensioners varies between countries, but Norwegian disability pensioners seem to be in poor health most often, compared to Denmark and especially to Finland. This may be due to the fact that the Finnish and Danish disability pension may be awarded using less strict medical criteria for older employed people (see note [1] later). In all three Nordic countries the perception of health is better among older people who are employed than among the early retirees. The Finnish early retirees and employed older people seem to have weakest perception of their health compared to the Danish and Norwegians. In the comparative studies it has been often supposed that Finns have less good health compared to other Nordic people and the British (Lahelma and Arber, 1994).

Table 12.2: Current state of health[a] among disability pensioners, early retirees and older employed people (55-64 years old) (%)

	Good health	Fair health	Poor health
Finland			
Disability pensioners	14	60.3	25.8
Early retirees	42.2	51.6	6.2
Older employed people	56.8	36.8	6.4
Denmark			
Disability pensioners	28.4	35.6	36.0
Early retirees	71.4	22.0	6.6
Older employed people	80.6	16.5	2.8
Norway			
Disability pensioners	8.5	38.5	53.0
Early retirees	68.6	29.3	2.1
Older employed people	78.3	18.8	2.9

Note: [a] The respondents were asked, "How would you describe your current state of health: very good, good, fair, poor, or very poor?". The distinctions in the good and poor categories were merged to provide one category each.

Table 12.3: Possession of social, political and economic resources (%)

	Social resources[a]	Political capability[b]	Economic resources[c]
Finland			
Disability pensioners	74.3	86.2	60.9
Early retirees	75.3	87.8	70.8
Older employed people	73.8	93.3	81.0
Denmark			
Disability pensioners	73.9	91.8	85.1
Early retirees	73.9	96.4	94.9
Older employed people	77.0	95.9	92.6
Norway			
Disability pensioners	69.6	90.1	58.1
Early retirees	79.0	94.1	90.0
Older employed people	83.3	98.5	90.6

Notes:

[a] Proportion of those who replied 'yes' to "Do you have a reliable friend outside your family whom you can talk to?"

[b] Proportion of those who reported being able to write a letter of complaint or who could get help with writing one, if they were mistreated by public officials.

[c] The respondents were asked, "Has your household had difficulties paying necessary expenses during last year?". The table shows the proportion of those who reported that they have not had economic difficulties (other options to this answer were: yes, but rarely; yes, sometimes; and yes, often).

The second dimension of welfare resources investigated was the social support provided by other persons. According to the data (Table 12.3) social resources in the Nordic countries are relatively good and do not vary greatly between the countries or different groups. Approximately one fourth of the older employed people, early retirees and the disability pensioners lacked a reliable friend outside the family. In Norway, the social resources of older people who are employed and the early retirees seem to be a little higher compared to Finland and Denmark, whereas Norwegian disability pensioners more often lack a reliable friend.

Political resources are measured as a capability to influence one's own situation. The respondents were asked if they would be able to write a letter of complaint or get help to write one, if they were mistreated by public officials. The majority of the respondents reported that they would be able to do so, or at least to get help to do so. This indicates that older people have a good chance of influencing their situation. These political resources are lowest among the disability pensioners compared to older employed people and early retirees. In Finland the early retirees also seem to have notably lower political capabilities than older people who are employed.

Economic resources are one of the most important resources for individuals. Economic resources vary more between the investigated groups and countries than the resources previously examined. Economic problems seem to threaten more disability pensioners than other early retirees and older people who are employed. Norwegian disability pensioners in particular often reported having very weak economic resources. It is noteworthy that economic problems in Finland are relatively common. This may be a reflection of the deep recession at the beginning of the 1990s.

Connections between different dimensions of welfare

The interest in studying well-being is to discern the degree to which the different dimensions of welfare problems overlap: in other words, the connection between the different dimensions of welfare resources. Table 12.4 displays the gamma coefficients between these different welfare problems. The first thing to notice is that the coefficients are positive, which indicates that well-being accumulates. Following that, it can be said that having one welfare problem increases the risk of having additional welfare problems (an exception are older people who are employed, among whom low economic resources are not connected to a lack of social resources). Among the disability pensioners

Table 12.4: The connections between the lack of social, political and economic resources (gamma coefficients)

Employed (n=547)	Lack of social support	Lack of political capability	Lack of economic resources
Lack of political capability	0.66**		
Lack of economic resources	−0.11	0.51	
Health problems	0.12	0.18	0.52

Early retirees (n=1,501)	Lack of social support	Lack of political capability	Lack of economic resources
Lack of political capability	0.33**		
Lack of economic resources	0.08	0.45**	
Health problems	0.32**	0.38	0.14

Disability pensioners (n=1,174)	Lack of social support	Lack of political capability	Lack of economic resources
Lack of political capability	0.43***		
Lack of economic resources	0.15*	0.37***	
Health problems	0.22**	0.28**	0.29***

Note: Coefficient is significant at the: * 0.05 level, **0.01 level, *** 0.001 level.

and other early retirees the coefficients are statistically significant, whereas among the employed they rarely reach the level of significance. Among older people who are employed a lack of social and political resources is strongly correlated. Health problems seem to be connected with economic problems, which are also connected with political incapability, although these coefficients are not significant. Among the early retirees these connections are more often significant. It is interesting that among older people who are employed health problems are not significantly connected with a lack of social support, but among early retirees this connection is significant, although it is not strong. Among disability pensioners all welfare problems are significantly connected, although not strongly so, which indicate that they have a cumulative nature. The weakest connections are found again between a lack of economic and social resources.

How much do these different dimensions of welfare overlap? This is investigated next. Cumulative welfare problems can be regarded as the ultimate measure of well-being and integration: the more people lack welfare problems, the better the situation is. As a corollary, if there are many people with many welfare problems, the situation becomes problematic.

The index of cumulative welfare problems is done simply by

computing the dichotomous indicators of welfare problems (lack of social, political and economic resources and ill health) together. Because health plays a crucial role, especially among disability pensioners, two different indexes were calculated. The first index does not include ill health as a welfare component, but the second does. This way it is possible to investigate the importance of health in the process of cumulative diswelfare. Table 12.5 displays the proportions of those having increased welfare problems in the groups examined in each country. Individuals are classified as having welfare problems if they have at least two of the above-examined welfare problems.

The examination reveals that especially among the disability pensioners the proportion of those having welfare problems increases significantly due to the health factor. In the other examined groups the effect of ill health as a component of diswelfare is relatively small. However, it is worth noticing that the proportion of older Finnish employed people with welfare problems is 6% when health is excluded. When health is included as a component of diswelfare, their proportion increases to 10%. This suggests that among older employed people are a number of those who suffer from ill health.

In the Nordic countries the cumulative nature of welfare problems is relatively weak, which means that the proportion of those with additional welfare problems is relatively low. Very few older people who are employed have many welfare problems. Finland displays a slight exception, mainly due to individuals' experiences of economic difficulties. Cumulative welfare problems are more common among early retirees and disability pensioners than among the employed, which

Table 12.5: Proportion of older people who have at least two welfare problems

	Health excluded	Health included
Finland		
Disability pensioners	16.1	28.1
Early retirees	12.1	13.9
Older employed people	6.4	10.2
Denmark		
Disability pensioners	5.8	19.7
Early retirees	3.2	5.3
Older employed people	4.5	4.8
Norway		
Disability pensioners	19.1	40.6
Early retirees	7.1	7.8
Older employed people	0.7	2.2

speaks in favour of the notion that labour–market marginalisation is related to the accumulation of other welfare problems. However, the results in Denmark do not unanimously support the notion that early retirement is related to diswelfare. When health is excluded from the definition of diswelfare, the proportion of early retirees with welfare problems is even smaller than the proportion of the employed with welfare problems. Norwegian disability pensioners stand out in this comparison as having a high proportion of diswelfare. This difference can partly be explained by institutional differences in the different countries, as noted above.

When examining the cumulative effect of diswelfare it is important to know who are these people suffering from cumulative welfare problems. Do different kinds of people use different pathways out of the labour force, resulting in the fact that their welfare outcomes are different? Tables 12.6 and 12.7 display the results of logistic regression analysis,[3] where gender, civil status and socioeconomic status are also included in the analysis. The aim was to investigate whether having additional welfare problems is related to being an early retiree or a disability pensioner, or whether it is more likely to be related to gender, civil status, socioeconomic status or health. Two models have been formulated for all three countries, which are presented in Tables 12.6 and 12.7. In Table 12.6 health is excluded from the definition of having additional welfare problems, and is used instead as an explanatory variable. In Table 12.7 health is included in the definition of having additional welfare problems.

The results indicate that when health is not included in a definition of welfare problems but rather used as an explanatory variable, only in Norway do the disability pensioners and early retirees have a higher risk of cumulative welfare problems. This means that having welfare problems is not related to being an early retiree or disability pensioner in Finland and Denmark. The strongest predictor of having additional welfare problems in all three countries is ill health. In Finland high socioeconomic status is related to welfare. In the other Nordic countries socioeconomic status does not play a role in defining welfare among early retirees, disability pensioners and older people who are employed. In Denmark being unmarried increases the risk of having additional welfare problems.

When health is included in the definition of having additional welfare problems, disability pensioners have the highest risk of having additional welfare problems in all three countries, whereas the other early retirees do not differ significantly from older employed people. This implies that early exit per se is not related to having welfare problems. In

Table 12.6: Respondents with at least two welfare problems. Logistic regression analysis, odds ratios (health is excluded from the welfare problems and used as an explanatory variable)

	Denmark	Finland	Norway
Disability pensioner	0.69	1.79	9.93*
Early retired	0.58	1.79	8.94*
Employed	1	1	1
Gender			
Female	0.80	0.66	1.21
Male	1	1	1
Civil status			
Unmarried	1.84*	0.91	1.32
Married	1	1	1
Socioeconomic status			
Higher white collar	0.30	0.50*	0.36
Lower white collar	0.89	0.67	0.74
Unskilled worker	1.46	1.09	1.36
Self-employed and farmers	0.52	0.68	1.07
Skilled worker	1	1	1
Health	–	–	–
Bad	1.86	3.66***	5.22**
Fair	2.13*	1.92*	2.34
Good	1	1	1

Note: *** significant at 0.001 level, ** significant at 0.01 level, * significant at 0.05 level

Denmark and Norway the risk of having welfare problems is higher among unmarried than married people (in Finland the difference is not significant), which suggests that marriage protects individuals from welfare problems, especially when these include health problems.

Overall it can be concluded that having additional welfare problems is strongly related to ill health, which explains the differences in the risks of diswelfare between the employed, early retirees and disability pensioners. This means that the results do not support the idea that early exit per se is related to diswelfare.

Discussion

The aim of this chapter was to investigate the level of well-being among older people who are employed, early retirees and disability pensioners. The results indicate that social, political and economic problems are connected to one another, but do not totally overlap.

Table 12.7: Respondents with at least two welfare problems. Logistic regression analysis, odds ratios (where health is included as a welfare problem)

	Denmark	Finland	Norway
Disability pensioner	3.77***	2.91***	26.85***
Early retired	1.05	1.37	3.49
Employed	I	I	I
Gender			
Female	0.79	0.64**	1.29
Male	I	I	I
Civil status			
Unmarried	2.00**	1.36	1.69*
Married	I	I	I
Socioeconomic status			
Higher white collar	0.46	0.61	0.71
Lower white collar	0.82	0.70	0.76
Unskilled worker	1.55	1.18	1.24
Self employed and farmers	0.65	1.06	0.93
Skilled worker	I	I	I

Overall the accumulation of welfare problems is not very common in the Nordic countries. The connections between the different dimensions of dis-welfare are stronger among the disability pensioners and the early retirees, that is, among those outside the labour force rather than among older people who are employed. However, the risk of having cumulative welfare problems is strongly related to health problems, not to the labour-market marginalisation in the form of early retirement.

The results suggest that at the beginning of the new millennium cumulative welfare problems are more common in Finland than in Denmark and Norway. Mainly the lower level of well-being was due to economic problems and ill health. Among Norwegian disability pensioners cumulative welfare problems were also found to be relatively common. This can be partly explained by institutional differences. In Finland and Denmark the analysis included also those disability pension schemes that can be awarded on less strict medical criteria.

The results indicate that the labour markets are not the only determining factor of well-being. The early retirees are not only likely to have cumulative welfare problems compared to the older employed, when gender, civil status and socioeconomic status are controlled for. Instead the results stress health as the determining factor of well-being which further proposes that the well-being of the disability pensioners should be investigated in more detail in future studies.

The results support the practised policy in the Nordic countires as the outcomes of early retirement are not related to diswelfare. It can be argued that mainly the policy has been able to maintain the level of well-being among older people outside the labour force. However, the results suggest that more emphasis could be put on policy targeting to maintain the health of older employed people, because health is a key factor determining not only the overall level of well-being, but also the length of the working career.

This chapter investigated the outcomes of early retirement in terms of well-being. Some studies have suggested (for example Saurama, 2004) that individuals' own perception of the experience of early exit may be an important factor in determining the level of well-being. In this study the experience of exit was not investigated as the interest was mainly in the comparison between the early retirees, disability pensioners and older employed people. However, the experience of early exit in relation to the institutional exit arrangement could also be approached in future studies.

Notes

[1] In Denmark there is an early retirement scheme, which allows people over 60 to exit early from the labour force. Until the mid-1990s there was also a scheme that entitled ageing long-term unemployed to exit at the age of 60, but this was later abolished. In Norway there is also a preretirement scheme for those who are 60 years old and older who wish to exit early, but there is no unemployment pathway. The Finnish early retirement legislation is more complicated. There are also preretirement schemes in Finland (early old age pension, part-time pension and special pension for farmers), which allow individuals to withdraw early from the labour force on a more voluntary basis, as in Denmark and Norway. The Finnish peculiarity is their unemployment pension scheme, which entitles those over 60 years old who have been unemployed long term to withdraw early from the labour force (this scheme is going to be abolished). In all these countries there is also a disability pathway. In Denmark and Finland the disability scheme is more flexible for older workers. In Finland there has been a special individual early retirement scheme, which is a special form of the disability scheme, targeted at ageing employed people, where the medical criteria are less strict (this scheme is also going to be abolished). The Danish disability scheme also uses less strict medical criteria in the case of older employed people.

[2] For more information about the Danish data see Clement (2002), for the Norwegian data, see Blekesaune and Øverbye (2001) and for the Finnish data, see Saurama (2001).

[3] Logistic regression analysis produces odd ratios. The reference category gets a probability of one for the incidence to occur. The other categories are compared to this so that, if the probability is greater than one, welfare problems are more likely in that category than in the reference category. Comparatively, if the probability is smaller than one, welfare problems are less likely in that category compared to the reference category.

References

Åberg, R. and Nordenmark, M. (2000) 'Arbetslöshet och levnadsvillkor under 1990-talets krisår' in J. Fritzell (eds) *Välfärdens förutsättningar. Arbetsmarknad, demografi och segregation*, Stockholm: Antologi från Kommittén välfardsbokslut SOU 37.

Blekesaune, M. and Øverbye, E. (2001) *Levekår og livskvalitet hos uførepensjonister og mottakere av avtalefestet pensjon, NOVA,* vol 10, no 01.

Burchell, B. (1994) 'The effects of labour market position, job insecurity, and unemployment on psychological health', in D. Gallie, C. Marsh and C. Vogler (eds) *Social change and the experience of unemployment*, Oxford: Oxford University Press, pp 188-212.

Casey, B. and Laczko, F. (1989) 'Early retired or long-term unemployed?', *Work, Employment and Society*, vol 3, no 4, pp 509-26.

Clement, S.L. (2002) 'Teknisk rapport til undersøgelsen "Arbeidsløshed, tilbagetrækning og medborgerskab"', Aalborg University, Centre for Comparative Welfare Studies: CCWS Technical paper no 1.

Gallie, D., Gershuny, J. and Vogler, C. (1994) 'Unemployment, the household, and social networks', in D. Gallie, C. Marsh and C.Vogler, (eds) *Social change and the experience of unemployment*, Oxford: Oxford University Press, pp 231-63.

Goul Andersen, J., Halvorsen, K., Jensen, P.H., Johannessen, A., Kangas, O., Ologsson, G., Svallfors, S. and Øverbye, E. (1998) 'Unemployment, early retirement and citizenship: marginalisation and integration in the Nordic Countries', Aalborg University: CCWS Working paper no 4.

Gould, R. and Saurama, L. (2004) 'From early exit culture to the policy of active ageing: the case of Finland', in T. Maltby, B. de Vroom, M.L. Mirabile and E. Øverbye (eds) *Ageing and the transition to retirement. A comparative analysis of European welfare states*, Aldershot: Ashgate, pp 67-92.

Gould, R. and Solem, P.E. (2000) 'Change from early exit to late exit. A Finland/Norway-comparison', Paper presented at the meeting of COST A13 Ageing and work, Rome 13-14 April.

Guillemard, A.-M. and van Gunsteren, H. (1991) 'Pathways and their prospects: a comparative interpretation of the meaning of early exit', in N. Kohli, M. Rein, A.-M. Guillemard and H. van Gunsteren (eds) *Time for retirement: Comparative studies of early exit from the labour force*, Cambridge: Cambridge University Press, pp 362-89.

Halleröd, B. and Heikkilä, M. (1999) 'Poverty and social exclusion in the Nordic countries', in M. Kautto, M. Heikkilä, B. Hvinden, S. Marklund and N. Ploug (eds) *Nordic social policy: Changing welfare states*, London: Routledge, pp 185-214.

Hytti, H. (1998) *Varhainen eläkkeelle siirtyminen - Suomen malli*, Helsinki: KELA, Sosiaali- ja terveysturvan tutkimuksia 32.

Jensen, P.H. (2004) 'Ageing and work: from "early" to "late" exit in Denmark', in T. Maltby, B. de Vroom, H.L. Mirabile and E. Øverbye (eds) *Ageing and the transition to retirement: A comparative analysis of European welfare states*, Aldershot: Ashgate, pp 41-66.

Kolberg, J.E. and Hagen, K. (1992) 'The rise of disemployment', in J.E. Kolberg (ed) *Between work and social citizenship*, New York, NY: M.E. Sharpe, Inc., pp 112-42.

Lahelma, E. and Arber, S. (1994) 'Health inequalities among men and women in contrasting welfare states: Britain and three Nordic countries compared', *European Journal of Public Health*, vol 4, no 3, pp 213-26.

Marshall, T.H. (1950) *Class, citizenship and social development*, Cambridge: Cambridge University Press.

Møller, I.H. (1995) 'Marginalisering på arbetsmarknaden', *Socialvetenskaplig tidssrift*, vol 1-2, pp 24-43.

Mutran, E. and Reizes, D.C. (1981) 'Retirement, identity and well-being: realignment of role relationships', *Journal of Gerontology*, vol 36, no 6, pp 733-40.

OECD (2002) *Labour force statistics 1981-2001*, Paris: OECD.

Pixley, J. (1993) *Citizenship and employment. Investigating post-industrial options*, Cambridge: Cambridge University Press.

Ritakallio, V.-M. (1991) *Köyhyys ei tule yksin*, Helsinki: National Board for Welfare and Health, Research report 11.

Saurama, L. (2001) 'Description of the Finnish survey data for the research programme unemployment, early retirement and citizenship: marginalisation and integration in the Nordic Countries', University of Turku: Department of Social Policy, series C:8.

Saurama, L. (2002) 'Départs anticipés du marché du travail au Danemark et en Finlande', *Les Politiques Sociales* (Nouvelles précarités), vol 61, nos 3 and 4, pp 83-99.

Saurama, L. (2004) *The experience of early exit: A comparative study of reasons for and consequences of early retirement in Finland and Denmark in 1999-2000*, Helsinki: Finnish Center for Pension Studies.

Solem, P.E. and Øverbye, E. (2004) 'Norway: still high employment among older workers', in T. Maltby, B. de Vroom, H.L. Mirabile and E. Øverbye (eds) *Ageing and the transition to retirement. A comparative analysis of European welfare states*, Aldershot: Ashgate, pp 18-40.

Walker, A. (1985) 'Early retirement: release or refuge from the labour market?', *Quarterly Journal of Social Affairs*, vol 1, no 3, pp 211-29.

THIRTEEN

Early exit from the labour market, social exclusion and marginalisation in the UK

Philip Taylor

This chapter considers the issue of early exit and marginalisation from a British perspective. The UK can be described as having a liberal welfare regime (Esping-Andersen, 1990). According to Esping-Andersen (1999, p 74): "liberal welfare regimes in their contemporary form reflect a political commitment to minimise the state, to individualise risks, and to promote market solutions." In terms of labour-market policy, this is exemplified by the dominance of needs-based and means-tested unemployment benefits as well as the relatively high importance of occupational pensions. Moreover, liberal social policies favour a passive approach to employment management and largely unregulated labour markets.

Building upon Esping-Andersen's work, a taxonomy of different unemployment welfare regimes has been developed (Gallie and Paugam, 2000). For an overview see Plougmann (2002). This taxonomy is based on the following three indicators:

- the proportion of unemployed people covered by insurance benefits;
- the level and duration of the benefits;
- the scope of active labour-market policy.

The UK belongs to the category of a liberal regime with minimum protection, where only a few unemployed people are supported by the unemployment benefit system, the amount of compensation is limited and active labour-market policies are weak.

Early exit from the labour market: a history

At a time when the UK's population has been ageing rapidly, there has been a marked decline in the labour-force participation of those aged 50 and over. Between 1979 and 1984, the rate of economic inactivity among people aged between 50 and the state pension age increased dramatically, from below 20% to over 30%. While inactivity among this group fell slightly in the late 1980s as the UK economy grew, this did not last, reaching 32% by the mid-1990s (Her Majesty's Treasury, Department for Work and Pensions, 2001).

Table 13.1 shows trends in labour-force participation rates among older workers over the last two decades. There has been a marked decline in participation rates among older men. Recently, this trend has reversed for the 55-59 and 60-64 age groups, though the rates are some way below 1984 levels. By contrast there has been increasing labour-force participation among older women.

Accounting for the situation of older workers

What accounts for the changing fortunes of older workers? The general consensus is that, in the UK, the shift to inactivity was not on the whole reflective of older people taking advantage of their increasing wealth to retire voluntarily. Instead, it was largely the result of a lack of employment opportunities (Campbell, 1999; Her Majesty's Treasury, Department for Work and Pensions, 2001). Changes in the nature of work, new organisational forms and changes in the aggregate supply of employment (or demand for labour) have had a central influence on the relationship between ageing and work, although a reduction in the supply of older labour has also played a part. For much of the last two decades unemployed older workers have largely been left to take their chances in the labour market or have been encouraged to leave it permanently, while governments focused on labour-market entrants. However, recently, reflecting the realities of current and

Table 13.1: Labour-force participation rates among older people (%)

Age	1984	1989	1994	1999	2002
Men					
45-54	94.5	92.2	90.2	88.2	88.1
55-59	82.8	80.2	76.1	75.2	76.1
60-64	57.5	54.6	50.9	50.4	50.8
Women					
45-54	69.2	72.0	75.0	75.7	77.0
55-59	51.7	54.1	55.4	55.8	59.6
60-64	21.8	22.8	25.5	25.0	28.5

Source: OECD (2003)

predicted labour shortages and demographic changes, there has been a clear departure from policies based primarily on the provision of 'social security' to 'active' policies which provide the main support and protection to older workers through employment-focused initiatives. This has been part of a policy of reversing the trend towards early retirement or 'early exit'.

Since the 1970s economic and structural changes linked to worldwide shifts towards liberal economic thinking have had a marked effect upon the ability of older people to sustain their position in the labour force. Within the public sector, and especially throughout the 1980s and early 1990s these structural changes have been accommodated by the wholesale privatisation of public utilities, the tightening of public expenditure and the imposition of a 'value for money' rhetoric that has adversely affected the complexion and nature of employment for many. A drive for increased productivity and efficiency savings has taken the form of workforce reduction exercises, the removal of organisational hierarchies and the outsourcing of some functions and activities. 'Downsizing' and other initiatives have had a disproportionate impact on older workers (Arrowsmith and McGoldrick, 1997).

Thus, the main factors explaining the growth of early exits among British older workers are on the demand side, particularly the recessions of the mid-1970s and early 1980s and the massive restructuring of parts of the public and private sectors over the last two decades (Walker, 1985; Trinder, 1990). In fact, it has been argued that this 'early retirement' is better understood as a form of unemployment rather than as a form of retirement (Casey and Laczko, 1989). For example, regarding inactive men in the 55-64 age group, the 1995 European Labour Force Survey found that in six out of 15 countries, over half claimed that the reason was normal or early retirement. By contrast, in Finland, Spain, Sweden and the UK the picture was somewhat different. In Finland and the UK a high proportion of involuntary departure was split equally between dismissal and redundancy and illness or disability (Auer and Fortuny, 1999).

Looking over the post-war history of older workers in the UK labour market reveals a pattern that is akin to their use as a reserve army of labour. They were encouraged to remain in employment in times of boom but were among the first to be jettisoned during periods of recession. Thus in the boom of the late 1950s older people were encouraged to work on to achieve a 'happier old age' while in the recessions of the mid 1970s and early 1980s older people were actively encouraged to take early retirement (Walker, 1985). In both periods social policies were used to assist the retention or the displacement of older workers.

The rise of early retirement

In the 1970s and 1980s, a period of simultaneous contraction of full-time employment and historic high points in the numbers entering the labour force, the problem of youth unemployment was given high priority by government. Moreover, early retirement as a tool in delayering and rationalising exercises has been popular among employers, employee representatives and the wider community, as it has reduced the need for compulsory redundancies among those with domestic commitments by encouraging people near retirement age to withdraw from their jobs (Casey, 1992).

In 1982 the House of Lords Select Committee on Unemployment and the House of Commons Select Committee on Social Services both came out in favour of a reduction in the male pension age. The Social Services Committee emphasised the motivation behind the widespread interest in early retirement: "Our inquiry arose from awareness of a growing demand for state male pension age to be lowered in order to ease the unemployment situation; and of a growing movement towards early retirement" (House of Lords Select Committee on Unemployment, 1982, p 1, ix).

The promotion of early retirement as a means of tackling unemployment had become official policy in 1977 with the introduction of the job release scheme (JRS). Though intended as a temporary measure introduced to alleviate unemployment among younger workers it was stepped up in the early 1980s with an extension of the eligible age ranges. At its peak, in 1984, some 90,000 older people were receiving JRS allowances (compared with 55,000 in 1979).

Moreover, older people were discouraged from seeking work by Job Centre staff and experienced considerable discrimination from employers. Thus, in this context, the pressures on older workers through the policies of employers, unions and government were generally in the direction of exclusion from the labour force in preference for younger workers.

So early retirement increased rapidly and found favour with virtually everyone as a means of tackling unemployment. Yet two quite distinct groups of older workers were affected by this consensus. On the one hand there were those who could choose relatively freely, from a position of economic security, whether or not to take early retirement.

On the other hand there were those who had no choice and were effectively forced or coerced into early retirement by a combination of redundancy, ill health and financial insecurity.

Early exit and marginalisation

A study carried out in the 1980s by the Department of Sociological Studies at the University of Sheffield of 400, mostly older, redundant steel workers indicated two paths to early retirement depending primarily on socioeconomic status (Walker, 1985; see also Walker, 1982). On the one hand there were those who saw early retirement as a positive option and were relieved to give up employment. On the other hand there were those who gave up work reluctantly and would have preferred to have continued to work if they could but found themselves discouraged from doing so, through their experiences in looking for work with employers and Job Centre staff. A similar pattern was observed in a study of hourly paid and salaried male retirees from the chemical industry (Cliff, 1989). Other research using data from the General Household Survey for the years 1980-82 and from the Labour Force Survey of 1983 showed that ill health was a less important reason for retirement than previous studies (Parker, 1980) had suggested (Laczko et al, 1988). This study, carried out using data from the General Household Survey for the years 1980-82 and from the Labour Force Survey of 1983 also found that those who retired early are clearly divided by socioeconomic status: manual workers being more likely than non-manual workers to retire early because of redundancy and also more likely than the latter to be living on very low incomes. Echoing these findings, Taylor and Urwin (1999) considered the situation of older workers from different occupational groups in the first half of the 1990s. Based on secondary analysis of the British Labour Force Survey they conclude that, for men who had formerly worked in higher occupations, there are two main non-work categories in addition to unemployment: long-term sickness or disability and retirement. In the case of the other occupational groupings there is only one: long-term sickness or disability. Research has also shown that older non-employed workers have a more negative perception of their own labour-market position in terms of the probability of them regaining employment (Laczko, 1987a) and may prefer to define themselves as disabled or early retired (Walker, 1985; Piachaud, 1986; Bytheway, 1987; Laczko, 1987b).

Orientations to work and retirement among older people are governed by a number of factors identified as pertaining to health, economic and structural elements (Johnson, 1989). While ill health has been identified as one of the most important reasons for retirement (Parker, 1980; Walker, 1985) other influences, such as income, wealth and labour-market considerations can be equally important. Pull factors associated with the attractiveness of life in retirement, such as opportunities to take up a secondary career, undertake voluntary work, or to enjoy new hobbies can be important for some older people: push factors, including the negative attributes of a current job can be important for others in their decision to remain in or to leave the labour force. Some commentators have suggested that declining employment rates among older workers are related to the wage levels they can command. While employers may be reluctant to employ older workers if the wages paid do not reflect their productivity levels, work is likely to be less attractive to people whose potential wage is relatively lower than it used to be, or lower than that of colleagues. Nevertheless, for older people without adequate assets in terms of property, pensions or other sources of income, the cessation of employment may not be a viable option.

Due to the difficulties encountered by older workers in accessing employment opportunities, particularly during periods when labour markets are slack, some commentators (such as Laczko, 1987b) have argued that more older workers are being discouraged and that they drop out of the labour force during periods of increasing unemployment. They may regard themselves as retired, sick or disabled as a strategy for dealing with their situation until there is an upturn in the market or, alternatively, remain external to the system. Others have disputed the discouraged worker hypothesis, asserting that recent labour-market trends, such as the economic boom of the late 1980s, had no discernible effect on flows from disability benefits (Campbell, 1999).

Some insight into the general area of retirement decision-making has been provided by a study carried out by Maule et al (1996). Comparisons of occupational groups revealed differences between salaried and hourly paid employees in the roles played by push and pull factors in the early retirement decision. While the retirement decision for hourly paid employees was dominated by push factors – the negative aspects of their current job, such as shift work, as well as factors including ill health and fears over their future health – salaried employees were attracted by the positive potential offered by retirement opportunities, such as starting a new career or developing new hobbies or interests.

Another study (Tanner, 1997) found that ill health provided an explanation for early retirement for over one quarter of men (26%) and women (28%). Voluntary severance, with reasonable financial terms, accounted for a further quarter of men (24%) leaving employment early, but was less important for women (7%). One in six men (15%) and over one in seven women (14%) cited 'involuntary redundancy' as the reason they had left employment. The relevance of the family context to retirement behaviour, especially among women, is evidenced by their retiring to spend more time with their families (11%), to coordinate giving up work with their partners (6%) or because of the ill health of others (6%).

More detailed analysis of the early retirement data revealed major differences between those with and without occupational pensions. Men without occupational pensions (23%) were almost twice as likely as women without (14%) occupational pensions to leave their jobs involuntarily. Among women little difference was noted between the two categories. Men without an occupational pension were more likely to cite ill health as the reason for retiring early (39%) than those with an occupational pension (26%). Similarly, men with an occupational pension were more likely to report their early retirement being 'individual instigated' (40%) than those without one (18%). For women, the situation was reversed: 35% of women with occupational pensions and 29% of women without occupational pensions reported ill health as the main determinant of their early retirement. With regard to occupational differences (among those employed prior to retirement), those in professional and white-collar occupations were more likely than those from other occupational groups to leave the labour force voluntarily. This was particularly pronounced among women.

Other research has considered transitions from unemployment to retirement and employment among British older men. Jackson and Taylor (1994) examined the relationship between present employment status and previous financial and psychological well-being and employment commitment among a group of 175 men aged over 50 to examine the factors associated with employment status. Respondents were interviewed at three time periods and the researchers used data collected at Time 1 when all were unemployed to compare those who remained unemployed, those who subsequently retired and those who were re-employed at Time 3, one year later. They report that both the retired and early retired groups felt more in control of their lives and reported a lower employment commitment than the other groups at Time 1. There was also a difference in terms of the financial strain reported by respondents, with both the retired groups but also a group which had been unemployed for a shorter period of time reporting lower levels of financial strain than a re-employed group and a longer-term unemployed group at Time 1. On the other hand, psychological well-being and self-reported health status did not differ between groups at Time 1, indicating that pre-existing differences in physical and psychological health could not account for subsequent changes in employment status.

There are thus important differences in orientations to retirement depending on socioeconomic group.

Among older, largely male workers opting for early retirement, UK research (Maule et al, 1996) has found that, with regard to their labour-market orientation, one in five respondents (22%) said they intended looking for part-time work after retiring; one in 14 respondents (7%) intended looking for a full-time job and one in 20 respondents (5%) intending investigating opportunities for self-employment. Two out of three respondents said they intended taking full retirement. When asked the reason for continuing employment, the majority (39%) attributed this to the inadequacy of the financial package they had been offered; a third wanted to be able to afford small luxuries and 18% said they wanted to use their time productively.

Similarly, research based only on those from the higher socioeconomic group has in general found a favourable view of early retirement (McGoldrick and Cooper, 1980). As noted by Hawkins (1984), while some professional older workers may leave employment on relatively favourable terms, older workers in semi-skilled or unskilled jobs may enter a period of unemployment with little more to live on than social security payments and a modest redundancy settlement. Such workers may remain anxious to find employment. McGoldrick and Cooper, for their sample of early retirees, report numerous reasons for the decision to take early retirement. That the finances were right was the most frequently cited reason, followed by feelings that they had worked long enough and deserved retirement, a desire for more free time and health. Unsatisfactory job factors were also cited and these included job changes, insecurity, management and stresses and strains of the job. According to McGoldrick and Cooper (1980, pp 859-64):

> While the majority felt that they had made their decision in an entirely unpressurised way, certain influences were noted by retirees. Some had felt influenced by company pressure or the feeling that they were not indispensable, pressure from union or fellow workers and the belief that they were expected to retire to prevent younger workers

being made redundant. Close-downs and redundancies caused insecurity. Volunteers sometimes felt that they might later be forced to leave with reduced financial benefits, or at a time when it would be more difficult to find alternative employment.

It is useful for policy purposes to make a clear distinction between these two groups of early retirees. The first group consists of those who see early retirement as a positive option and are often relieved to give up employment. Health is an important determinant of the decision to retire early – hence improvements in health are often reported subsequently – as is the feeling that they have done their bit and now want to retire and make way for young people. Others in this group retire at the same time as their spouse. Many think it unlikely that they will need to work again because of relatively high non-employment incomes although some do voluntary work. For others, their close proximity to the state pension age on being made redundant lead them to conclude that it would not be worth seeking alternative employment and so they define themselves as early retired.

This first group of non-employed older people might be considered to correspond to what is usually meant by the term 'early retired'. The following are some quotations from research among a sample of older people living in Sheffield:

> "It's only fair. Elderly people have had their chance. I took early retirement (under the job release scheme) because of it." (Man, 65)

> "I have had time to do things that I enjoy. Time to relax and feel healthy. My blood pressure has gone down. I welcomed it. I was disillusioned with teaching. If you are ready to leave and 50 and can afford to why not do so?" (Man, 62)

Turning to the second group, the involuntarily retired; in contrast to the first group they gave up work reluctantly, having been forced into non-working through redundancy, in order to care for someone or through ill health and they would have preferred to have continued to work if they could. These older people tend to live on low or much reduced incomes compared both to their own earnings when in employment and to the incomes of the first group of retirees.

Not surprisingly, for many in this group the experience of non-working is often very distressing, although many become resigned to it and adapt to their situation. The loss of the status that work provided is felt deeply by many. Most felt discouraged from seeking employment and think that their prospects of finding work again are poor. Some feel that they have already effectively retired despite being in their 50s or early 60s and become resigned to the fact that they will not work again. The commitment to regaining employment remains high but the expectations of finding work are low.

The following quotations give an idea of the sort of responses we obtained from this second group of people who were reluctantly driven into early retirement:

> "I'd been in the job for 28 years and knew it off by heart. I wanted to keep on working and not feel idle." (Man, 60)

> "The more I look at jobs and the age requirements the more I consider myself at retirement age now." (Man, 58)

As these quotations indicate, despite a continuing commitment to employment, older people in this second group are being denied access to employment. Their unemployment or premature retirement is itself often the product of age-discriminatory labour-market policies which, for example, put a premium on the redundancy of older workers as opposed to younger workers. In addition, once thrown back into the labour market to search for jobs, older workers in this group are likely to experience discrimination on the part of employers.

A greater number of potential working years, better paper qualifications, greater adaptability and lower costs of employment are cited by older people as reasons employers might give for preferring to employ younger people. Many older people also feel that the only jobs open to them are extremely low paid and part-time ones.

The problem of age discrimination cannot be dismissed as being merely the result of overly pessimistic attitudes on the part of older workers. In fact, there is evidence that older workers have very realistic perceptions of their re-employment prospects. A study of redundancy in the Sheffield steel industry found that age was an important determinant of unemployment across all socioeconomic groups. For example, among the skilled manual group the average number of months spent unemployed, in a three-year period following redundancy was three times greater for those aged 60 to 64 than the under 40s. Among the higher non-manual group the differential was four times between these two age groups (Westergaard et al, 1989).

Here are some examples of what older people said about age discrimination from the more recent Sheffield survey:

"A higher management team came in, all about 40. Said I'd be made redundant. I threatened them with court proceedings and in the end they said the job was redundant, not me. We went from 15 of us in the same status down to just six in three years. Some were re-deployed but they wanted me to go out of Sheffield but wouldn't say where. I was utterly disgusted with the whole set up. Reason was always 'we are looking to build up a future'." (Man, 58)

"When I have 'phoned someone you can tell people discriminate against age." (Woman, 60)

"Too many youngsters still leaving school looking for jobs who are cheaper to employ. You might be lucky and get a part-time job like night-watchman or security guard." (Man, 64)

A striking feature of some of the responses concerned treatment by official agencies. Some reported having been told that they were unlikely to find employment due to their age by staff at official Job Centres and had therefore stopped looking. These are some examples:

"They told me at the Unemployment Office not to bother now that I'd reached 60 – that I'd got no chance of a job anyway now. Nothing would prompt me now, having been told not to bother." (Man, 60)

"Only in for 10 minutes. Jobs were never discussed. Sixteen of us about the same age went in together. Just said, 'At your age don't bother and come back in six months'. They couldn't change anything. It all comes back to being too old at 60 for anything." (Man, 60)

"He agreed with me all advertisements just don't want anyone in my age group or too many hours needed or extremely low pay. It just qualified what I thought about my situation. Not getting work at all." (Man, 59)

These results indicate that for some there was a decision to leave work or not to seek work and for these people their experience of non-working was a positive one – a time to relax and to do new things. There was little desire to return to work, except in some instances on a voluntary basis. However, these people were very much in the minority. For many, the experience of non-working was often a negative one. Many would have preferred to work but there were factors against them. These included poor health and the fact that they are caring for a relative. For many, the negative experiences they have had in looking for work and in seeking retraining both with employers and with official agencies has led them to conclude that there was little point in them seeking employment – the typical discouraged worker. A feeling that their age was against them was a feature of most of the responses. Many had become resigned to their situation and doubted that they would ever work again.

The new imperative: an extension to the end of working life

Recently, European policy makers have shifted their focus away from early retirement to policies aimed at the (re-) integration of older workers. Far from being viewed as a burden, older workers are increasingly viewed as one of the solutions to the problem of labour shortages in the European labour market and for tackling issues regarding the sustainability of European pension systems (von Nordheim, 2004).

In only a few years, the British government's attitude towards older workers was transformed. From 1989 frequent references were being made by ministers, including the then Prime Minister and Secretary of State for Employment, to labour shortages and the loss of skills due to retirement. In contrast to statements made in the early 1980s, the then Secretary of State for Employment, Norman Fowler, referred to the government's desire to "encourage the elderly to lead healthier lives and work longer". The government's dramatic change of heart reflected the twin pressures of demographic change, leading to an ageing workforce and European directives on equal treatment.

Accompanying this change of attitude have been changes in policies towards the older worker. A whole raft of policies and initiatives concerning the employment of older workers have emerged in the UK over the last few years under the 'welfare to work' banner, though the extent of this should not be overstated: expenditure on active labour-market policies for older workers is considerably less than elsewhere in Europe (see Frerichs and Taylor, forthcoming). Increasingly, the emphasis of policy makers is on reactivating those classified inactive, many of whom are older workers claiming disability-related benefits (Department for Work and Pensions, 2002). However, older workers may perhaps be forgiven for being sceptical about the motivations behind the sudden interest in them among policy makers.

Conclusions

This chapter has considered early exit and its consequences for marginalisation in the UK. In contrast to the case of the Nordic countries discussed elsewhere in this volume, early exit from the labour market has been a major cause of social exclusion and marginalisation, though not for all. In fact, it has often been aspired to and welcomed by many, though a minority who are primarily from higher socioeconomic groups.

This review of the position of British older workers shows that they are vulnerable to redundancy. This redundancy is often involuntary and even if a person is re-employed, such employment has often been of low status and remuneration. This review also shows that older workers are over-represented among the long-term unemployed and are more likely to have been claiming disability benefits for longer.

The long-term decline in the participation in the workforce of older people, particularly older men, cannot be attributed to changes in the individual characteristics of older people themselves – their health, attitudes to work and so on. Nor can this trend be understood simply on the basis of the preferences expressed by older workers. In the UK retirement has been used by employers, including government, to reduce and restructure their workforces in response to both the constant pressure to increase productivity and cyclical changes in the demand for labour.

In the post-war period employers have used redundancy, like retirement, to restructure their workforces by 'buying out' those regarded as less efficient. This restructuring has been concentrated on older workers and, as we have seen, for some it has effectively reduced their retirement age. In Britain this process has been encouraged by public policy because redundancy payments have been based on a formula which awarded greater amounts the longer the period of service. This has both encouraged the view that it is more acceptable to make older workers redundant than younger ones and has legitimated the use of age by employers and trade unions as a basis for redundancy. There is evidence that older people often come under immense managerial and peer group pressure to take redundancy or early retirement.

Age discrimination operates across all socioeconomic groups but its impact is greatest on the manual group. Redundancy thus has the effect of exposing the disadvantages associated with social class that influence other aspects of a person's economic life, such as poor working conditions (resulting in ill health), low levels of education and training and lack of opportunities for skill enhancement and promotion, as well as opening the door to new age-related ones.

That some older people retain any kind of attachment to the labour market is perhaps remarkable. Yet, for many as has been shown, there is little choice. They are caught in a painful dilemma: on the one hand, the pressures associated with poverty and low incomes and the force of the employment ethic of capitalist societies push them to search for a job or to accept an insecure one and, on the other, there is the reality of an age-segmented labour market. In other words, the economic insecurity experienced by older workers is to a large extent a function of social policies with regard to employment, social security and retirement (see Guillemard, 2003 for a discussion). The end result of this socially constructed relationship between old age and the labour market is the economic hardship and psychological distress experienced by older people and their families, which is outlined earlier in this chapter.

Yet, amid current proposals concerning active labour-market policies aimed at older workers, the protection afforded by early retirement should not be overlooked. Far from the downward trend in participation rates among older workers pointing to failings of western Europe in tackling the economic problems confronting it in the 1970s and 1980s, an alternative view is that mass early retirement protected older workers from the vagaries of the labour market during this period (Taylor, 2003). Viewed from this perspective, some early retirement may in fact be considered integrative rather than marginalising, in that it facilitates a transition with dignity and a degree of security from employment to retirement, rather than a situation where older workers are required to participate in a disinterested labour market. It seems highly unlikely that many of the current generation of older workers will make an easy transition from old to new economy employment. Therefore, for some, early retirement will remain the better alternative if the only other is unemployment.

References

Arrowsmith, J. and McGoldrick, A. (1997) 'A flexible future for older workers?', *Personnel Review,* vol 26, no 4, pp 258-73.

Auer, P. and Fortunay, M. (1999) *Ageing of the labour force in OECD countries: Economic and social consequences,* Geneva: ILO.

Bytheway, B. (1987) 'Redundancy and the older worker', in R.M. Lee (ed) *Redundancy, layoffs and plant closures,* Beckenham: Croom Helm, pp 84-115.

Campbell, N. (1999) 'The decline of employment among older people in Britain', CASE paper, London: LSE, Centre for Analysis of Social Exclusion.

Casey, B. (1992) 'Redundancy and early retirement: the interaction of public and private policy in Britain, Germany and the USA', *British Journal of Industrial Relations,* vol 30, no 3, pp 425-43.

Casey, B. and Laczko, F. (1989) 'Early retired or long-term unemployed? The situation of non-working men aged 55-64 from 1976 to 1986', *Work, Employment and Society,* vol 1, no 4, pp 509-26.

Cliff, D.R. (1989) 'Quality of life in early retirement: differences in the experience of hourly paid and salaried male retirees from the chemical industry in the West Riding of Yorkshire', Paper presented to the British Sociological Association Annual Conference, Plymouth.

DWP (Department for Work and Pensions) (2002) *Simplicity, security and choice: Working and saving for retirement,* Norwich: The Stationery Office.

Esping-Andersen, G. (1990) *The three worlds of welfare capitalism,* Princeton, NJ: Princeton University Press.

Esping-Andersen, G. (1999) *Social foundations of postindustrial economies,* Oxford: Oxford University Press.

Frerichs, F. and Taylor, P. (forthcoming) *Labour-market policies for older workers and demographic change: A comparative study of policy approaches in Germany and the United Kingdom,* London: Anglo-German Foundation.

Gallie, D. and Paugam, S. (2000) *Welfare regimes and the experience of unemployment in Europe,* Oxford: Oxford University Press.

Guillemard, A.-M. (2003) 'Concluding remarks. Company practices and public policies regarding age: lessons drawn from comparisons', *Geneva Papers on Risk and Insurance,* vol 28, no 4, pp 673-6.

Hawkins, K. (1984) *Unemployment,* Harmondsworth: Penguin.

Her Majesty's Treasury, Department for Work and Pensions (2001) *The changing welfare state: employment opportunity for all,* London: Her Majesty's Treasury.

House of Commons Select Committee on Social Services (1982) *Age of Retirement*, HC 26, London: HMSO.

House of Lords Select Committee on Unemployment (1982) Volume 1: report, HL 142, London: HMSO.

Jackson, P. and Taylor, P. (1994) 'Factors associated with employment status in later working life', *Work, Employment and Society*, vol 8, no 4, pp 553-67.

Johnson, P. (1989) 'The labour force participation of older men in Britain, 1951-81', *Work, Employment and Society*, vol 3, no 3, pp 351-68.

Laczko, F. (1987a) Discouragement, *Unemployment Bulletin*, Issue 24, Summer.

Laczko, F. (1987b) 'Older workers, unemployment, and the discouraged worker effect', in Di Gregoria, S. (ed) *Social gerontology: New directions*, London: Croom Helm, pp 239-51.

Laczko, F., Dale, A., Arber, S. and Gilbert, G.N. (1988) 'Early retirement in a period of high unemployment', *Journal of Social Policy*, vol 17, no 3, pp 313-33.

Maule, A.J., Cliff, D.R. and Taylor, R. (1996) 'Early retirement decisions and how they affect later quality of life', *Ageing and Society*, vol 16, no 2, pp 177-204.

McGoldrick, A. and Cooper, C.L. (1980) 'Voluntary early retirement taking the decision', *Employment Gazette*, August, pp 859-64.

Parker, S. (1980) *Older workers and retirement*, OPCS: Social Survey Division, London: HMSO.

Piachaud, D. (1986) 'Disability, retirement and unemployment of older men', *Journal of Social Policy*, vol 15, no 2, pp 145-62.

Plougmann, P. (2002) 'Internalisation and the labour market of the European Union', in J.G. Andersen and P.H. Jensen (eds) *Changing labour markets, welfare policies and citizenship*, Bristol: The Policy Press, pp 15-39.

Tanner, S. (1997) 'The dynamics of retirement behaviour', in R. Disney, E. Grundy and P. Johnson (1997) *The dynamics of retirement*, London: HMSO, pp 25-70.

Taylor, P. (2003) 'Age, labour market conditions and male suicide rates in selected countries', *Ageing and Society*, vol 23, no 1, pp 25-40.

Taylor, P. and Urwin, P. (1999) 'Recent trends in economic activity rates among older workers', *Geneva Papers on Risk and Insurance*, vol 24, no 4, pp 551-79.

Trinder, C. (1990) 'Employment after 55', National Institute for Economic and Social Research Discussion Paper no 166.

Von Nordheim, F. (2004) 'Responding well to the challenge of an ageing and shrinking workforce. European Union policies in support of member state efforts to retain, reinforce and re-integrate older workers in employment', *Social Policy and Society*, vol 3, no 2, pp 145-54.

Walker, A. (1982) 'The social consequences of early retirement', *Political Quarterly*, vol 53, no 1, pp 61-72.

Walker, A. (1985) 'Early retirement: release or refuge from the labour market?', *Quarterly Journal of Social Affairs*, vol 1, no 3, pp 211-29.

Westergaard, J., Noble, I. and Walker, A. (1989) *After redundancy*, Oxford: Polity Press.

FOURTEEN

The emergence of social movements by social security claimants

Rune Halvorsen

In public debates on unemployment and social protection, the unemployed and beneficiaries of social security schemes have often been considered as passive clients who need to be activated by others. It has been assumed that their lack of resources, and especially labour power, turns them into passive victims and objects rather than active actors and subjects (Offe, 1973; van Berkel, 1997; Williams, 1998; Williams et al, 1999). However, over the last two decades we find a number of empirical cases of social mobilisation of and by social security claimants in several western European countries (Halvorsen, 2001). This is a relatively new welfare-policy condition that requires greater understanding. It appears that our conception of the prospects for self-help activities and initiatives from and among social security claimants and the welfare-policy relevance of these initiatives have to this point been underdeveloped.

By analysing the emergence of social-movement organisations initiated by social security claimants in Norway during the 1990s, we ask whether it is possible that social-movement organisations established by and composed of social security claimants may have been successful and have had an impact on public-welfare policy, even if many of them have been short-lived and unstable.

Demands of new actors and policy measures in western European welfare regimes

The ongoing welfare policy reforms in many western European countries are focused not only on the choice of the most efficient welfare-policy measures and management problems. They also focus to a considerable extent on changing relations between the citizen and the state and on questions of participatory or deliberative democracy. Arguably many of the challenges that western European welfare states face today involve citizens not seeing themselves simply as passive costumers but as willing to take an active part in the deliberation and implementation of public-welfare policy, and more generally act as co-responsible for the development and governance of society. It has been assumed that the information and knowledge society requires its citizens to be in a position to keep updated and respond adequately to new and changing problem conditions, with the requisite condition that they are informed, make competent choices and contribute as best they can to the lives of their communities.

Uncertainty about the effects of existing welfare-policy measures and the perceived need to restructure western European welfare states have prompted the belief that alternative welfare-policy strategies are needed (Esping-Andersen et al, 2002). This includes the prospects of achieving better social inclusion and a higher degree of participation from people with no connection or only a marginal one to the labour market, including those who have been excluded, and preventing further exclusion from the labour market. One measure has been to stimulate increased user involvement, self-help activity and the systematic participation of recipients of public help and assistance in deliberating public-welfare policy and policy in each individual case. Such user involvement may be from individuals or small groups, or more collectively through interest organisations and social movements.

Since the early 1990s, the European Commission's Directorate-General for Employment and Social Affairs has granted significant financial support to a number of organisations established by and composed of the traditionally vulnerable social categories and target groups of the policy. They have established fairly intensive systems for contact and counselling with representatives of participants and participants themselves in these organisations. It appears as if the European Commission has gone further in this regard than many of the member states. The directorate has had direct and continuous dialogue with these organisations, and has also invited them into broad and more formal forums for exchanging opinions. In this way the Commission has created allies to help push reluctant member states to introduce new and more demanding standards for goods and services (Bouget and Prouteau, 2002). The member states are also expected to involve social partners and target groups in the preparation and evaluation of national action plans on employment and social inclusion. This amounts to significant ongoing processes of political structuring in the European political system (Porta et al, 2002).

However, it is questionable whether the political and administrative elites in Western Europe have managed to respond adequately to stimulate increased cooperation, participation, initiatives and self-government on the part of the recipients of help and assistance. We ask what policy lessons can be learned from the social mobilisation of social security claimants in Norway during the 1990s. We seek a stepwise answer to this by addressing three questions:

* What have been the reasons for this mobilisation?
* What have these social-movement organisations achieved and what problems have they faced?
* What are the future prospects for and welfare-policy potential of organisations and self-help activities established by and involving social security claimants?

United against public-welfare policy?

In a Norwegian study from 1995-99 we managed to identify 25 organisations, nodes and networks that claimed to represent recipients of welfare benefits and other types of assistance from the public services. The movement was composed of small horizontal networks that were more or less coordinated between individuals and small groups rather than hierarchical organisations. The participants were occupied with issues of social risk and the encoding of everyday life, or what has been referred to as 'life politics' (Giddens, 1991). This included concerns about the conditions for receiving social security benefits and society's modes of handling unemployment. The aim was partly social mobilisation for the recognition of social security claimants as responsible citizens. The participants also pursued traditional socioeconomic issues, such as access to gainful employment, a predictable income, access to an adequate material standard of living and health and measures against poverty. The movement encompassed thus both a political-economic dimension and a cultural-valuation one that were not neatly cordoned off from one another. Both economic disadvantage and cultural devaluation impeded equal participation in the making of society, in the public sphere and in everyday life (Fraser, 1995).

Overall, the experience of control, unreasonable demands, importunity and wrongful treatment at the hands of the politicians or first-line services helped to unite the social security claimants. Such concerns were to a large extent reflected in how the organisational efforts came about and their raison d'etre. Participants complained that the public authorities tried to force people into activities they were not interested in. Obligations to participate in recurrent short-term courses to qualify for labour-market participation and courses in how to apply for jobs were to a certain extent viewed as a nuisance and as punishment rather than assistance. The participants strongly expressed the view that the individual help they were given and their applications for support or compensation were associated with a large degree of social control and inspection.

The organisations tended to define themselves in relation to the welfare state's services and provisions. To a considerable extent they tried to act as subjects with a collective voice by presenting themselves as objects of specific measures or as service recipients and not as poor or financially destitute people. Arguably, the emergence of the welfare state, or more generally the collectivisation of care and assistance, opened the way for a social movement of people who perceived themselves as in need of help or as controlled by the assistance services. The new institutional structures that were established after World War II laid the groundwork for the construction of claimants' organisations; a type of framing of claims that is difficult to imagine could have emerged before the war (Halvorsen and Hvinden, 1998; Eriksson, 1999).

These organisational efforts were not the result of direct opposition to an official commitment to a high level of employment as the guiding principle behind the Norwegian social security schemes (Drøpping et al, 1999), although several of the participants expressed ambivalence towards the domination of this approach in Norway. As the majority of the participants had difficulties achieving sufficient or permanent work, a unilateral emphasis on paid work would imply the devaluation of their own position. At the same time most of them had work experience and had been socialised into the dominant mode of classifying human activities according to their attributed value for society as a whole. To a considerable extent, the claimants shared the dominant judgements and views on what was recognised as 'work'.

However, growing access to information and a higher average level of education in the population appears to have increased general competence in and expectations of being able to make one's own individual choices, or at least to make the opportunity to influence social issues of importance to one's own life, participation and realisation of a meaningful life. Individuals and social groups feel to a greater extent nowadays than formerly that the state should not behave paternalistically, or deny them recognition and respect. In this respect the welfare state appears to be encountering more demanding and less submissive recipients of assistance. At the same time, such changes in competence and expectations are most likely to have reinforced the feeling on the part of the claimants that the control aspects inherent in the social security system are less legitimate and tolerable.

Individual negotiations with the public authorities

The temptation of individual claimants to ask for special treatment promoted defection and undermined the goals of the organisations to unite and achieve improvements they all could benefit from. Although the participants tended to agree that more rule-oriented, rights-based, transparent and predictable services were preferable, individual-case processing led them to focus on their own personal merits in courses and education and on their own individual accounts for their claims to social security benefits. More rule-based services would limit the scope of the discretion of officials and thus the power of the staff in the first-line services and make it easier to predict the outcome. It would then also be easier to compare one's case with others and check that the disbursements were being fairly distributed. But when the services are more rule-based you cannot expect much understanding for your individual plight. It was therefore tempting to stress aspects that made them unique and comparisons between themselves and other claimants irrelevant and to eschew ordinary requirements and eligibility criteria ('my case is different'). More individual consideration and discretionary service provision was necessary to ensure that all relevant circumstances in one's own individual case were taken into consideration. In their efforts to negotiate access to benefits with the public authorities, the claimants might emphasise what made their case unique to appear the most deserving and needy in comparison with others.

The defensive function of appeals to a person's own uniqueness represented the possibility of alleviating the requirements other claimants were exposed to. In this way they could attempt to negotiate with the staff in the public-help services. At the same time it became more difficult to compare themselves with other claimants and work for common goals in and through the organisations. This ambivalence on the part of the claimants probably reflected real but contradictory needs on their part. These were both needs for discretion and for being followed up individually and predictability.

This contradiction gave them a good strategic position for negotiations with staff in the help services. If the welfare officials referred to the rules, the claimants could complain that they were 'insensitive', 'too strict' or 'dogmatic'. When the officials used their discretion, the claimants could complain they were 'ignorant of the rules', 'unfair' and 'inconsistent'. From the perspective of the officials, this could possibly be experienced as a Catch-22 situation. The claimants complained about lack of justice in the distribution system and lack of efficiency in the bureaucracy, while their experience of paternalism and social control elicited arguments about human values and morality. This is not an experience, a dilemma or a coping strategy that is unique to welfare bureaucracy. On the contrary, it probably reflects quite common experiences with bureaucratic organisations and reactions to them (Mathiesen, 1965).

Time and ambiguity of status

There is often a fear that the claimants might become too accustomed to a social status that is supposed to be temporary. This tended to increase the ambivalent approach of the political and administrative elites as to how much time and energy able-bodied social security claimants of working age should invest in claimant organisations. The socially expected duration of the status as social security claimant has been partly formalised and institutionalised in the social-protection systems and these expectations have had something of the character of informal norms and collective common sense (Merton, 1984). As helpers, politicians and staff in the welfare bureaucracy were inclined to sympathise with the initiatives to organise. But as controllers, they feared that claimants would become too accustomed to their status as social security recipients. The public authorities therefore tended to perceive these organisations as an expression of resistance to accepting help and advice from others, or even unwillingness to accept paid work.

Similar considerations were reflected in and had consequences for the adaptation and coping strategies of the claimants. The organisation and the individual claimant appeared to have contradictory interests when it came to the length of time they were affiliated to the organisation. This led to ambivalence in activists when other users and activists obtained jobs. Participants in the organisations reported that many people were only interested in solving their own specific and individual problems and withdrew as soon as they had achieved this. This was also a source of moral censure. In discussions between themselves, some activists condemned others who left the organisation when they obtained a job and labelled this behaviour a betrayal, deceitful and lacking in solidarity.

At the same time, the activists also argued that this short-term and temporary perspective could be an advantage. For instance, the remaining activists in one of the organisations mentioned that several members of the first local boards had obtained new jobs within three to four months. When we asked them whether or not they saw this as something that impeded self-organising efforts, they replied that it did not, even if it meant that many of the local boards were short lived. One activist in another organisation even stated that it could be seen as a positive development that many of the claimants' organisations were short lived, if this implied that people became re-employed. It was, after all, a sign of the organisation's success. When the organisation contributed to re-employment or did not impede re-entrance into the labour market, it became a victim of its own success.

Several of the activists claimed that they were in a transition phase in their lives, such as that they were waiting for court cases against former employers, intending to finish their education or trying to become re-employed. Some of the core activists we interviewed left the organisation after a short time. In other cases, participants became less active during periods of vocational training, subsidiary and unreported income-providing activities and employment, but repeatedly returned to the organisation.

> "Now I'm going to renovate a loft. I work [in x organisation] just now. Somebody has to take care of business here too. [The person who usually is here] is attending a vocational training course in how to establish new enterprises now. So he isn't here during the daytime just now. I live a bit on the edge. I don't always have much money. I visit the social-services office at times." (from interview with participant in Organisation I, April 1997)

> "I have realised that I have to start taking care of my own life at least. I can probably use the experiences I have had here, work experience as they call it. Now I don't want to go in that direction [organisational work]. If I don't move on I'll be stuck here. I've been almost schizophrenic about this. In the worst moments I just want out and away from this. It's hard only to give and not get any fuel. On the other hand, I know that what we do is very important. That keeps me going. But I have to take care of myself and then I will have to pull out a bit." (from interview with participant in Organisation II, May 1996)

In some cases, the participants maintained a connection with the organisation for a longer period of time than they had first intended. But since they assumed that they were in the process of leaving, they did not want to become too involved in organisational matters and therefore had only a peripheral connection. Core activists also assumed that others would leave as soon as they were applying for job opportunities. Consequently, they often invested only minimal effort in involving other claimants in more demanding and time-consuming activities. The expected duration of an unemployed person's status and their expectations of social mobility promoted claimants and service recipients to participate less in other and alternative arenas during the intervening period of time. Committing oneself to joint efforts with others in similar situations or persons in what was assumed to be a temporary social environment appeared, to a large extent, to conflict with improving one's own individual status and returning to a working life. Joining the organisation tended to be conceived as betraying one's hope and aspiration for achieving paid work.

Ambiguous relations to professional helpers

Paradoxically, several of the organisations had a certain level of contact with the national trade union for social workers. They appeared together with them in the mass media and in meetings with the central authorities and sometimes accepted social work students who had had vocational training in these organisations. As long as the welfare offices were perceived as help services the claimants could seek alliances with the social workers and support claims for more resources for the improvement of their services. The social-services offices had the dual objective of providing both income maintenance and professional help to promote self-sufficiency through paid work. Social workers and claimants appeared to have joint interests in increasing the financial resources and the number of staff in the social-services offices, and in achieving more generous and standardised social-assistance benefits. From the claimants' perspective, the latter would facilitate more predictability and certainty about their entitlements. From the perspective of social workers, it would relieve them of the discomfort and negative self-image associated with assessing in detail the financial circumstances of claimants and it would also provide better opportunities for more active help and assistance.

Many social workers have identified with and wanted to work for the benefit of their clients. However, from the claimants' point of view, social workers were easily seen as representatives of the official authorities, that is, as the immediate oppressor or enemy, as in some ways social workers acted as gatekeepers to social-assistance payments. In several cases the claimants said that they limited their contact with social workers as much as possible or gave them as little information as possible. Similarly, as a controller, a social worker might keep in mind that the client could attempt to manipulate the information provided. Hence, the contradictions inherent in the structural position of the social workers as both gatekeepers to income-maintenance benefits and providers of help and advocacy contributed to the ambivalence with which the social workers and claimants viewed each other (Merton et al, 1983). The control function they had been assigned appeared to a certain extent to make the exercise of their help and service functions more difficult.

Strained relations with government representatives

The national welfare policy reinforced the ambivalence of the organisations to establishing contact with representatives of the public authorities. Several of the most active members in the organisational efforts stated that they wanted to have a greater impact on political decisions that affected their social status, or recognition as subjects with a legitimate right to have an influence on the social-policy measures they were dependent on. On other occasions they claimed it was not an important goal that should be accepted by politicians. At the same time, they complained that they were excluded from participation. Nevertheless, the efforts to seek contact and establish a dialogue with government representatives were not given high priority: they were few and far between or only followed up in part.

The claimants were to a large extent not recognised as autonomous subjects and this made the relationship between the organisation participants and the public authorities more similar to an adversarial one. Their perception of the central authorities was often characterised by large social distance, scepticism and even mistrust. The university colleges, social workers, mass media and the ministries were sometimes perceived as part of the same oppressive state machinery en bloc. For instance, when a university college wanted to participate in an evaluation of the social services offices in 1997, they were rejected as state representatives and as not being really independent by some participants in one of the organisations. On other occasions it was assumed that newspaper editors had received orders not to write about them: that there was a deliberate suppression of information on the real number of people out of work, as well as hidden obstructions and delays and assumptions about secret alliances between some officials high up in the public administration system and the political elites.

Several participants were uncertain about the consequences of applying for financial support from the government, choosing instead to stand outside and confront the government. They demanded absolute and immediate changes. Willingness to seek compromises and cooperation was construed as weakness. They wanted to be loyal to their own position and immovable, holding fast to their beliefs ("will not sell our souls"). This was not only their own subjective feeling, but was also built into their social position. If they became involved in the decision-making process, it would serve to undermine their presentation of themselves as victims of circumstances outside their own control. They would to a larger extent be co-responsible for policy development and lose or diminish the opportunities that self-presentation as an innocent victim could provide in negotiations on access to resources and in avoiding the withdrawal of these resources.

For the defenders of the social democratic welfare state project, these organisations were disturbing reminders of the imperfections and the social problems they had not yet been able to solve. There has also been awareness of the risks of free riders in the wake of a generous welfare state and the officially endorsed work ethic has had a moralistic effect. The organisation's efforts to seek recognition as representatives of social security claimants were sometimes redefined or denied by the staff in the public administration and the first-line services (not as 'homeless' people but as 'people with psychiatric problems'). Staff in social-services offices and labour-exchange offices asserted that the claimants had problems other than just unemployment (such as drinking or drug problems, or physical or mental-health problems) or they claimed that the participants of the organisation did not deserve assistance. The public officials questioned whether the claimants' organisations were representative or claimed claimants should be treated individually (as they were a 'non-homogenous group'). It was also argued that the first-line services had contact with a broader spectrum of the clients and thus had a better overview of the needs and interests of social security recipients.

There was also some evidence that the largest confederation of trade unions (Landsorganisasjonen) was ambivalent towards or even disapproved of organisations of the unemployed and social security claimants. The labour movement has been an explicit representative of paid work as a crucial signifier of identity, societal participation, respect and honour. The accumulation of economic capital has not been the rationale for their high legitimacy in society. Rather, it has been the virtues of drudgery, patience, endurance and self-denial. The dignity associated with the virtues of hard toil has been an explicit part of their self-representation. This appeared to reinforce their ambiguous attitude towards having the unemployed as allies. Seeing the unemployed as part of the labour force, as part of the larger 'we' of the labour movement, appeared to contradict their self-understanding and self-presentation.

Paradoxically, it appeared to be easier to achieve recognition, financial and moral support for some of the organisations during a period when a conservative coalition government was in power (since 1997). The second conservative coalition government, in power since October 2001, dominated by the Conservative Party, has set goals of combating poverty while at the same time limiting state bureaucracy and cutting budgets. The government's intention has been to concentrate more public services and social security schemes on the provision of basic security and to a larger extent leave other and additional service provision to charity foundations, voluntary associations and market forces (Ministry of Social Affairs and Health, 2002). They have claimed that too large a welfare state should be avoided and services should be concentrated more on those who really need help. A central objective has been to develop more 'targeted measures' and a more cost-effective strategy to solve the potential financial crisis in the welfare state.

For a long time it has been a prevalent and dominant assumption that poverty did not exist in Norway and that it had been eradicated by the creation of the welfare state. For all intents and purposes poverty appears to have been a taboo word for a long time (Aubert, 1970). Norway has neither had an officially recognised poverty line, nor standardised criteria for determining what is required to meet the basic needs of human existence and when the public authorities should assume responsibility for basic needs. Norway has instead maintained its residual system for means-tested and discretionary social assistance. However, as part of the new discourse on poverty, the Ministry of Social Affairs (2001) circulated recommendations for minimum social assistance to the municipalities in 2001.

For the Conservative and Christian Democratic parties the renewed focus on poverty and the existence of organisations of 'the poor' could serve as proof of the failures and flaws of social-democratic policy. This represented new opportunities for the organisations under discussion to apply for financial resources. Support for these organisations could serve to demonstrate that they were more inclusive, attentive and concerned about solving the problems for people out of work. The new focus on poverty was probably also reinforced by the

European Union's decision in 2000 to adopt the method of open coordination of national action plans on social inclusion and Norway's decision to take part in that process. Furthermore, some of the Norwegian organisations achieved more legitimacy and financial support from the Norwegian government from their contact with and moral support from the European Anti-Poverty Network in Brussels.

Media as unreliable allies

Several organisations managed to take advantage of these opportunities. They managed to liberate themselves from their hesitation in contacting central authorities and from shying away from public visibility. By appearing in the mass media, participating in meetings with politicians and governmental ministries, mobilising moral support from outside supporters employed in the universities and adapting to the formal requirements for applying and receiving financial support, they managed to gain more financial support from the central authorities, the local authorities and charities and to recruit passive users.

In a sense the media contributed to creating the opponent by presenting the organisational efforts as if they were representative voices of all social security claimants. The mass media appeared to be less interested in the number of people the organisational efforts represented; which was something that was of much greater concern to the government. This is not to say that the journalists fabricated their evidence, even if they were helping to create the reality that they maintained they were only describing. In practice, some of the organisational efforts assumed the characteristics of 'virtual organisations'.

The agenda-setting function of the mass media represented a source for greater influence on the part of the disadvantaged vis-à-vis the public authorities. Media coverage could improve the chances of reversing decisions in individual cases and could be the springboard for change in public-welfare policy. Organisations could gain public attention when their interests corresponded with and served the interests of the media. By appearing in the mass media, they could also strengthen their position vis-à-vis the government prior to meetings with the authorities. This represented an extra possibility for appeal outside the bureaucratic channel.

The possibility of personalisation and the intensification of conflict was the basis for these organisations' uneasy alliances with journalists. Individual life-projects and the expressive claims of many of the claimants appeared to correspond well with the journalists' desire and need for individuals to illustrate and personalise their case. The organisations made it easier for the journalists to recruit interviewees from social security claimants. Moreover, the mass media has its own interest in presenting social conflicts, deficiencies and disagreement as severely as possible, as the media compete for attention from readers and viewers (Puijk et al, 1984).

These alliances represented the possibility of self-assertion, protest and influence on the policy agenda. This use of media emerged as a prevalent and significant element in the dynamic between the providers and recipients or claimants of welfare-policy measures. But the media coverage depended on the journalists' own account of the issue. The disadvantaged risked being misrepresented by the journalists or presented as more victimised than they would have chosen to be themselves. The lack of experience with the mass media and the lack of continuity among journalists who covered welfare-policy issues made it difficult to control the outcome of the alliances on the part of the disadvantaged.

Concluding remarks

Despite their other problems, several of the organisational efforts successfully sought a high media profile, especially in the local press. Through appearance in the media, the organisation participants managed to make unsolved issues visible in public and contributed to placing new needs and demands on the welfare-policy agenda. The organisation representatives produced and advocated alternative interpretations of the social world and the redefinition of social problems, and provided new examples and material of their situation to the media. But it was sometimes questionable whether the organisations were subjects, or objects used by the mass media and other critics of the social democratic welfare state project. On the one hand, the media coverage could be interpreted as evidence that the claimants were objects of other people's concern, help and control and objects the mass media could make use of and even present as 'the others' among us. On the other hand, this also gave the claimants the opportunity to break their silence and become more visible in the public.

Change in public policy emerged as the measure of success in which they had achieved the lowest scores so far. This does not necessarily differ from interest organisations that are much more established. Even in the case of larger and more permanent interest organisations with a high legitimacy, the symbolic dimension of participation can sometimes be the more important contribution: the organisations become recognised as parties in negotiations with the political system, as having the right to receive information and express their opinion, give a voice to the subject population and keep this population visible in the public sphere. What substantial or tangible results the organisations achieve may vary and also change over time.

Many of the organisations' problems were related to their lack of recognition and whether it was appropriate for them to have a collective voice. Entrenched modes of thinking about welfare-policy measures and too narrow a focus on the ultimate goals of achieving a higher employment rate prevented the consideration of alternative and more flexible measures of social inclusion. The dominant welfare policy appeared to limit participation in areas other than the labour market and preclude more active citizenship on the part of people who temporarily or on a more long-term basis were out of work. This prevented the development of a more vital participatory democracy in Norwegian society and undermined the opportunity for social security beneficiaries to act as co-responsible citizens who could pursue their own life-goals, rather than being trapped in the role of 'customer', 'client' or 'user' of public help and assistance.

There are two crucial reasons that explain why self-help initiatives established and run by social security claimants are important. People with the same background, identity or experience may in certain contexts be better conversation partners and advocates than professional helpers and these initiatives can be a means to increase the self-confidence of the participants. Ideally, self-help contributes to the empowerment of the participants so that the public authorities face more self-confident claimants demanding help. At the same time, the government gains more articulated and systematic feedback from the users of public services. Participation in self-organised activities and self-help groups may provide opportunities to attain a larger degree of dignity and pride, and reduce the shame and stigmatisation of these participants and others in a similar situation.

Social security claimants may have little confidence in the public authorities or certain professions en bloc, or they may have little interest in traditional party politics and bureaucratic work methods. When, in spite of such features, they seek to represent their own interests, we may see the organisations as contributors to the development and reinforcement of democracy as an institution. These self-help initiatives may represent their first efforts to articulate their own interests and serve as a point of departure for developing a dialogue between the professions and the beneficiaries of the services and assistance schemes, and possibly over time also develop a common understanding of the problem. We could also argue that placing too large an emphasis on consensus and avoidance of conflicts could be counterproductive. Open, limited and substantial conflict between social security claimants and the public authorities can help us to give greater attention to how welfare-policy measures and services are experienced and perceived by the recipients or users. This, in turn, can lead to the development of more targeted and effective policy measures by the public authorities. If the beneficiaries of the help and assistance services are given real opportunities to have more equal and symmetric participation, there will be fewer reasons to perceive the government as an adversary that one has the moral right to resist. In this way it will most likely be easier to obtain more committed and independent initiatives from the users and recipients of the services.

References

Aubert, V. (1970) 'Rural poverty and community isolation', in P. Townsend (ed) *The concept of poverty*, London: Heinemann, pp 236-50.

Bouget, D. and Prouteau, L. (2002) 'National and supranational government-NGO relations', *Public Administration and Development*, vol 22, no 1, pp 31-7.

Drøpping, J.A., Hvinden, B. and Vik, K. (1999) 'Activation policies in the Nordic countries', in M. Kautto, M. Heïkkilä, B. Hvinden, S. Marklund and N. Ploug (eds) *Nordic social policy*, London: Routledge, pp 133-58.

Eriksson, L. (1999) 'De arbetslösas förening: förutsättninger för mobilisering och handlingsutrymme 1919', in A. Berge, W. Karpis, J. Palme, S.-A. Stenberg and K. Åmark (eds) *Välfärdsstat i brytningstid*. Special supplement of *Sociologisk Forskning*, Stockholm.

Esping-Andersen, G., Gallie, D., Hemerijck, A. and Myles, J. (2002) *Why we need a new welfare state*, Oxford: Oxford University Press.

Fraser, N. (1995) 'From redistribution to recognition?', *New Left Review*, no 212, pp 68-120.

Giddens, A. (1991) *Modernity and self-identity*, Stanford, CA: Stanford University Press.

Halvorsen, R. (2001) 'The paradox of self-organisation among disadvantaged people', unpublished PhD, Trondheim: Norwegian University of Science and Technology.

Halvorsen, R. and Hvinden, B. (1998) 'Collective action of clients and claimants in Norway', in R. van Berkel, H. Coena and R. Vlek (eds) *Beyond marginality?*, Aldershot: Ashgate, pp 177-202.

Mathiesen, T. (1965) *The defences of the weak,* London: Tavistock Publications.

Merton, R. (1984) 'Socially expected durations: a case study of concept formation in sociology', in W. W. Powell and R. Robbins (eds) *Conflict and consensus,* New York, NY: Free Press, pp 262-83.

Merton, V., Robert, K. and Barber, E. (1983) 'Client ambivalence in professional relationships: the problem of seeking help from strangers', in B. DePaulo (ed) *New directions in helping,* New York, NY: Academic Press, pp 13-14.

Ministry of Social Affairs (2001) *Statlige veiledende retningslinjer for utmåling av stønad til livsopphold etter sosialtjenesteloven,* Rundskriv 1-13/2001, Oslo.

Ministry of Social Affairs and Health (2002) *Tiltaksplan mot fattigdom,* White Paper. St.meld.nr. 6 2002-2003, Oslo.

Offe, C. (1973) 'Politische Herrschaft und Klassenstrukturen Zur Analyse spätkapitalistischer Gesellschaftsysteme', in G. Kress and D. Senghaas (eds) *Politikwissenschaft,* Frankfurt am Main: Fischer.

Porta, D. della, Kriesi, H. and Rucht, D. (eds) (2002) *Social movements in a globalizing world,* Houndmills: Palgrave.

Puijk, R., Østbye, H. and Øyen, E. (1984) *Sosialpolitikk eller sosialpornografi?,* Oslo: Universitetsforlaget.

Van Berkel, R. (1997) 'Urban integration and citizenship, local policies and the promotion of participation', in M. Roche and R. Berkel (eds) *European citizenship and social exclusion,* Aldershot: Ashgate, pp 185-200.

Williams, F. (1998) 'Agency and structure revisited: rethinking poverty and social exclusion', in M. Barry and C. Hallett (eds) *Social exclusion and social work,* Lyme Regis: Russell House Publishing, pp 13-15.

Williams, F., Popay, J. and Oakley, A. (1999) *Welfare research,* London: University College of London Press.

FIFTEEN

Conclusion: policy change, welfare regimes and active citizenship

Jørgen Goul Andersen and Anne-Marie Guillemard

In the 1990s, there was a widespread belief in the inertia of the welfare state. In contrast, we now observe quite far-reaching changes in welfare policies, and several possible directions seem to be open for tomorrow's welfare states. In brief, we are in the midst of a thoroughgoing reform of welfare systems. Welfare policies are changing in response to new challenges, new actors and changing power relations. We also face new discourses about welfare that are disseminated across the rich welfare states.

Current conceptualisations and explanations of welfare state change are not always very helpful for analysing these often quite ambiguous changes. In the first place, explanations of changes have tended to focus too much on the problems of cost containment or competitiveness, failing to acknowledge other sources of change. Secondly, they have seen change too one-sidedly as a matter of retrenchment and failed to recognise that current changes also involve the expansion of social rights. Furthermore, the criteria used to assess change depend too much on the welfare state architecture that developed in the second half of the 20th century; in particular, they usually focus too narrowly on the state versus the market dichotomy, and too much on cash transfers rather than services. Finally, analyses of change often put too much emphasis on formal institutions and too little on outcomes.

Although analyses and interpretations along these lines have provided valuable insights, we must find a new vantage point for looking at the reforms under way and devise new standards of measurement for assessing current reforms and their eventual effects. In this book, we have suggested as a starting point for this analysis a broader notion of societal change; we have suggested assessing welfare reforms mainly from an outcome perspective and we have suggested focusing on the effects of such reforms on citizenship – while acknowledging at the same time that citizenship itself is being redefined.

Challenges and change: beyond retrenchment

During the 1990s, following Pierson's (1994) pioneering work, welfare state reform was mainly seen in terms of retrenchment. This view highlighted economic pressures as the major cause of change and provided extremely valuable insights into the politics of blame avoidance. But it paid too little attention to other sources of change (such as long-term economic pressures, changes in culture and values and political power relations); it took public opinion too much for granted and overestimated resistance to change and it underestimated the degree of change (not least the accumulated effects of incremental reforms).

As demonstrated in the first four chapters of this book, changes have in fact been quite far-reaching, and we seem to be in the midst of a major restructuring of the welfare state. This is acknowledged by Pierson (2001) who has suggested a distinction between cost containment, recommodification and recalibration and specified the different reform strategies needed for different welfare regimes. However, we need a broader perspective on the determinants of reform and we need a more detailed assessment of the extent and direction of change. In a governance world with new institutional mixes between state, the market and other actors, it is difficult to assess the extent and direction of reforms from a purely institutional perspective. It is necessary to put more emphasis on outcomes and we have chosen citizenship as our main criterion for gauging these outcomes. This criterion will also help to decide whether, as Gilbert (2002) maintains, reforms are converging in spite of institutional differences or whether, as we tend to think, they are diverging in spite of institutional similarities.

It is interesting to notice that, as regards the economic factors at work, attention has shifted from acute economic pressure and more or less radical measures of cost containment to long-term economic issues such as globalisation and ageing. Given the high degree of uncertainty about the impact of these long-term challenges, discourses and perceptions inevitably come to play a more important role. For example, Garrett and Mitchell's (2001) empirical study of the impact of globalisation concludes that it is not even possible to demonstrate an association between corporate taxes and foreign direct investments. In their view, what triggered the downward spiral in corporate taxes was not globalisation as such but discourse about it and the impact of the latter on the perceptions of political decision makers. Needless to say, such discourses are related to interests and power resources: discourses about the challenges of globalisation and ageing serve to justify major welfare reforms in countries where these challenges appear relatively small. This is not to say that ageing, in particular, is not an important problem for most welfare states. But one should not forget that in politics, solutions are always looking for problems.

However, our focus takes into view more than the economy. Family patterns, for example, are coming apart, as Birte Siim (Chapter Ten) and Birgit Pfau-Effinger (Chapter Eleven) have described. This affects the life course of both men and women. Men are no longer just breadwinners and women are more than housewives. Care for children is shared by both spouses and ensuring care for children (in the family or in childcare institutions) has increasingly become an obligation for the state. As Pfau-Effinger has pointed out, we currently find a significant expansion of social rights in the field of care, but in quite a different shape across the different welfare regimes.

Changes in the life course, and the breaking up of traditional family patterns, however, also reflect other and equally profound social changes, as pointed out by Anne-Marie Guillemard (Chapter Four) who speaks of a more general destandardisation of the life course in post-industrial society. Changes in the life course are also visible in the way work and non-work activities are distributed over the life span. The tripartite life-course model typical of industrial society is coming undone. Work is more fragmented and individualised, and paid work and non-work are ideal-typically mixing up during each stage of life instead of work being concentrated in adulthood and non-work lodged at the two ends of life: training for youngsters and retirement for old age.

The life-course is being changed by several forces, but one process that is affecting it is increasing individualisation. This process also represents a challenge to the adaptability of the welfare state. As the sociological literature about late modernity (for example, Giddens, 1991) has emphasised, individualisation does not mean that people become more egoistic or greedy or that they lack concern for others. It means that they are increasingly free to choose their own social networks, their own identity, their own life project. It is not only an option; it is instead an obligation. As Giddens has put it, the only choice you cannot have is the choice not to choose. To adapt the welfare state to a new type of citizen is a major challenge facing contemporary welfare states. How do individualism and freedom of choice combine with solidarity? How can the welfare state help enhance, rather than restrict, the opportunities provided to individuals to make choices?

Individualisation of social risks, or tailoring welfare to individualistic, active citizens

As we have seen from the first four chapters, current welfare reforms are somewhat ambiguous. On the one hand, most reform efforts may be interpreted as having roots in a neoliberal ideology or strategy. This interpretation would take as evidence the obvious emphasis of these reforms on incentives and the inclination to see welfare arrangements basically as distortions that hinder the smooth operation of the market. As Adrian Sinfield points out in Chapter Two, further evidence is the changed welfare mix with an increasing privatisation of certain social risks such as pensions (usually subsidised by tax deductions). To pursue Sinfield's line of inquiry, such reforms have become increasingly hegemonic, as evidenced by the use of phrases like 'active' versus 'passive' or 'dependency ratio', and by their relabelling retrenchment as welfare 'reform'.

However, quite a few current welfare reforms have also included a strengthening of social rights. This is observable not only in the field of care but also (at least in principle) in some activation reforms, as pointed out by Born and Jensen in Chapter Nine. Strengthening the individual's opportunities to choose may also contain an element of empowerment. Even the increasing private provision of social welfare in the field of retirement pensions does not unconditionally mean recommodification: on closer inspection, there are huge differences between multi-tiered or 'multipillar' pensions systems in terms of risk sharing. In principle, at least, a multipillar or multi-tiered pension system might lead to the same outcome as a fully public system. Ambiguity is found also at the European level. As Alan Walker has pointed out in Chapter Three, the European Union officially pursues a 'European social model' that is different from the American model and from neoliberal ideals. But it is ambiguous and the substance of this model is still a bone of contention.

Clearly, institutions are changing in contemporary welfare states, often in direction of somewhat more 'private' or 'individualistic' arrangements. However, if we skip the important discussion of whether institutional dynamics or new actors will eventually pull such changes in one direction rather than another in the long run, the question remains: what will be the outcome? Ambiguity is also a keyword when we consider welfare state changes in relation to the de-standardisation of the life course, as described by Anne-Marie Guillemard in Chapter Four. De-standardisation is an empirically observable trend, but how should the welfare state adjust to it? And how should we interpret the adjustments actually being made? As pointed out in Chapter Four, there are clearly dangers of a privatisation of the social sphere. But welfare states cannot avoid adapting to the fact that their citizens have become much more individualistic. Obviously, too, the welfare state's actions in this respect will have repercussions on society and the behaviour of citizens.

These are but a few examples of the ambiguity in the changes now under way in the welfare state. To assess their direction and impact, we must take into account the whole mix of public and 'private' arrangements and the interplay between them. We must certainly not ignore the fact that such institutional changes could have far-reaching dynamic implications, as actors, power relations, perceptions, norms and behaviour change as well. But in any case, such changes must be evaluated from an outcome perspective. This also means that we must consider how such changes are actually implemented.

We suggest that changes are evaluated in terms of their impact on citizenship, which is a broader criterion than alternatives such as equality. However, this brings up yet another problem, namely that citizenship itself is being redefined in quite ambiguous ways.

New citizens and varieties of active citizenship

As mentioned above, welfare states have to adapt to more individualistic citizens with larger capacity to act. This is not an insurmountable task. In welfare services, the empowerment of users by providing not only more voice opportunities, but also more choice opportunities, has been a major line of reform in many welfare states, in particular the Nordic ones (Andersen and Hoff, 2001). There is also widespread agreement about the necessity to avoid the 'clientilisation' of people in need of social security; but there is certainly no consensus about how to avoid this.

This is also among the key points where new discourses on active citizenship are formulated. But these discourses refer to a variety of meanings and practices. In the theoretical literature we also encounter changes in the conceptualisation of citizenship. Whereas the main emphasis used to be on social rights (and obligations), two other dimensions of citizenship (which were embryonic in Marshall's seminal work) are increasingly attracting attention: participation and orientations (or identities in the broad sense), as pointed out by Andersen (Chapter Five) and Siim (Chapter Ten). This change in emphasis involves a shift of focus towards the outcome side; towards the effects: beyond equality, does the welfare state help 'empower' its citizens? And how could it do so?

The task is more difficult when it comes to social security transfers where similar pressures are felt but where the dangers of individualising social risks are larger. Adapting social transfers to the process of individualisation is more complicated than, as in the past, providing standardised protection under social security. The individualisation of social rights may potentially involve the individualisation of social risks. For instance, there has been talk about 'social drawing rights' or a 'citizens' account' (see Guillemard, Chapter Four). But such accounts, if actually created, would very likely be in the red for people with a weak position in the labour market and provide a surplus for people with a strong position. In short, the differences that currently haunt performance-based and achievement-based welfare systems could be made even worse. Combining flexibility and solidarity is a major challenge.

Nonetheless, the welfare state has to take into account the fact that its citizens have far larger resources than they had previously and that they want to have more control over their own situation. Nor can it avoid addressing the question of the avoidance of 'clientilisation'. This is also one of the reasons why new discourses about active citizenship have come into being – and have come to stay.

The current redefinition of (active) citizenship has many other aspects. Implicitly, it was originally linked to the position of male breadwinners, as pointed out in feminist research. Alongside the breakdown of the male breadwinner model, citizenship has not only been defamilised and individualised; active citizenship has also come to include a number of social rights in relation to care, such as the guarantee for state-provided childcare in some countries, or the introduction of a 'social right to care' in others (Pfau-Effinger, Chapter Eleven). As mentioned earlier, this is perhaps the best illustration that the current transformations of the welfare state and the redefinition of citizenship is not only a matter of the retrenchment and erosion of social rights.

Furthermore, traditional notions of citizenship are challenged by migration. Traditionally, citizenship meant state citizenship. Today, citizenship rights are also expanding at the European level, and to a large extent, they are also granted to residents with state citizenship outside Europe. Even here, in a long-term perspective, it is reasonable to speak of an expansion of citizenship rights. In most countries, citizenship in the past was originally confined to a culturally homogenous population. With multiculturalism, citizenship also becomes a question of recognition as pointed out by Calloni (Chapter Six) and Siim (Chapter Ten).[1] Immigration is also one of the changes that has triggered discourses about active citizenship: the citizenship of immigrants, according to such discourses, should not only mean a modicum of civil, political and social rights, but also their active participation in the labour market, their active participation in society at large and some orientation towards the political community.

A very important change is the shift of focus in the new discourses of citizenship. From a focus on social rights to a focus on participation and empowerment – and on the duty to participate. What contributes to participation and empowerment is an open question. In the classical interpretation, generous social protection was the main precondition (Andersen, Chapter Five). Indeed, there is no lack of empirical findings supporting this interpretation. For instance, economic factors were pointed out as the most important in the study of Gallie and Paugam (2000), as well as in a Scandinavian study (Andersen, 2002). But in many current discourses, this is underemphasised or ignored in favour of a rather mechanical emphasis on labour-market inclusion. The ideal citizen is pictured as a self-supporting individual, and often social protection is portrayed as 'passive support'. The right to social protection is replaced by the right to become self-supporting. Although elements of such discourses are found in most countries, the content of active citizenship is markedly different between one welfare regime and another. Below, we summarise a few central findings.

Active citizenship and activation of social protection

The most important field where the notion of active citizenship has become dominant is in labour-market policies. As pointed out by Barbier (Chapter Seven), active labour-market policies form part of an even broader movement towards activation of social protection with the aim of bringing people into some sort of paid employment, also including all sorts of 'making work pay' policies. However, as Barbier underlines, this broad movement and the accompanying notion of active citizenship, despite some similarities in discourse and procedures, covers highly contradictory and divergent tendencies. The context and actual implementation are essential for the assessment of such policies. In other words, it is essential to focus on substance and on outcomes. Barbier distinguishes between two ideal-types. The first is the liberal type – mainly found in Anglo-Saxon countries – with an emphasis on incentives, sanctions and in-work benefits. The other is the universalistic ideal-type, which also provides a variety of services for those who are unemployed, establishes a sort of negotiation between the individual and the system and guarantees rather generous protection against poverty. In various shapes, this ideal-type is found mainly in the Scandinavian countries. The continental welfare states have not developed a distinct pattern but seem to combine elements from these two ideal-types, or to oscillate between them. In Scandinavia as well, however, there is an ongoing battle about substance which may pull in both directions.

Born and Jensen (Chapter Nine) elucidate the potentials of the individual action plans in Denmark which presuppose the client as an active player, equal to the caseworker. This is a very important new principle of negotiation, resulting in the writing of a contract, which means an entirely new role construction and can be seen as a great leap forward in expanding and adapting social rights to changing preconditions in society. It not only means empowerment of those who are unemployed; it is also an example of the individualisation of social rights which is by no means in conflict with solidarity. In many ways, it is a prototypical example of an empowering active citizenship.

Needless to say, the actual implementation of this principle may be different. As pointed out by Larsen (Chapter Eight) in his overview of research on the effects of active labour-market policies in Denmark, such policies may sometimes be quite counterproductive and lead to even harder clientelisation in actual practice. If the principles of equality and negotiation are disregarded, it means that the terms of a far-reaching contract are dictated from above – an issue pursued by Halvorsen in Chapter Fourteen about resistance to such treatment among long-term unemployed in Norway during the 1990s. Further, implementation in this instance is not only a matter of administrative bodies not following the intentions of law makers; indeed, as a maneouvre of blame avoidance, law makers may deliberately seek to change implementation rather than change the law.

Halvorsen's chapter shows how the constellation of the driving force in welfare programmes is being reconfigured. A social movement organised by and for social security claimants has arisen in Norway; it is evidence that these beneficiaries are no longer merely passive recipients who need to be stimulated to act. This social mobilisation, despite ambiguities, signals a willingness to be recognised as responsible citizens capable of self-help. Public authorities have thus had to listen to their demands and opinions. Halvorsen draws attention to the ability of these claimants to form alliances with social workers and the media. Ultimately, these organisations of welfare beneficiaries are capable of playing an active part in reconfiguring the relations between citizens and the state. This again serves to illustrate the fact that, at all levels, the content of 'active citizenship' is a battlefield between competing political interests.

Active citizenship, family and care

All over Europe, the post-war male breadwinner model which underpinned social policy as well as family policy has been eroded, partly in response to changing aspirations among women, partly in response to increasing political emphasis on the responsibilities of all adults to engage in paid work (see Siim, Chapter Ten). However, there are large differences between countries in their policy response in terms of providing childcare facilities or other arrangements that can compensate for the care deficit which has emerged, and there are nearly everywhere problems of adapting social rights to this change as defamilisation of social rights often tend to generate new gender inequalities or new class inequalities among women. Even here, there has been a 'politics of recognition' in order to have care work in the family recognised as equally important as paid work, not least in relation to social rights like pensions rights which are based on individual contributions (see Pfau-Effinger, Chapter Eleven).

Although often with considerable delay, the transition of women to active labour-market participation has been followed by increasing public responsibility for care, and the right to care has increasingly become a new social right alongside traditional ones. But there has also been increasing emphasis on the right to leave the labour market temporarily with public support, and with the right to return to the same job afterwards. Thus, the social right to care takes two directions: the provision of public care facilities, and the provision of semi-formal forms of family childcare, treating family care as equal to paid work (Pfau-Effinger, Chapter Eleven). In some countries, this is provided simply by the state, in others, by various combinations of the state and agreements between social partners. Formally, this involves a privatisation of social responsibilities, but in terms of effects, it is often equivalent to a purely public arrangement.

So far, it is uncertain whether this leads to a convergence in European social and family policy towards support for working mothers and families. Divergence was perhaps until recently the most visible, but in the last 10–15 years, converging trends are also observable. Also, although there remain big differences in take-up of such rights between men and women, both legal arrangements and behavioural changes may tend to undermine the classical gender division of labour in this respect.

Active citizenship and early retirement

A major trend in European societies during the past 20 years has been the early withdrawal of older wage-earners from the labour market. For the sake of saving jobs in a context of widespread unemployment, many European countries until recently chose to encourage older workers to exit early from the world of work. As a result, the employment rates of 55- to 64-year-olds dropped some 35-40 percentage points between 1971 and 1995 on the continent, including in Finland. In Scandinavia and the UK, this drop after the age of 55 can also be observed, but on a lesser scale. The contributions of Saurama (Chapter Twelve) and Taylor (Chapter Thirteen) inquire into the impact of this massive early exit trend on individuals. Did it lead to the social marginalisation of those pushed out of the labour market and to rising social insecurity for older workers or, on the contrary, have these wage-earners been able to maintain their role as full citizens and their level of security? The conclusions of these two chapters, the one on the Nordic countries and the other on the UK, shed light on the complexity and ambivalence of this trend. Strictly speaking, this trend does not just signal either complete exclusion and a disenfranchisement of citizenship or an improvement in the well-being and social rights of older persons still working. For the UK, Taylor concludes that "by contrast to the case of the Nordic countries, early exit from the labour market has been a major cause of social exclusion and marginalisation". He also points out that, in a way and to a degree, early exit schemes have protected older employees from labour-market fluctuations and opened up a less chaotic pathway from work towards retirement. How can these diverging consequences of early retirement be explained? They must be related to the scope and diversity of opportunities offered to older wage-earners either to stay in employment or to pass towards inactivity thanks to social benefits. The impact on individuals and their well-being depends on the dialectics between, on the one hand, the level of early retirement coverage provided by welfare programmes and, on the other, active employment policies, specifically the incentives they provide for remaining in the workforce at an advanced age (Guillemard, 2003).

Except for Finland, the Nordic countries are characterised by what they offer to older wage-earners at the levels of both employment and welfare. Their active employment policies open possibilities for ageing employees to remain working and their generous welfare entitlements open up the possibility for them to withdraw early from the labour market in the case of serious health problems or work-related disability, or even by personal choice. Till the late 1990s, Finland was in a somewhat different situation and was closer to the 'continental welfare regime' in its treatment of older wage-earners. This type of welfare system passively provides a generous level of compensation for the risk of losing a job or not finding work. Given the scarcity of active employment policies, this sort of system provides few opportunities for keeping older employees in their jobs. In Finland as well as in Scandinavia, older employees have a relatively enviable welfare status, which replaces their status as wage-earners when, for various reasons, they are pushed out of the labour market. This status enables them to maintain both their well-being and full economic, political and social rights as citizen. Laura Saurama's empirical results in Chapter Twelve bear this out. This contrasts sharply with the plight of older wage-earners in Great Britain. The liberal welfare state regime there offers a less than advantageous status to whoever is pushed out of the labour market. Furthermore, this country does not have active employment policies for preventively maintaining such employees in the labour market or helping them return there. As Barbier has shown (Chapter Seven), the means provided by this type of welfare system mainly amounts to welfare-to-work programmes. The exclusion of older workers from the world of work thus leads to their social disenfranchisement. The loss of an occupational status triggers the loss of social status and plunges the person into economic insecurity with the stigmatised status of welfare beneficiary. In all industrialised countries, given globalisation and the advent of the knowledge-based society, age has become a standard for dispensing with older wage-earners and prodding them out of their jobs. Although this process has set off a spiralling depreciation of ageing wage-earners, its impact varies depending on the type of welfare system in the country. Where welfare provides generous benefits in the form of compensation for economic inactivity and a status recognised under social security, the massive exclusion of older wage-earners from the labour market has not entailed a loss of citizenship and well-being. Under the continental welfare regime, as in Finland, an explicit right to retire early has taken shape. An 'early exit culture' has emerged in these countries. Early withdrawal from the labour market has been seen as a form of social progress and all parties in the labour market, for different reasons, strongly support it. This explains why the new turn taken by employment policy in the EU, a turn toward 'active ageing', has encountered so many difficulties in its application in several countries.

The new face of welfare

What lessons can we learn from this tour of European welfare states and of the changes they are undergoing?

First of all, these welfare states are obviously not 'immovable objects' (Pierson, 1998). The changes reported here run very deep. We can detect hardly a single, homogeneous meaning in them, for example a convergence towards a liberal or residual model of welfare corresponding to a 'retrenchment' of 'social rights' and 'social citizenship'. All the comparative chapters here have pointed to the diversity and 'path dependence' of the changes that have been adopted. But they have also drawn attention to the disparity of practices in implementing new social policies. Beyond the many differences observed, we can detect a common minimal basis of changing welfare policies. Reforms pursue the same objective, but one that has taken different forms depending on the country and its welfare state regime with its specific pathology. This objective is to develop an active rather than a passive citizenship. Social citizens are no longer taken to be recipients of benefits and services as a counterpart to the obligations they must meet. They must become active in their own lives. This new requirement has arisen as the social compromise worked out in industrial society has worn down. This compromise was based on the wage-earner's subordination to the employer in exchange for extensive protection against risks. This compromise is out of phase with the exigencies of a post-industrial or knowledge-based society, where careers and biographies are being individualised and destandardised. The individual is gaining more freedom, mobility and control over time, but this is in exchange for greater responsibilities and reduced guarantees of security.

In this new context, welfare policies have been assigned the global objective of contributing to the empowerment of these new – free, autonomous and responsible – individuals by granting them more opportunities for voicing their point of view and for making choices about how to guarantee their own security. However the ways of designing and building this new 'enabling social state' that has turned towards 'social investment' (Esping-Andersen, 1996) and empowerment, are not at all alike. They differ widely, depending on whether they emphasise individuals and their autonomy and responsibility, or whether they pay attention to the collective structures and regulations that can help individuals make choices and ensure co-responsibility for managing the risks of insecurity.

Here, Barbier (Chapter Seven) has brought to light the radically distinct forms of activation. By doing so, he has been able to formulate a recommendation that holds for this book as a whole and for future research on welfare state reforms. We cannot be satisfied with analysing only the new institutional rules and regulations. We must also – and above all – examine concrete practices as closely as possible at the level of individuals and their demands. Beyond ideologies, such an approach will help us penetrate the significance and meaning of the reforms under way in terms of the outcome they have on individuals and their well-being. The contributions to this book have pointed out that the new arrangements being made in welfare converge towards a common objective. This objective is to move beyond the rationale of effecting a cure or reparations by compensating victims for specified risks; a rationale on which the welfare state and its conception of 'entitlements' have been grounded. The new objective is to invest preventively in developing human and social capital throughout an individual's life-course. The intention is to preserve the autonomy of individuals by leaving them room for making choices. But how can this freedom be made compatible with security? This is the dilemma that the new welfare states are facing. Given the process of individualisation and the new, diverse needs that have arisen, welfare states can no longer operate by following standardised rules and regulations. They have responded to this new situation by trying to find more flexible, optional forms of social intervention. But this risks leaving individuals to fend for themselves on their own, without any collective environment to guide them in making decisions. As a consequence, they are stalked by insecurity. For instance, investment in training for a lasting integration in the labour market is costly. The formulas that have proliferated (such as 'training credit') tend to assume that all persons are equally capable of planning their own investment in training. But as we know, not all wage-earners are as capable as each other of acting like rational, responsible individuals and not all know how to make plans – this depends very much on the person's initial schooling. Under these conditions, the programmes of asset-based welfare (which provide for the egalitarian distribution of training credits) for making people autonomous actors responsible for their own lives might well turn out to be ill-adapted and inefficient. Ultimately, they might even make inequality worse, opening new opportunities and freedom of choice for the strong, but (intentionally or unintentionally) strengthening obligations, sanctions and subordination for the weak, thus putting them in an even more dependent situation.

'Active citizenship' is a way to summarise the new face of welfare. The notion of active citizenship is an ambiguous one, and the new face of welfare may even be a Janus face. But perhaps it is more appropriate to use the metaphor of a battlefield, where there are a variety of possible outcomes. Probably, this is one of the main reasons why interpretations of the current changes in welfare states are so difficult. The new battlefield opens new potentials as well as new threats for social security. It may lead to increasing polarisation between the weak and the strong, but this is not inevitable. The changes include an expansion of social rights as well as retrenchments. But it is a new battlefield and it cannot be evaluated mechanically using the institutional criteria of the past. We believe that it is in this context that current welfare reforms should be discussed.

Note

[1] Although there were differences between class cultures and perhaps some struggle about recognition, Marshall did not find it difficult implicitly to take British upper-class culture as the ideal for the working class.

References

Andersen, J.G. (2002) 'Coping with long-term unemployment: economic security, labour market integration and well-being. Results from a Danish panel study, 1994-99', *International Journal of Social Welfare*, vol 11, no 2, pp 178-90.

Andersen, J.G. and Hoff, J. (2001) *Democracy and citizenship in Scandinavia*, Houndmills: Palgrave.

Esping-Andersen, G. (1996) 'After the golden age? Welfare state dilemmas in a global economy', in G. Esping-Andersen (ed) *Welfare states in transition: National adaptations in global economies*, London: Sage Publications, pp 1-31.

Gallie, D. and Paugam, S. (2000) *Welfare regimes and the experience of unemployment in Europe*, Oxford: Oxford University Press.

Garrett, G. and Mitchell, D. (2001) 'Globalization, government spending and taxation in the OECD', *European Journal of Political Research*, vol 39, no 2, pp 145-77.

Giddens, A. (1991) *Modernity and self-identity: Self and society in the late modern age*, Cambridge: Polity Press.

Gilbert, N. (2002) *Transformation of the welfare state: The silent surrender of public responsibility*, Oxford: Oxford University Press.

Guillemard, A.-M. (2003) *L'âge de l'emploi: Les sociétés à l'épreuve du vieillissement*, Paris: Armand Colin.

Pierson, P. (1994) *Dismantling the welfare state*, Cambridge: Cambridge University Press.

Pierson, P. (1998) 'Irresistible forces, immovable objects: post-Industrial welfare states confront permanent austerity', *Journal of European Social Policy*, vol 5, no 4, pp 539-60.

Pierson, P. (2001) 'Coping with permanent austerity: welfare state restructuring in affluent democracies', in P. Pierson (ed) *The new politics of the welfare state*, Oxford: Oxford University Press, pp 410-56.

Index

Page references for notes are followed by n